Before the Pharaohs

Before the Pharaohs

Exploring the Archaeology of Stone Age Egypt

Julian Maxwell Heath

PEN & SWORD
HISTORY

First published in Great Britain in 2021 by
Pen & Sword History
An imprint of
Pen & Sword Books Ltd
Yorkshire – Philadelphia

ISBN 978 1 52679 041 5

A CIP catalogue record for this book is
available from the British Library.

Typeset by Mac Style
Printed and bound in the UK by CPI Group (UK) Ltd,
Croydon, CR0 4YY.

Pen & Sword Books Limited incorporates the imprints of Atlas,
Archaeology, Aviation, Discovery, Family History, Fiction, History,
Maritime, Military, Military Classics, Politics, Select, Transport,
True Crime, Air World, Frontline Publishing, Leo Cooper, Remember
When, Seaforth Publishing, The Praetorian Press, Wharncliffe
Local History, Wharncliffe Transport, Wharncliffe True Crime
and White Owl.

For a complete list of Pen & Sword titles please contact

PEN & SWORD BOOKS LIMITED
47 Church Street, Barnsley, South Yorkshire, S70 2AS, England
E-mail: enquiries@pen-and-sword.co.uk
Website: www.pen-and-sword.co.uk

Or

PEN AND SWORD BOOKS
1950 Lawrence Rd, Havertown, PA 19083, USA
E-mail: Uspen-and-sword@casematepublishers.com
Website: www.penandswordbooks.com

Contents

Acknowledgements

S everal organizations and individuals have made generous contributions to this book and, as a result, have made its completion an easier task. I thank you all but in particular I would like to express my gratitude to: Professor Wouter Claes, Professor Joel D. Irish, Professor John McKim Malville, Professor Pierre Vermeersch and Dr Francis Wenban-Smith.

Introduction

Ancient Egyptian civilization is rightly renowned for its remarkable archaeological legacy, with the magnificent monuments and treasure-filled tombs of pharaonic Egypt an enduring source of fascination for countless numbers of people around the world. However, while the spectacular allure of ancient Egypt is hard to deny, it is not with its archaeology that this book is concerned, but rather with that of the shadowy peoples of prehistoric or Stone Age Egypt. Admittedly, the archaeological evidence from the Egyptian Stone Age may often appear 'primitive' alongside that of ancient Egypt, particularly that from the earlier periods of Egyptian prehistory. However, this does not lessen its importance and, as we will see, this evidence has provided many compelling insights into life (and death) in Egypt's distant past. It is also worth bearing in mind that the prehistoric communities of Egypt ultimately set in motion the major social changes and processes that led to the emergence of one of the world's greatest ancient civilizations in the Nile Valley, some 5,000 years ago.

Countless traces of Stone Age life can be found scattered throughout the Egyptian landscape. These were left by a complex cultural milieu of Palaeolithic ('Old Stone Age') and Neolithic ('New Stone Age') communities who inhabited not only the Nile Valley and Delta, but also the flanking Western and Eastern Deserts, with these two deserts forming the eastern edge of the Sahara (the Western Desert is alternatively labelled the 'Libyan Desert'). It was Sir John Lubbock,[1] the Victorian banker, politician and polymath, who first introduced the terms 'Palaeolithic' and 'Neolithic' to define these two major periods of prehistory in his classic monograph *Pre-Historic Times as Illustrated by Ancient Remains and the Manners and Customs of Modern Savages* (published in 1865). *Pre-Historic Times* was hugely popular (its final, seventh edition, was published in 1913) and as has been said of Lubbock: 'he has come to be seen as one of the most influential figures in prehistoric archaeology.'[2]

Of course, archaeology has come a long way since its formative years in the nineteenth century, when the early archaeologists or 'antiquarians' began to investigate in earnest the archaeological remains of the Stone Age,

Egypt from space: photograph taken by Nasa's *Terra* Satellite. (*Jacques Descloitres, Creative Commons*)

and there is now a much greater understanding of the diverse mosaic of prehistoric cultures that lived during the Palaeolithic and Neolithic. Thanks to the advent of radio-carbon dating in the late 1940s and the ever more sophisticated battery of dating techniques that archaeologists have at their disposal, more sound chronological frameworks with various subdivisions have also been established for the Palaeolithic and Neolithic. However, looking at Palaeolithic and Neolithic peoples at a basic level, the former were hunter-gatherers who followed a mobile lifestyle for many thousands of years, living in seasonal camps, their lives dictated by wild food resources, while the latter rejected this deeply ancient way of life and began settling down in permanent farming settlements where life revolved around domesticated crops and animals.

The Lower Palaeolithic

The story of the Egyptian Stone Age begins in the Pleistocene Period (c.2.5 million to 10,000 BCE) years ago, in the Lower Palaeolithic, with the earliest 'unambiguous evidence' for a human presence found at sites in the Western Desert dating to c.300,000 BCE,[3] although Egypt's earliest Stone Age inhabitants very probably arrived well before this time. The evidence garnered through geological research is less ambiguous, revealing that during the Egyptian Lower Palaeolithic, there were lengthy periods when the Western and Eastern Deserts were not the barren and inhospitable places that for the most part they are today:

> To imagine what it must have been like in those times, we must picture some of the rolling semiarid savannahs of eastern and southern Africa today, such as the Serengeti Plain. Giraffes, gazelles, and even hippopotami abounded on the now arid margins of the Nile Valley during the periodic rainy or pluvial periods that prevailed in the Southern Hemisphere as glacial advances and retreats in the north altered world-wide patterns of rainfall during the Pleistocene [more commonly known as the 'Ice Age']. Our ancestors followed the game and plant life and congregated around good fishing holes, expanding and contracting their wanderings in response to the pressures exerted by local climatic conditions.[4]

These 'good fishing holes' were the lakes, pools and springs created as a result of the significant amounts of rain that fell in Egypt during the Lower Palaeolithic pluvial periods. It is also worth noting that at this time, the famous River Nile would have been somewhat different in appearance: 'the Protonile, the river flowing through Egypt at this time, was a braided, intertwined network of river channels rather than a single channel like today's Nile.'[5]

The hunter-gatherer groups that roamed the Egyptian landscape in the Lower Palaeolithic used a distinctive Stone Age toolkit that archaeologists

Savannah landscape in Taita Hills Wildlife Sanctuary, Kenya. (*C.T. Cooper, Creative Commons*)

refer to as the 'Acheulean' industry or tradition (after the type-site of Saint-Acheul in the Somme Valley, northern France). The Acheulean handaxe (Plate 1) is the stone tool that defines this industry and these striking pear-shaped or oval objects, which often display rather elegant symmetry in their design, have become an icon of early prehistory, and 'Indeed, they are so distinctive that they are probably the one artifact that all archaeologists, whatever their period of interest, are capable of identifying.'[6]

Hundreds of thousands of Acheulean handaxes have been recovered from many sites in Africa, Asia and Europe and they are generally assumed to have been made by two early human species that have long since disappeared from the face of the earth: *Homo erectus* and *Homo heidelbergenis*, although the numerous examples found in Egypt are attributed to the former. The characteristic features of an Acheulean handaxe have been described thus:

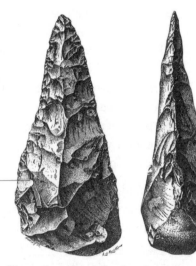

Illustration of an Acheulean handaxe found in the nineteenth century at Saint Acheul, France, by the French prehistorian Gabriel de Mortillet. (*Creative Commons Public Domain*)

Handaxes are bifacially flaked tools [worked on two sides], often teardrop or pear-shaped in outline. They are usually flaked around all or most of their circumferences, and the edges are normally carefully flaked and fairly sharp near the tips, an effort evidently made to thin the tools at this end.[7]

'Picks' and 'cleavers' were also made by *Homo erectus*: the former were handaxes with a narrow, pointed top and the latter handaxes with a straight chisel-like cutting edge at the top. Archaeologists quite commonly use the general term 'biface' for all three types; smaller flakes that came off the stone 'cores' during the production of handaxes, picks and cleavers were also used as simple but handy tools.

The Middle Palaeolithic

The succeeding Middle Palaeolithic period in Egypt is of considerable importance as it was during this time that modern humans first arrived on the scene, marking the beginning of the long road that would eventually lead to the great civilization of the pharaohs. Most (but not all) human evolution experts or 'palaeoanthropologists' favour the idea that *Homo sapiens* emerged in sub-Saharan Africa around 200,000 years ago, subsequently spreading around the rest of the world and replacing earlier *Homo erectus* and Neanderthal populations: the 'Out of Africa' theory.[8] A notable site in respect of this theory is site 8-B-11 on Sai Island in northern Sudan (c.7.5 miles long by c.3.5 miles wide), which is home to a rich collection of archaeological sites spanning many thousands of years. Archaeological excavations here in the 1990s uncovered an archaeological layer dated to about 200,000 years ago, containing both late Acheulean handaxes, stone 'core-axes' and other lithic artefacts of the 'Sangoan' industry, which is associated with the emergence of early modern humans in sub-Saharan Africa. This evidence points towards 'the coexistence of two different population groups in this region around 200 ka [200,000 years ago] and is interpreted as the replacement of a local late Acheulean [*Homo erectus*] population by *H. sapiens* groups.'[9]

However, fossil evidence has been found to suggest that things may not have been so straightforward and that the emergence of *Homo sapiens* was 'a complex pan-African process [that began] before or around 300,000 [thousand years ago].'[10] This evidence was found at Jebel Irhoud in Morocco, a former cave-site where the remains of at least five early Stone Age individuals were found alongside numerous stone tools and animal bones (mostly from gazelle) during the various excavations undertaken here in the 1960s and

2000s. Using thermoluminescence and electron spin resonance dating on fire-heated tools from the site and a child's mandible respectively, Jean-Jacques Hublin (director of the most recent excavations at Jebel Irhoud) and his colleagues at the Max Planck Institute for Evolutionary Anthropology, Leipzig were able to ascertain that the human fossils from Jebel Irhoud were at least c.300,000 years old. Furthermore, 'Hublin and his team used state-of-the-art micro computed tomographic scans and statistical shape analysis based on hundreds of 3D measurements to

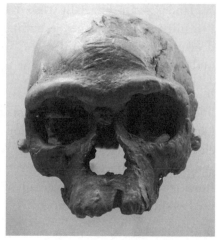

Early *Homo sapiens* skull from Jebel Irhoud. (*Ryan Sommer, Creative Commons*)

show that the facial shape of the Jebel Irhoud fossils is almost indistinguishable from that of modern humans living today.'[11] For Jean-Jacques Hublin the fascinating fossil evidence from Jebel Irhoud is compelling: 'It looks like our species was already present probably all over Africa by 300,000 years ago. If there was a Garden of Eden, it might have been the size of a continent.'[12]

It was during the early Middle Palaeolithic in Egypt, and many parts of the Old World, that the long-lived Acheulean tradition, which had persisted for many thousands of years, was replaced by a new and distinctive way of working stone tools known by archaeologists as the 'Levallois technique' or the 'Levalloisian' (after the Paris suburb of Levallois-Perret where it was first recognized in the nineteenth century).[13] Archaeologists have also identified a 'classical' and 'Nubian' Levallois technique, with the latter focused on the production of pointed stone flakes known as 'Levallois points'. The Levallois technique basically involved the careful preparation of a stone core, from which flakes were subsequently removed and used to make a much wider variety of stone tools, marking an important leap forward in Palaeolithic stone-tool technology:

> The advantage of the Levallois technique was that it represented an advance over older methods which either demanded that a large hunk of raw material be flaked down to form a single core tool, or that the highly varied flakes produced in this fashion be retouched [secondary working to produce a sharp or blunt edge on a stone tool] or used as is. With the Levallois technique, however, thin, sharp flakes of predictable

and standardized shape could be made and later retouched from one (unifacial) or both (bifacial) directions, creating a more diversified tool kit in which individual tool types were more effectively standardized.[14]

The most significant of these tools was the Levallois point (Plate 2), also known as Mousterian points after 'the most prevalent industrial complex'[15] of the Egyptian Middle Palaeolithic, the Mousterian. Although they may look rather unimpressive to modern eyes, the significance of these simple stone artefacts, which were probably mounted on wooden shafts as spearheads, cannot be overstated. As has been said, the Levallois point 'heralded a new efficiency in hunting that must have been of revolutionary importance…the superiority of stone projectile points over the old fire-hardened wooden spear must have permitted a great increase in hunting tactics and strategies.'[16] It has also been suggested that some Levallois points were used as arrowheads, although most archaeologists think this is unlikely.

Spears tipped with Levallois points 'could be used as a thrusting weapon, but could also be thrown at prey, thus reducing the risk of injury during the hunt and enabling the hunting of animals previously out of range.'[17] At times, the 'prey' may well have been human rather than animal, for as we shall see later, archaeological evidence has revealed that people's lives in Stone Age Egypt were sometimes shattered by episodes of deadly violence.

That Levallois points were used as projectile weapons has been confirmed by a rare discovery made at the multi-period prehistoric site of Umm el Tlel in Central Syria. In one of the site's Middle Palaeolithic levels, a Levallois point fragment was found embedded in the third cervical vertebra of an unfortunate wild ass (*Equus africanus*). However, although discoveries such as this reveal the efficiency of Levallois points in hunting, it seems

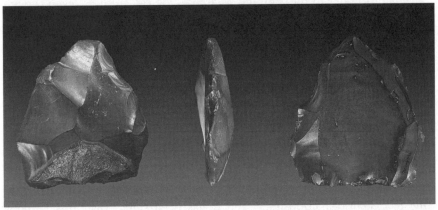

Levallois core found in the Valley of the Kings. (*Didier Descouens, Creative Commons*)

that at least on occasion they had other functions, as 'microwear analysis' (examining use-wear traces under a high-powered microscope) carried out on some examples has revealed that they were used as knives for cutting various materials.

In the European Middle Palaeolithic, the Mousterian industry is associated with the famous Neanderthals,[18] who in the nineteenth and earlier twentieth centuries were commonly portrayed as 'brute savages' of low intelligence – providing the classic caricature of the club-wielding caveman – an image that we now know is far from the truth. It is thus not surprising that some scholars have seen the stone tools of the Egyptian Mousterian industry as also being the handiwork of Neanderthal communities who inhabited Egypt during the Middle Palaeolithic. However, the consensus among palaeoanthropologists is that Neanderthals 'never occupied the African continent'[19] and so far, no convincing evidence has turned up to suggest that they are wrong.

There are two other notable stone tool industries from Middle Palaeolithic Egypt: the Aterian and the Khormusan, both of which 'produced tools that utilized the Levallois technique to greater or lesser extents in producing their lithic artefacts.'[20] These Stone Age 'technocomplexes' may indicate that in Middle Palaeolithic Egypt there were distinct ethnic groups with separate cultural traditions existing alongside one another. On the other – perhaps more plausible – hand the Aterian and Khormusan 'may reflect no more than minor differences in behaviour; there is no reason to believe that they represent self-conscious social entities.'[21] Nevertheless, the fact remains that from the Middle Palaeolithic onwards, there were contemporary Stone Age groups in Egypt who, although living the same lifestyles, do show some differences in their material culture and ways of life. Therefore, it remains convenient to refer to these groups as archaeological 'cultures', even though some modern archaeologists are wary of using this term.

Earlier twentieth-century archaeologists thought that both the Aterian and Khormusan industries dated to the Upper/Late Palaeolithic c.30,000–15,000 BCE, although it is now known they emerged at a much earlier date in the Middle Palaeolithic. Dates obtained on material (ostrich eggshell and charcoal) found at the type-site of the Khormusan industry – site 1017 on the banks of the Khor Musa River in what is now northern Sudan – gave a range of c.55,000–42,000 years ago and the age of the Khormusan has now been estimated 'to be between 45,000 and 55,000 years ago'.[22] It has been argued, however, that the Khormusan dates back further in time to c.85,000–65,000 BCE,[23] and it has been stated that 'this is likely to be a reliable estimate as it is based on environmental, geological and stratigraphic correlation.'[24] The Aterian, which unlike the Khormusan is found throughout North Africa, has been dated to c.145,000–30,000 BCE. Although the date of the emergence of the Aterian in Egypt is uncertain, radiocarbon and other scientific dating methods (e.g. uranium-series and thermoluminescence dating) have pushed back its Egyptian origins to well before 45,000 years ago. In fact, dates obtained from the important site of Bir Tarfawi in the Western Desert have suggested that the Aterian industry may well have been present in Egypt around 100,000 years ago.

The Khormusan industry seems to have been confined to an area near the modern-day border of Egypt and northern Sudan (which archaeologists often refer to by its ancient name of Nubia) and only a handful of Khormusan sites have been discovered. Nonetheless, these have been very informative, yielding rich assemblages of archaeological material comprising the remains of ancient hearths and thousands of stone tools and animal bones. The latter are badly preserved and we can thus 'only make a very cautious reconstruction of the fauna: large herbivores [aurochs], donkeys, hippopotami, gazelle, rodents and Nile fowl.'[25] It is evident that the stone tools of the Khormusan industry were made from a wide variety of raw materials (i.e. sandstone, quartzite, rhyolites, quartz, chalcedony, agate) and that certain types of stone were used for specific tool-types. For example, the numerous burins (small tools with a chisel-like edge) found at the Khormusan sites, were probably used for working wood, reed, and bone, and were commonly made from chalcedony. Numerous fragments of ground haematite have also been discovered at Khormusan sites (most noticeably at the site of Jebel Sahaba) and, more rarely, tools made from bone or wood.

Aterian point from Zaccar, Algeria. (*Michel-Georges Bernard, Creative Commons*)

The Aterian was first defined by the archaeologist Maurice Reygasse in 1919, after his discoveries at the type-site of Bir el Ater in Algeria. The industry is characterized by the stem or tang seen on the base of certain stone tools such as the distinctive Aterian tanged points. It has been remarked that this represents a 'technological breakthrough [that] was devised to enhance the hafting of stone tools'.[26] Aterian tanged points, like the similar Levallois points, are often assumed to have been projectile points hafted as spearheads (or less likely, arrowheads). However, some researchers have argued that they were used as 'tanged scrapers [for working animal hides] or knives'.[27] Rare discoveries such as that made at the cave site of Dar es-Soltan 1, on the Atlantic coast of Morocco, also reveal that not all Aterian tools were made from stone, as a bone knife-like artefact was recovered from a layer in the cave that dates to about 90,000 BCE.

Archaeologists have long been aware that Aterian tanged points somewhat resemble the stemmed points of the Upper Palaeolithic Solutrean industry (c.20,000–15,000 BCE), which is found in various parts of Europe, including southern Iberia. Therefore, the similarities seen between the two led some scholars to propose that 'Aterian people' from North Africa crossed the Strait of Gibraltar to Spain and Portugal. In the mid-twentieth century, for example, the English archaeologist Gertrude Caton Thompson,[28] who made a significant contribution to our knowledge of the Egyptian prehistoric period, postulated that there had been an 'Aterian Invasion' of Iberia. More recent scholars have not been as dramatic, but have still argued that actual migration or 'artefact diffusion', from the coasts of north-western Africa, introduced the Aterian 'culture' to southern Iberia in the Upper Palaeolithic. However, in truth, the Aterian and Solutrean points are not as similar as some scholars have suggested, and furthermore, radiocarbon dates obtained from sites of the Aterian industry indicate that it died out in northern Africa about 10,000 years before the emergence of the Solutrean in Europe.

Several Middle Palaeolithic quarries, where the raw materials for various stone tools were extracted, have also been investigated by archaeologists working in Egypt, with the work of the Belgian Middle Egypt Prehistoric Project of Leuven University particularly noteworthy in this regard. Chert cobbles were mainly extracted by the Middle Palaeolithic groups who came to these quarrying sites, which are located on escarpments above the River Nile floodplain. Although yielding abundant waste material or 'debitage' (i.e. cores and waste flakes) from the production of stone tools, these sites are generally lacking in the latter. This is because most finished tools must have been removed to be used at the living sites or settlements of the groups who worked the quarries. Unfortunately, these sites have not been located, probably because they have been buried or washed away in later times by the annual flooding of the Nile (with the completion of the Aswan High Dam in 1970, the annual Nile floods came to an end).

The Middle Palaeolithic rainy or pluvial periods occurred between c.175,000–70,000 BCE, with permanent 'palaeo-lakes', some of which were more than 7 metres deep, formed in a desert basin or depression, appearing in the Western Desert as a result. Archaeologists and geologists refer to the remnants of these ancient lakes as 'playas'. As has been pointed out: 'The associated faunal [animal] remains from the Middle Palaeolithic indicate that there was perhaps as much as 500mm of rain a year and that the lakes existed in a savanna or wooded savanna landscape which supported wild animals such as rhinoceros, giant buffalo, giraffe, giant camel, wild ass and various antelopes and gazelles.'[29] Fish were also present in the lakes, and animals such as hare, porcupine and wild cat were also on the Middle Palaeolithic menu. It is also likely that there were rich plant resources available to the Middle Palaeolithic groups who lived around the lakes, but unfortunately the evidence for these is lacking. It is also likely that these groups did not linger around lakesides at night because of the dangers posed by wild predators, probably removing themselves to camps located on higher ground. Much the same could be said for the people who lived in Egypt's Western (and Eastern) Desert during the Lower Palaeolithic rainy periods.

When the Middle Palaeolithic pluvials ended some 70,000 years ago, the Egyptian deserts became inhospitable: their savannah-type grasslands that had supported both humans and animals began to dry up as hyper-arid conditions returned to the Sahara, and lakes, springs and pools were gradually choked by sand. Thus, there was a prehistoric 'exodus' as the deserts were emptied of both their human and animal populations, and the Nile Valley subsequently became the principal place of prehistoric habitation for many thousands of years. Of course, this also remains the case in modern-day Egypt.

The Upper and Late Palaeolithic

In the early stages of the Upper Palaeolithic, there was another significant change in the way that Egyptian Stone Age communities made stone tools, with the Levallois technique disappearing during this time. Basically, when detached from the core of flint, chert or other type of stone providing the raw material, the Levallois technique produced wide, flat flakes [or 'blanks'], which were subsequently fashioned into different tool-types. The new stone-tool technology that emerged in the Upper Palaeolithic focused instead on the production of narrower and longer flakes, and 'made more efficient use of raw material [resulting] in blanks or "blades" that were more consistent in shape and size; the latter may be a major factor in the increased standardization evident in the retouched tools of the Upper Palaeolithic.'[30] This new technology had its roots in the Late Middle Palaeolithic and can be observed at some Egyptian sites dating to this time, such as Al Tiwayrat and the more well-known Taramsa-1, near Qena in Upper Egypt.

In contrast to the Middle Palaeolithic, Upper Palaeolithic sites are scarce in Egypt, with the deserts lacking human settlement because of the hyper-arid conditions that existed there during this period. Some Upper Palaeolithic sites are known in the Nile Valley, however, the earliest and most important of which is Nazlet Khater-4 dated c.33,000 BCE, with the next oldest sites attributed to the 'Shuwikhatian' industry, the type-site of which (Shuwikhat-1) has been dated to around 23,000 years ago. Nazlet Khater-4 is one of the oldest known examples of an underground mine in the world and Shuwikhat-1 seems to have functioned as hunting and fishing camp located on the Nile floodplain.

At the beginning of the Late Palaeolithic around 20,000 BCE another significant change is seen in the Egyptian hunter-gatherer toolkit, with the large blade tools of the Upper Palaeolithic replaced by 'microlithic' (i.e. about 1–2cm long by 0.5cm wide) bladelet tools, some of which feature the pleasingly named 'Ouchtata' retouch on their edges. These tools would have been used as armatures on composite weapons such as harpoons and spears,[31] with several bladelets being inserted into their shafts to make them more deadly.

Several Egyptian Late Palaeolithic stone-tool industries have been identified by archaeologists such as the Fakhurian (c.20,000 BCE–18,000 BCE) and the Kubbaniyan

Composite bone harpoon with microlithic barbs. (*José–Manuel Benito Álvarez*)

(c.18,000 BCE–16,000 BCE), which is the oldest known from this period. Perhaps the most intriguing of these Late Palaeolithic industries is the Sebilian (c.12,000–10,000 BCE), which was discovered by the young French archaeologist (and chemist) Edmond Vignard, as a result of his excavations at prehistoric sites in the Kom Ombo Plain, in the early 1920s (Vignard named the industry after the nearby town of Sebil). This was a significant discovery, and many fascinating finds were made by Vignard during his excavations at the Sebilian sites. For example, there were the remains of numerous hearths and 'kitchen middens', formed from heaps of mussel shells and wild animal bones, polished bone tools, a *Corbicula consobrina* (freshwater clam) shell that had been perforated to be worn as jewellery, and sandstone pestles and mortars. Some of the latter still contained traces of red ochre and it is quite possible that people had used this ochre to decorate their faces and bodies.

In 1962–63, a Canadian archaeological expedition conducted rescue excavations at Sebilian settlement sites in the Kom Ombo Plain, which were being destroyed by modern agricultural activities. At one site (Gebel Silsila 2a) that was rich in stone tools and other artefacts, they made the rare discovery of a partial frontal bone (the forehead) from an adult male skull and smaller fragments from at least two other skulls. Radiocarbon dates obtained on flecks of charcoal and freshwater clam shells recovered from the site suggested that the skull fragments were probably about 13,000 years old.

It is also quite possible that the Sebilian industry was brought to Egypt by immigrants from further south in Africa:

> Suddenly, about 14,000 years ago, many small Sebilian sites appear, from the Second Cataract to the Qena bend, in which most of the tools are large, wide, flat flakes (struck from Levallois or discoidal cores) retouched into geometric shapes never or rarely seen in earlier sites. Furthermore, Sebilian tools were preferentially made on quartzitic sandstone, diorite and other basement rocks, instead of the Nile chert and agate pebbles preferred by earlier Late Palaeolithic groups. Only in Upper Egypt did the Sebilian people use flint, in those areas where there is no sandstone or basement rock.[32]

Exactly where these 'intrusive groups' hailed from is not clear, but several researchers have noted the similarities seen between the Sebilian industry and the Late Palaeolithic/Later Stone Age Tshitolian industry, which has been found by archaeologists working in Angola, Congo and Gabon. These three countries lie a significant distance from Egypt, although this does not totally rule out the possibility that the Sebilian industry was brought by migrants from one of these places.

The archaeologists of the Canadian expedition also uncovered several settlement sites containing a previously unidentified Late Palaeolithic microlithic stone-tool industry during their excavations in Kom Ombo Plain, with these sites dating to c.14,000 BCE. They named this new industry the 'Silsilian' and interestingly, it bears a close resemblance to the Ballanan industry of northern Sudan, with a 'Ballanan-Silsilian culture' thus proposed by some archaeologists. At one of the Silsilian sites excavated by the Canadian archaeologists 'two...intimate relics of human presence were found'[33] and comprised a milk tooth from a child aged under 7 and a lump of hardened mud that, incredibly, still bore the palm-print (probably an adult's) of a Late Palaeolithic hunter-gatherer who had lived some 15,000 years ago.

Archaeological evidence recovered from Egyptian Late Palaeolithic sites along the Nile Valley has revealed that people had a more diverse diet than in the preceding Upper and Middle Palaeolithic. Fish apparently provided a major source of protein at this time, as large quantities of bones from various species of fish have been recovered (although catfish seems to have been a favourite), as well as pits containing large amounts of charcoal that were probably used for smoking and preserving fish. It is also evident that freshwater shellfish and various water birds often featured on the Egyptian Late Palaeolithic menu, along with various fruits, berries and nuts.

As in the Middle and Upper Palaeolithic, Late Palaeolithic groups in Egypt, like more recent hunter-gatherer societies around the world, must have 'built brush huts, windbreaks or light tents [made from animal hide], shelters that would have left few traces'.[34] The ravages of time and the environment have doubtless put paid to a wide array of other Palaeolithic artefacts made from perishable materials: objects such as wooden and bark containers, fishing nets and fish traps, the wooden handles and shafts in which stone tools and weapons were mounted, and clothing.

Also found at Egyptian Late Palaeolithic sites are the remains of edible plants that grew along the edge of the Nile, such as club-rush and camomile; the grinding stones found at some sites were probably used to crush out the toxins and break up the tough fibres found in plants such as nut-grass. Many sites from this time have also yielded the bones of wild animals such as hartebeest, wild cattle and dorcas gazelle, showing that hunting was still important to Late Palaeolithic communities, even though the subsistence base became more diverse during this time.

As we will also see later, evidence uncovered in the 1960s, at the famous cemetery-site of Jebel Sahaba near the modern-day Egyptian/Sudanese border, showed that relations between the hunter-gatherer communities who lived in the Nile Valley at the end of the Late Palaeolithic were, at least on occasion, far from friendly.

The Epipalaeolithic

Archaeologists have also identified an 'Epipalaeolithic' (c.8500–6500 BCE) period in Egypt, during which time some prehistoric groups were essentially still living a Late Palaeolithic lifestyle, using microlithic toolkits and subsisting from hunting, fishing and gathering, and living somewhat nomadic lives. The two best-known Epipalaeolithic cultures from Egypt are the Elkabian and the Qarunian (also known as the 'Fayum B' culture). Sites of the Qarunian, or 'Fayum B' culture, are found near Lake Moeris in the Fayum Oasis (a large depression located in the Western Desert, south-west of Cairo), with excavation of Qarunian or Fayum B sites clearly revealing that fish played a major part in the diet of its communities. Excavations carried out in the northern Fayum in 1968–69 by the Combined Prehistoric Expedition also unearthed an important Qarunian burial containing the skeleton of an adult (probably female), who was estimated to be c.160cm (5ft 3in) high and about 40 years of age, which would have been considered 'elderly' by the people of this time.

The Elkabian has only been found in the Nile Valley at the important multi-period site after which it is named: Elkab. The Elkab Epipalaeolithic site was excavated by the Belgian archaeologist Pierre Vermeersch[35] from 1968–75 and the remains of several hunter-gatherer campsites, that were still in situ on an ancient bank of the Nile, were unearthed. These sites yielded more than 4,000 stone tools, numerous fish and other animal bones (e.g. aurochs, dorcas gazelle and hippo), ostrich shell beads (that people had used as jewellery) and several different types of grinding stones, with the larger examples – somewhat remarkably – still bearing red pigment stains on them (probably from the grinding of red ochre).

Evidence of the Elkabian culture has also been found at the remote Eastern Desert site of 'Tree Shelter', which was named after the lone acacia tree that grew next to it. As has been noted, the presence of the Elkabian at this important site 'suggests that the Elkabians should be viewed as nomadic hunters, following east-west routes with wintertime fishing and hunting in the Nile Valley and exploitation of the desert during the wet summer.'[36] Tragically, however, Tree Shelter was basically destroyed by limestone quarrying in 2012. The exceptional site of Sodmein Cave, which contains 4m of stratified Stone Age deposits dating from the Middle Palaeolithic to the Neolithic, only lies about 2.5 miles from Tree Shelter and faces the same threat of destruction from modern quarrying, although so far, thankfully, the cave appears to have survived intact. It is worth noting that Sodmein Cave has yielded the earliest evidence yet known for domesticated sheep and goats in Egypt (the sheep and goat bones date from at least 6200 BCE), with the extensive dung deposits also found in the cave by archaeologists of the Belgian Middle Egypt Prehistoric Project of Leuven University, revealing that Neolithic herders penned their animals here.

Evidence of an intriguing Epipalaeolithic culture known as the Masara has also been found by archaeologists working at Dakhla Oasis in the Western Desert. Unusually, most of the Masara sites that have been investigated feature small, circular or oval rings of stone, representing the remains of stone huts (c.2–4m in diameter), most of which are semi-subterranean and have sunken floors. The processing and storage of wild plant foods at Masara sites is revealed by the presence of grinding slabs, and by the storage pits associated with the stone dwellings, with the discovery of the bones of wild animals such as gazelle, hare and hartebeest providing evidence of hunting. Taken together, the archaeological evidence uncovered at these Masara sites suggests that they were the base camps of Stone Age groups, who were somewhat sedentary in nature.

The Egyptian Neolithic

Without the emergence of the Neolithic or New Stone Age, the remarkable civilization of ancient Egypt would never have existed and indeed, neither would our incredibly complex and over-populated modern world. Although it was a complex and long, drawn-out process that took thousands of years, during the Neolithic Egypt's prehistoric communities gradually turned to a sedentary life centred on permanent settlements and domesticated crops and animals.

The first Neolithic settlements in Egypt emerged in the Western Desert, as a result of the onset of the 'Holocene Wet Phase' that replaced the hyper-arid conditions of the previous Pleistocene period (c.2,500,000–10,000 BCE), and brought significant amounts of rainfall to the desert. As has been noted, during the Early Holocene (the current geological epoch in which we live), 'the tropical summer rain front moved about 700–1,000km northward... which initiated more humid conditions in the Eastern Sahara.'[37]

Most of these Early Neolithic settlements are small seasonal camps, although substantial examples are known from the Middle and Late Neolithic. These larger sites may, perhaps, have been occupied all year round and are located near the permanent lakes that formed in the Western Desert because of the arrival of wetter conditions in the early Holocene which, as in the Middle Palaeolithic, led to the creation of a savannah-like environment here. Wells and storage pits, presumably for storing wild plant foods, have also been found at some Neolithic settlements in the Western Desert.

To a large extent, however, these ancient desert communities still followed the semi-nomadic, hunter-gatherer lifestyle of their Palaeolithic forebears, with wild animals and plants providing the main subsistence base, and microlithic toolkits still used during the earlier stages of the Western Desert Neolithic. However, new stone tools and weapons such as fine bifacially-flaked flint knives and arrowheads subsequently emerged, and pottery – a hallmark of the Neolithic lifestyle – is found at most sites from the Early Neolithic onwards, although not in large quantities. Much more commonly found are ostrich eggshells, which must have been used as convenient, ready-made containers for water, milk and blood. For much of the Western Desert

Neolithic, the pottery was of the 'Saharo-Sudanese' or 'Khartoum' tradition, comprising well-made deep bowls, often decorated over the entire surface with patterns of impressed lines and points created by cord or combs. Archaeologists think that these bowls probably mimicked basketry, and they show no signs of having been used for cooking. It therefore seems likely that this pottery 'must have had great social significance – and because of the decoration – probably also symbolic meanings.'[38] It has also been plausibly suggested that pottery vessels 'were used for storage and serving in social or religious settings, perhaps related to the specific period of intensive plant gathering.'[39]

Grinding stones have also been recovered from many Western Desert Neolithic sites, which would have been used for the processing of wild plants. Rare examples of wild grasses, wild sorghum and *Ziziphus* fruits have been found at sites such as E-75-6 in the Nabta Playa basin, an area of the Western Desert that has several fascinating and important Neolithic sites. Also found are mollusc shells from the River Nile and sea-shells from the Red Sea (which borders the Eastern Desert), indicating wide-ranging contacts between the Western Desert and these areas.

Agriculture is not attested for the Western Desert Neolithic, although it is possible that people may have been herding and keeping wild cattle (*Bos primigenius*) in the Early Neolithic. However, this is a controversial issue that continues to cause academic debate, which we will return to look at in more detail later. The presence of pottery and the lack of domesticated crops have led some scholars to suggest that 'ceramic' is a more apt term for the 'Neolithic' groups of the Western Desert. Whatever term is preferred, 'Domesticated cattle are attested with certainty in the Western Desert Neolithic from the mid-6th millennium BCE onwards.'[40] Domesticated sheep and goats were also imported from the Levant during this time, although 'Wild animals remained the main source of protein; and hunting equipment, especially arrowheads, was still the major component of the lithic industries.'[41]

After c.5000 BCE, and particularly from c.4500 BCE onwards, the Egyptian Sahara became a hostile place to live because of the onset of the very arid climate that characterizes it today, and this led to a large-scale, Stone Age 'exodus' from the desert, which corresponded to the rise of sedentary, Neolithic farming communities along the Nile. However, not everybody headed to greener pastures, due to the fact that there were a handful of ecological niches (e.g. oases such as Dakhla, and the Nabta Playa-Bir Kiseiba region) that still allowed for human habitation. It was at this time that a new and distinctive pottery appeared somewhat abruptly, replacing the long-lived Saharo-Sudanese and Khartoum wares, and perhaps representing the arrival of a new people in the Western Desert. Known rather prosaically as 'desert black-topped' pottery, it was evidently used for cooking as revealed by the clear traces of burning seen on the exteriors of vessels.

The earliest evidence for 'fully-fledged' Neolithic communities in Egypt comes from the Fayum Oasis, with archaeological research carried out here in the earlier twentieth century revealing the existence of the Neolithic Fayum A culture (c.5450–4400 BCE). Its communities grew emmer wheat and six-row barley (also introduced from the Levant) and also kept domesticated sheep, goats, cattle and pigs, with the large storage pits for grain also found at many sites used to stockpile grain, probably for the whole community. However, fishing and hunting still played an important role in the diets of these communities, who also made simple and undecorated pottery vessels that were utilitarian in nature.

In the distinctive Delta region of Upper Egypt, there is the Merimde culture, named after the site of Merimde Beni Salama, which was mainly excavated by the German archaeologist Hermann Junker between 1929 and 1939.[42] This large settlement, which covers some 2,0000m², comprises five levels of occupational debris measuring an average c.2.5m in depth, with dates obtained from the site spanning much of the fifth millennium BCE. The numerous archaeological remains recovered from the site included grain that had somewhat remarkably been preserved through burning and the remains of small oval houses made from straw-tempered mud, which had sunken floors and roofs made from reeds and branches. Pottery decorated with a herringbone pattern was used by the 'Merimdens' and the faunal remains included the bones of domesticated sheep, cattle and pigs, with dogs also evidently living alongside the people at Merimde Beni Salama.

An important Neolithic culture also existed in the Nile Valley and is known as the Badarian after the site of el-Badari in Upper Egypt where it was first discovered by the English archaeologist Guy Brunton in the early twentieth century. The Badarian culture has been dated to c.4500–4000 BCE, and as noted by Béatrix Midant-Reynes, although not all archaeologists agree, it 'now tends to be considered as a regional development of the Tasian nomadic culture, which occupied the southern part of the Egyptian deserts and the Sudan during the fifth millennium [BCE].[43] Badarian communities were the first farmers of southern or Upper Egypt growing crops, keeping domesticated animals and living in small settlements, some of which were probably seasonal herding or fishing camps. They also buried their dead in simple pit-graves, with bodies often placed on mats and lying on their left sides. The excavation of Badarian burials has also clearly revealed that some were more richly furnished than others, pointing to the social stratification that became increasingly marked in the succeeding Late Predynastic/

Naqada Period. The commonest item placed in Badarian graves was pottery, with some of the distinctive products produced by Badarian potters of the highest quality and revealing their great technical skills.

The Predynastic/Naqada Period c.4000–3000 BCE

The fourth millennium BCE in Egypt marks the final chapter in the long and complex story of Stone Age Egypt, and also represents the final and most significant phase of the late prehistoric period c.5500–3100 BCE, with the earlier phase (c.5500–4000 BCE) represented by the first 'fully-fledged' Neolithic farming communities of the Fayum, Nile Valley and Delta. In truth, every one of Egypt's Stone Age cultures could be classed as 'Predynastic', as they all preceded the ancient Egyptian state and its ruling pharaonic dynasties.

Leaving aside such semantic quibbles, it was at the beginning of the fourth millennium BCE that the seminal Naqada culture (c.4000–3000 BCE) emerged, which was first brought to light at the end of the nineteenth century by the famous Flinders Petrie, the 'Father of Egyptology' and the scholar who first proved the existence of Egyptian prehistory.[44] The significance of the Naqada culture cannot be underestimated, as it laid the foundations for ancient Egyptian civilization, with many of its major characteristics appearing in embryonic form during the time of the Naqada culture, hence the reason why the Late Predynastic Period is also referred to as the 'Naqada Period'. For example, elaborate tombs containing impressive assemblages of grave goods, which speak of powerful ruling groups or elites, appear for the first time, and large walled towns or urban centres containing thousands of inhabitants developed along the Nile. On the fine, decorated pottery and other artefacts made by Naqada artisans, 'the beginnings of the iconography that would eventually lie at the core of

Photograph of a young Flinders Petrie, taken in the late nineteenth century, c.1886. (*Creative Commons, Public Domain*)

pharaonic civilization[45] can also be seen. This iconography includes depictions of victorious warriors or leaders smiting their captured and bound enemies, appearing to provide the prototype for the iconography of the all-conquering pharaoh, which underpinned royal propaganda in ancient Egypt. It is also evident from the many superb artefacts that have survived from the Naqada culture that as in ancient Egypt, a skilled artisan class existed, who specialized in serving rulers and elite groups that displayed their wealth and power by including these fine objects in their burials.

In northern or Lower Egypt, another distinctive Late Stone Age culture appeared in the early fourth millennium BCE. Traditionally labelled the 'Maadi culture/Maadian cultural complex' (c.4000–3400 BCE), after the major site of Maadi and Buto, this culture is now more commonly known as the 'Lower Egyptian culture' because the discovery of new sites has extended its geographical range. The Lower Egyptian culture was eventually assimilated into the Naqada culture after its more powerful and influential southern neighbour expanded northwards from its homeland in Upper Egypt in the Naqada II period, and it has been argued that this assimilation was probably achieved 'by a mix of acculturation and coercion'.[46] As we shall see in the final chapter, although the archaeological evidence for the Lower Egyptian culture is less 'spectacular' than that of the Naqada culture, impressive discoveries have nevertheless been made at some of its sites, along with finds indicating that the Lower Egyptian culture had strong links with the southern Levant.

Chapter One

Hominids and Handaxes:
The First 'Egyptians'

The thousands of handaxes and other Lower Palaeolithic stone tools of the Acheulean industry found in Egypt provide an enduring testimony to communities who lived here many millennia before the emergence of ancient Egyptian civilization. Although, as yet, no skeletal evidence for the people who made and used the stone tools of the Acheulean industry has come to light – and there is only a slim chance that it ever will – it is generally assumed that they were small bands of the archaic human species, *Homo erectus* ('upright man') who had migrated from sub-Saharan Africa.[1] Various dates have been proposed for the emergence of the Acheulean industry over the years, but 'there is now evidence that the Acheulean appeared at least 1.75 Ma [million years ago] in the East African Rift Valley, which on an evolutionary scale coincides with the appearance of *H. erectus*.'[2]

Most researchers favour the idea that *Homo erectus* emerged in Africa and subsequently spread into many parts of Asia and Europe,[3] via the Sinai peninsula, proposing that these early hominid 'adventurers' travelled either along the Nile Valley corridor or the coastline of the Red Sea coast to get to Sinai. Some researchers have argued that *Homo erectus* took a more direct migration route out of Africa and crossed into the Arabian Peninsula via the Bab al-Mandab Strait which lies between the southern end of the Red Sea Coast and the Horn of Africa. Whatever the case, the site that has provided the best-known evidence for these early African migrants is Dmanisi, located in a beautiful rural corner of the Republic of Georgia. This hugely important site has been dated to c.1.77 million years ago, with five exceptionally well-preserved hominid skulls and various other bones (e.g. a femur and tibia, vertebrae, clavicles) representing the oldest hominid remains yet found outside Africa. Its early date has led some researchers to suggest that our early human ancestors emerged not in Africa, but on the European continent.

The Dmanisi hominid remains were discovered during the various archaeological excavations carried out at the site between 1991 and 2005, with numerous animal bones from species such as giant deer and ostrich, giraffe, jackal, sabre-toothed tiger, jaguar, rhinoceros and elephant also unearthed. It is worth noting that one of the Dmanisi hominids had lost all but one tooth several years before he/she died, and it has therefore been suggested that this individual would have needed to be cared for by other members of its group: 'Since it could only have consumed soft plant or animal foods, it seems likely that it would have needed support.'[4] The fossil remains at Dmanisi are generally attributed by experts to an

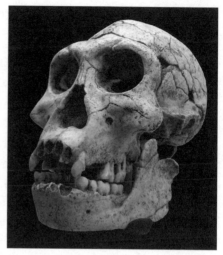

Early *Homo erectus* skull from Dmanisi, Georgia. (*Rama, Creative Commons*)

early or 'primitive' form of *Homo erectus*, although not all agree, arguing instead that these archaic humans should be reclassified as a new, separate species known as *Homo georgicus*.

Another important archaeological site that has provided evidence for early *Homo erectus* migration out of Africa is Ubeidiya in the Central Jordan Valley, not far from the Sea of Galilee, Israel. Archaeological excavations carried out at Ubeidiya in the mid-twentieth century uncovered two skull fragments and teeth alongside early Acheulean handaxes and various animal remains (e.g. gazelle, hippopotamus, wild cattle, antelope, leopard), with the site dated somewhat later than Dmanisi, to c.1.5 million years ago.

Of all the *Homo erectus* remains yet discovered, there is little doubt that those of 'Turkana Boy' (who is also known as 'Nariokotome Boy' after the river near where he was found) are the most important, as they give us an unrivalled idea of what these early humans looked like 'in the flesh'. Turkana Boy was discovered in 1984, when the famous 'fossil hunter' Kamoya Kimeu spotted a piece of bone in a gully near Lake Turkana, Kenya, with the site subsequently excavated by Richard Leakey (son of the famous palaeoanthropologist Louis Leakey), his wife Maeve and their colleague Alan Walker. Turkana Boy represents the almost complete skeleton of an adolescent male *Homo erectus* and potassium-dating carried out on the tuffs (volcanic ash layers) which lay above and below him suggest that he had died about 1.56 million years ago, with estimates of his age ranging from 8 to 12. When he died, Turkana Boy was about 5ft 3in tall, and may reached an impressive 6ft or more if he had survived into adulthood; it has been noted that 'His arms were no longer, relative to his legs, than in living people and he had a barrel-shaped chest over narrow hips. From a distance, he would have looked very similar to the lanky herders who live around Lake Turkana today.'[5] Ronda Graves and her colleagues, however, have argued that it is more likely that Turkana Boy 'would only have attained an adult stature of 163 cm [5ft 4in].'[6] Whatever his original height, it was Turkana Boy's face and skull that were strikingly different from modern humans:

> His braincase was long and low [containing a brain about half the size of our own], and the skull walls were exceptionally thick. His forehead (frontal bone) was flat and receding, and it descended to merge at an angle with the bony browridge over his eyes. His nose was typically human in its forward projection and downwardly orientated nostrils, and in this he differed from [other early hominids] who had apelike noses that were flush against the face. The nose aside, however, his face was striking for its great length from top to bottom, and his massive jaws were prognathic, projecting far to the front. These jaws contained chewing teeth that were significantly larger than our own.... The bone below his lower front teeth slanted sharply backwards, meaning that he was completely chinless.[7]

Reconstruction of a male *Homo erectus* in the Westfälisches Landesmuseum, Herne, Germany. (*Lillyundfreya, Creative Commons*)

The Oldowan Industry in Egypt?

None of the Acheulean handaxes, which were 'invented' by *Homo erectus*, were found at the site of Dmanisi; rather, crude stone tools belonging to the 'Oldowan' tradition or 'technocomplex' (also rather prosaically known as 'Mode 1'), revealing that in Georgia, early *Homo erectus* was still using a stone-tool technology that had emerged with the earlier hominids. The Oldowan was discovered in the mid-1930s in the earliest levels at the famous Olduvai Gorge, Tanzania, by the equally renowned Louis and Mary Leakey, who continued to work in the gorge for the next three decades, as a result, 'discovering an unparalleled prehistoric sequence spanning almost 2 million years'.[8] The Oldowan tradition is characterized by the simplicity of its stone tools, basically consisting of tools worked on one or two edges, which were used for chopping, scraping, cutting and pounding, with 'choppers' the most common artefact of this early hominid toolkit. Dating back to c.2.5 million years ago, 'The Oldowan represents the first instances of technological innovation in human history, wherein our ancestors first began to enhance their biological capabilities with the manufacture of stone tools.'[9]

Oldowan stone tools are rarely found in association with early hominid remains and thus it is hard to say for sure which of our early human ancestors were the first ones to make them. However, Louis and Mary Leakey discovered Oldowan tools alongside the remains of the two hominid species, *Paranthropus/Australopithecus boisei* and *Homo habilis* at Olduvai Gorge. It is possible that early hominids using Oldowan technology were living in Egypt long before *Homo erectus* groups arrived in the Nile Valley. As the French archaeologist Fernand Debono has noted:

> From 1949 onwards very early evidence of these hominids, in the shape of pebbles barely worked into crude tools, came to light at Nuri and Wawa, in the Sudan, but these isolated surface finds were not enough to amount to definite proof. It was not until 1971, following systematic research at Thebes [Luxor], that it was possible to be certain on this point. Here the exploration of twenty-five alluvial deposits dating from the early Quaternary yielded a rich harvest of these primitive tools. The discovery in 1974 of three stratified sites containing worked pebbles (choppers) yielded a wealth of information and swept away the last lingering doubts. The worked-pebble strata were below the early Acheulean [levels].... Very recently a hominid tooth was found in early alluvial strata in the Thebes mound, associated with choppers. It will be recalled that in about 1925 a similar sequence was found in alluvial strata at Abbassia, near Cairo [unfortunately, these strata are now covered by the city suburbs]; but at that time the worked pebbles were classified as eoliths [naturally chipped stones]. New light has most recently been thrown on this remote period as a result of our 1974 excavations at Adaima, in Upper Egypt...this is a new site that is still being studied, but is apparently similar to the previous ones.[10]

Not all scholars are convinced, however, that these Egyptian Oldowan tools are authentic. Stan Hendrickx and Pierre Vermeersch, for example, have argued that 'most of these published "artefacts" are probably not of human origin',[11] while Béatrix Midant-Reynes has noted 'that the identification of these tools are by no means certain, given that we currently only have the

Three views of an Oldowan chopper from Melka Kenture, Ethiopia. (*Didier Descouens, Creative Commons*)

published drawings rather than the tools themselves.'[12] Douglas Brewer has also commented that 'Unfortunately, these tools…have never been made available for scholarly study.'[13] Thus, it seems that the archaeological jury will remain out on this issue, unless these tools are indeed made available for study or new and irrefutable evidence for the Oldowan turns up in Egypt.

Acheulean Sites in Egypt

Whether or not the Oldowan industry was ever brought to Egypt by early hominids remains a matter of scholarly debate, but 'there is little disagreement surrounding the Acheulean…and its presumed creator, *Homo erectus*.'[14] The first Acheulean handaxes and other Stone Age tools recorded in Egypt were those discovered in 1869 at various desert sites along the edges of the Nile Valley (e.g. in the hills above the Valley of the Kings) by three French antiquarians: Adrien Arcelin, Ernest Hamy and François Lenormant. The publication of their discoveries was 'the first account of Palaeolithic chipped stone implements found in Egypt and launched the science of prehistoric archaeology in that country.'[15] Messieurs Arcelin, Hamy and Lenormant were of the opinion that these artefacts predated pharaonic civilization and belonged to the Egyptian Stone Age. However, not all scholars agreed, arguing instead that these artefacts were either natural or belonged to the time of the pharaohs, pointing out that similar worked flints had been found in some ancient Egyptian tombs. Sir John Lubbock, the English antiquarian who invented the term 'Palaeolithic' to define the Old Stone Age, decided to visit Egypt a couple of years after the discoveries of the three French antiquarians, keen to see for himself the sites where they had found the purported Stone Age artefacts:

> I was extremely anxious to visit these interesting spots, and by an inspection of the localities themselves, to form, if possible, an independent judgement.... Last autumn I was so fortunate as to visit Egypt.... I found worked flints [including three Acheulean handaxes] at various spots along the valley; especially in the Valley of the Tombs of the Kings, at Thebes, and at Abydos.... I am disposed to agree with... Arcelin and Hamy in considering that these flint implements really belong to the stone age, and are ante-Pharaonic.[16]

It would be several more years before it was fully accepted that there had been a pre-pharaonic, Egyptian Stone Age or prehistoric period. However, the initial discovery of Lower Palaeolithic tools by Adrien Arcelin, Ernest Hamy and François Lenormant marked the beginning of the end for the popular idea that Egypt had been devoid of prehistory.

Interestingly, for a large part of the nineteenth century, much of the Victorian scientific establishment held 'a view of ancient humanity [that was] largely framed, consciously or not, by the Book of Genesis.... And according to Genesis the human presence on earth began only half a dozen millennia ago.'[17] This view originated in the mid-seventeenth century with James Ussher, Archbishop of Armagh, and Dr John Lightfoot, Vice-Chancellor and master of Saint Catherine's Chapel, the University of Cambridge. Both men precisely calculated, from evidence in the Book of Genesis, that God created the world on 23 October 4004 BCE, with Lightfoot going one step further than Ussher and calculating that God created mankind on 23 October at 9 o'clock in the morning! Although it may seem absurd to us today that this idea still held sway in the nineteenth century, archaeology was in its

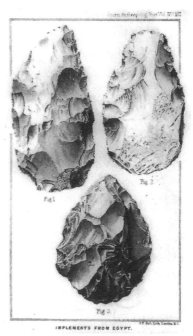

Acheulean handaxes found at Luxor and Abydos in the nineteenth century by Sir John Lubbock. (*After Lubbock 1873*)

infancy during this time and the scientific dating of archaeological sites was still many years in the future, meaning that the dogma of the church was more readily acceptable than it is today.

However, in the mid-nineteenth century, Jacques Boucher de Crèvecœur de Perthes '[smashed] the Biblical "time barrier" that denied the existence of Stone Age man.'[18] Boucher de Perthes was a well-to-do French customs official with a passion for the past who, in the mid-nineteenth century, turned up what we now know to be Acheulean handaxes alongside the bones of animals long extinct in Europe (e.g. elephant and rhinoceros) in river terraces in the Somme Valley, northern France. His claim that these handaxes and bones provided evidence that the human story began long before the Book of Genesis suggested was not well received and was basically ignored by the French scientific elite, who viewed Boucher de Perthes as something of a provincial crank, and it was not until 1859 that his peers began to take him more seriously. In the spring of that year, the antiquarian John Evans and the geologist Joseph Prestwich, intrigued by Boucher de Perthes' discoveries, crossed the Channel from England to visit the French scholar. On the afternoon of 27 April, after earlier visiting gravel pits at Abbeville (where many Acheulean handaxes and extinct animal bones had turned up) with Boucher de Perthes, Evans and Prestwich were taken to see a handaxe that had only recently been found by workmen, embedded in one of the walls of a gravel pit at Saint-Acheul in the suburbs of Amiens. A sepia-tinted photograph survives and shows two workmen in the bottom of the pit: one points to the in-situ Acheulean handaxe above his right shoulder, while the other sits on a wheelbarrow nearby and gazes towards the ancient artefact. The figures in the photograph may be somewhat stilted and posed, but this early photograph from the mid-nineteenth century is quite remarkable as it represents 'the first use of photography to support claims for prehistoric evidence and captures the moment that human antiquity was established.'[19]

On his return to England, Joseph Prestwich read a paper to the Royal Society on 26 May 1859, which had a rather ponderous title typical of scientific papers of the time: 'On the Occurrence of Flint Implements associated with the remains of extinct species in beds of a late geological period at Amiens and Abbeville and in England at Hoxne.'[20] However, as has been noted of Prestwich's lecture to the Royal Society in 1859: 'Now in the same year that Darwin's Origin of Species shook the foundations of Western science, [Boucher de Perthes] was exonerated before the Royal Society in a meeting attended by the greatest scientists of the day.'[21] The following year, Sir John Lubbock accompanied Joseph Prestwich on his second visit to the gravel pits of the Somme Valley and was obviously impressed by what he saw: 'I am sure no geologist could return from such a visit without an overpowering sense of the change which has taken place and the enormous time which has elapsed since the first appearance of man in Western Europe.'[22] The visits of Evans, Prestwich and Lubbock to the Somme Valley gravel pits and the exoneration of Boucher de Perthes sounded the death-knell for the idea that humanity only dated back some 6,000 years: 'After 1859, it was an inescapable fact that humans had lived in very ancient times, and the Bible ceased to provide the framework for the past of humankind.'[23]

Acheulean handaxe found at Saint Acheul in the nineteenth century. (*Didier Descouens, Creative Commons*)

Many of the Acheulean handaxes found in Egypt have been stray finds, with what may be the oldest example yet known recovered from the desert cliffs that lie opposite one of ancient Egypt's most famous monuments: the awe-inspiring temple of Ramesses II at Abu Simbel in the lower Nile Valley.[24] Although no definitive date has been obtained for this handaxe, it has been 'dated by geological association to sediments laid down by the river some 700,000 years ago.'[25] Also worth mentioning is the striking Acheulean handaxe made from 'Libyan Desert Glass', which was found in the Western Desert in 1979. Libyan Desert Glass is only found in the Egyptian half of the 'Great Sand Sea', a region of the eastern Sahara that straddles the Egyptian-Libyan border, and the glass varies in colour 'from clear to milky, straw yellow, light green, dark green or even black'.[26] This rare artefact was fashioned from a yellowish, translucent fragment of glass and measures some 12cm long by 6cm at its widest point and 'About one face of the tool, and a small part of the other face near the tip, have suffered abrasion caused by blown sand' ('sand polish' or 'sand-blasting').[27] Although it cannot be proved definitively, the style of the handaxe and the way it was made suggest 'that it is more likely to be of lower Paleolithic (Acheulean) origin than anything else.'[28]

It is interesting to note that most scientists favour the theory that the numerous fragments of Libyan Desert Glass found strewn throughout the Great Sand Sea of Egypt are the result of a meteor impact at some point in the far distant past, in this region of the Western Desert: 'When an asteroid or comet pummels a planet's surface, the immense energy of the impact can melt large volumes of rock and soil. If this liquid rock cools quickly enough, it hardens into a solid – impact glass ["impacite"].'[29] Scientific studies of Libyan Desert Glass suggest that it formed about 29 million years ago, and some researchers have suggested that rather than resulting from a meteor 'impact', it formed after a 100-megaton 'airburst'[30] when a comet exploded over the desert, producing temperatures hot enough (c.1,800°C) to melt the sand and turn it to glass. The fact that no geological evidence has been found in the Egyptian Great Sand Sea for a meteor impact crater perhaps lends support to this idea. Either way, it is worth noting that in 1996, Italian mineralogist Vincenzo de Michele and Egyptian geologist Aly Barakat discovered that a yellow gemstone, carved to depict a scarab beetle and set in the middle of a beautiful 'pectoral' (a type of necklace) that was found in the tomb of King Tutankhamen, was made from a yellow fragment of Libyan Desert Glass.

Sites where several Acheulean handaxes have been found grouped together are also not uncommon in Egypt, with one of the best-known of these handaxe concentrations unearthed near the village of Nag Ahmed el Khalifa on the West Bank of the Nile, near Abydos, Middle Egypt. The site was discovered by Pierre Vermeersch and his colleagues, who came across several handaxes lying in a waste dump from a modern gravel quarry, located in a wadi near the village, with their presence 'suggesting that the mined deposits were rich in handaxes'.[31] Subsequent excavation of the gravel deposits confirmed that this was indeed the case, as almost 100 handaxes were recovered as well as several chopping tools, along with the 'cortical' waste flakes that were struck from the rough outer surface or 'cortex' of the chert cobbles used for the handaxes and other tools. Vermeersch and his colleagues have dated the site to the late Lower Palaeolithic c.400,000–300,000 years ago, concluding that it 'attests the nearby presence of an occupation of which the type remains unknown [and that the handaxe-makers] were selective in choosing their raw material, testing a cobble before proceeding to the handaxe shaping.'[32]

An even more impressive concentration of Acheulean handaxes was discovered in 1931, during the second season of the Royal Anthropological Institute's Prehistoric Research Expedition to Kharga Oasis in the Western Desert. This expedition was led by the archaeologist Gertrude Caton Thompson and the geologist Elinor Gardner, two important names from the early days of Egyptian Stone Age archaeology. As has been remarked, the work of Caton Thompson and Gardner represents 'The first systematic investigation of Pleistocene geology and Acheulean artifacts in the Egyptian Sahara.'[33] The handaxes were discovered beneath a series of 'tufa' deposits that had been laid down by an ancient fossil spring:

A magnificent collection of 500 hand-axes contained within an area not exceeding 30 square metres, in mint condition but glazed, with their attendant flake industry and cores was collected. The glaze was almost certainly produced by the flow of sandy waters in the spring and is not due to desert exposure.[34]

Many of the handaxes were of the classic 'lanceolate' or pear-shaped type, but there were also 'cordate' and 'ovate' types in the assemblage, with these handaxes more oval in form. Caton Thompson also mentions that some of the handaxes are 'miniatures under 4cm'[35] and although the function of these

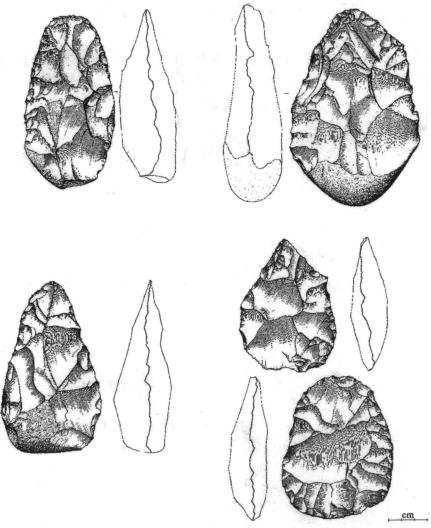

Acheulean handaxes from Nag Ahmed el-Khalifa. (*Professor Pierre Vermeersch*)

tiny handaxes is unclear, could it perhaps be possible that these intriguing artefacts from the distant past were children's toys?

Not long after Caton Thompson and Gardner unearthed the 'cache' of Acheulean handaxes at Kharga Oasis, the desert explorer and geologist Major Ralph Alger Bagnold led his third expedition to the Gilf Kebir region at the southern edge of the Great Sand Sea. The major wrote an evocative account of the 1938 expedition and its many interesting archaeological discoveries in *The Geographical Journal* (1939), which is well worth reading. The archaeologist Oliver H. Myers accompanied the major, and on the southern edge of the Gilf Kebir plateau, in the Wadi el Bakht, he 'discovered several Acheulean assemblages, characterized by abundant, sand-blasted handaxes.'[36] It seems that a long time was spent in the investigation of these assemblages as Myers recounts in the 1939 narrative of the expedition: 'Nearly three weeks were devoted to the clearance of an Acheulean surface site with instruments *in situ*.'[37]

In the early 1970s archaeological research carried out by the Combined Prehistoric Expedition in the Bir Tarfawi and Bir Sahara depressions in the Western Desert also discovered numerous Acheulean handaxes scattered around and in the remnants of ancient ponds and springs that had formed during an interval of significant rainfall in the Late Lower Palaeolithic or 'Upper Acheulean'. The scraps of equid bone (probably from a wild ass) and fragments of ostrich eggshell also found in one of the Bir Sahara springs indicate the presence of a savannah-type landscape. The Combined Prehistoric Expedition also carried out excavations at ancient fossil springs near the village of Mut, about 60 miles west of Kharga Oasis, and these springs 'contained an extremely rich assemblage of Upper Acheulean artifacts, including over a thousand handaxes.'[38]

In 1984–85, the US Geological Survey (USGS) and the Egyptian Geological Survey and Mining Authority uncovered numerous Acheulean sites in the Western Desert at Wadi Arid and Wadi Safsaf, which had once been river valleys in the Lower Palaeolithic (known as 'radar rivers' or 'palaeo-valleys'). These ancient valleys were discovered by the imaging radar (SIR-A) of the space shuttle Columbia in 1981, and 'backhoe excavations' carried out on the ground brought to light both isolated and small groups of Acheulean handaxes. The team that carried out the survey have also noted that on the southern margin of Bir Safsaf is a recorded but unstudied site (84M9-12), 'which stretches for at least 1.2km in a slightly irregular arc. Here hundreds or perhaps even thousands of handaxes form a discontinuous cover (lag) that…marks an ancient topographic feature – a river bank or terrace, an island, or possibly a former dry river channel.'[39]

More recent discoveries of Acheulean handaxes and other Lower Paleolithic tools have been made in the Western Desert. For example, in 1996 C. Vance Haynes and his colleagues found a cluster of three handaxes and twelve cleavers at the base of a plateau while investigating buried Lower Palaeolithic river channels[40] near Bir Kiseiba – 'a typical watering place on the ancient caravan route'[41] – in the south-west corner of the Western Desert. Returning to Bir Kiseiba in 1998, they discovered a further twenty-six additional Acheulean surface sites, although only one of these (KAS-15) was mapped, with thirty handaxes and thirty-eight cleavers identified, as well as a small number of choppers and picks. In 2000, the Abydos Survey for Paleolithic Sites (ASPS) found 'multiple, large thick and fairly crude handaxes'[42] at site ASPS-20, a high desert 'hammada' (a rocky plain or plateau) above Abydos. The survey also identified several other probable Lower Palaeolithic sites (e.g. ASPS-19), which 'are locales where stone raw material was tested for its usefulness in producing flakes to use as tools or to fashion into tools'.[43] Rather remarkably, at these sites it was discovered that it was possible to refit the flakes onto the stone cores from which they had been detached, revealing that the sites had remained undisturbed for many thousands of years.

Although it now lies just over the Egyptian border in northern Sudan, one of the most important and largest sites relating to Lower Palaeolithic life in the Nile Valley is Arkin 8 near the town of Wadi Halfa. This extensive site was discovered in wadi sediments on the Nile's West Bank and is thought to date to the Late Lower Palaeolithic. Several 'quarries' and 'workshops' yielding 3,400 crudely-made Acheulean handaxes (perhaps because they were unfinished) and other tools such as choppers and side-scrapers were excavated by the Polish archaeologist Waldemar Chmielewski in the mid-1960s. Also uncovered at Arkin 8 were two intriguing structures, one of which comprised a shallow oval depression measuring 1.8m by 1.2m, with flat sandstone slabs lining its floor; the other was less easy to define, consisting of a rough circular arrangement of large sandstone blocks. As has been said of these structures, 'From such finds it seems possible that at Arkin 8 we are dealing with the remains of one or more "tent rings" in which heavy rocks were used to tack down skins or brush that formerly were stretched over a makeshift frame.'[44]

The Acheulean Handaxe Enigma

Thousands of Acheulean handaxes may have been recovered from sites along the fringes of the Nile Valley and in the Western Desert but, like their counterparts scattered throughout the Old World, they remain something of a prehistoric puzzle. It has been pointed out that 'there is still much disagreement regarding the function of the Acheulean handaxe', [although] 'it appears to be universally agreed that one, although not necessarily the only, function was that of a heavy duty butchery tool.'[45] Indeed, even though examples have been found in association with butchered animal bones, it does seem likely that Acheulean handaxes, which were generally robust implements, would have been used for tasks other than butchery, such as digging, processing edible plants and chopping wood, leading to them jokingly being called the 'Swiss Army Knife' of the Lower Palaeolithic. Use-wear analysis of Acheulean handaxes lends support to the idea that they were used for a variety of tasks. For example, two chert handaxes recovered from Wonderwerk Cave in the Northern Cape Province, South Africa, displayed (under a high-powered microscope) 'microwear polish' that 'closely resembles that of experimental polish resulting from working plant material'.[46]

One interesting suggestion as to the function of Acheulean handaxes is that they were primarily designed as weapons: 'projectile weaponry would have allowed *H. erectus* (as it permits *H. sapiens sapiens*) to wound, maim, kill, etc., an animal while avoiding, delaying or eliminating the threat of physical retaliation or assault.'[47] Using a fibreglass replica of an Acheulean handaxe from the famous Kenyan site of Olorgesailie made by staff at the National Museums of Kenya, Eileen O'Brien conducted an experiment to test this theory at the University of Massachusetts discus/shot-put practice field in 1978, with 'discus-style' chosen as the most efficient method for throwing the handaxe. It was concluded from the experiment that 'As a projectile, the classic handaxe is functionally and efficiently designed. Experiments reveal that it can be used effectively this way…. When combined with the superior strength of *H. erectus*…the handaxe would have been an important weapon.'[48] This theory, however, has not found much favour with experts and the evidence does seem to argue against it: 'No characteristic throwing wear or impact damage has been proposed or identified for handaxes; what use-wear information is available supports interpretations of handaxes as multipurpose tools often used for butchering.'[49] Furthermore, 'The original [O'Brien] experiment…was flawed in its use of a fiber-glass replica – a sharp-edged handaxe is quite unpleasant to throw.'[50] Nevertheless, Acheulean handaxes may have been used – at least occasionally – as projectile weapons to kill or repel wild animals, and perhaps they were even sometimes used as weapons of 'war' by their makers as a handaxe could certainly inflict serious injuries – or even death – if wielded in anger.

The most puzzling aspect of Acheulean handaxes is why their makers often seem to have 'over-engineered' what were basically multi-purpose, workaday tools to produce symmetrical and finely-shaped artefacts, the basic form of which remained unchanged for well over a million years. As has been said, 'the finesse, exactitude and apparent aesthetic sense worked into what are essentially meat knifes demands an adequate explanation.'[51] Of course, any explanations about the 'meaning' of Acheulean handaxe form are open to question, but one controversial theory worth considering in this regard is that

> Those hominids...who were able to make fine symmetrical handaxes may have been preferentially chosen by the opposite sex as mates. Just as a peacock's tail may reliably indicate its 'success', so might the manufacture of a fine symmetrical handaxe have been a reliable indicator of the hominid's ability to secure food, find shelter, escape from predation and compete successfully within the social group. Such hominids would have been attractive mates, their abilities indicating 'good genes'.[52]

This idea 'that handaxes were products of sexual selection'[53] is a plausible one, but the 'Sexy Handaxe Theory' has not found favour with all experts. For example, it has been argued that 'Handaxes do not...make reliable indicators

of reproductive merit since they could easily be loaned out and may have circulated more as communal property than individual property, as is typical of almost all material possessions in simple hunter-gatherer societies.'[54] It could even be the case that scholars are over-complicating things in their attempts to unravel the enigma of why Acheulean handaxes were 'designed' in such a specific way: 'The simplest explanation for this is that hominin knappers experienced pleasure from this accomplishment.'[55] If so, the maker of the giant Acheulean handaxe or 'ficron' found at the site of Cuxton in Kent in 2005 must surely have derived pleasure from the remarkable artefact that he or she crafted, and it has been said of this ancient artisan: 'This is an individual knapper, recognizing his or

Giant Acheulean handaxe or 'ficron' from Cuxton. (*Copyright of Dr Francis Wenban-Smith*)

her skill and revelling in it.'[56] The Cuxton handaxe is huge (a pointed type known as a 'ficron' by archaeologists), measuring c.31cm long and c.12 cm wide, and 'Besides its extreme size, the workmanship of this new Cuxton find is exquisite, almost flamboyant.'[57] Several other Acheulean handaxes were recovered from the Cuxton site along with a very impressive cleaver measuring c.18cm long by c.13cm wide.

We will never be able to say for sure what Acheulean handaxes meant to their makers, but there is no doubt that they are 'one of the most iconic, analyzed and fiercely debated artefacts from the early prehistoric period.'[58] These ancient artefacts are also often rather beautiful in appearance and provide us with a striking reminder of our early hominid ancestors who walked the earth hundreds of thousands of years ago.

Chapter Two

Middle and Upper Palaeolithic Sites

R esearch carried out in the later twentieth century by the Belgian Middle Egypt Prehistoric Project of Leuven University[1] identified many Middle Palaeolithic quarrying and stone tool production sites along a stretch of the Nile Valley running from Asyut to Qena, an area noted for huge and impressive limestone cliffs that border the River Nile on either side. Like us, the people who opened up these prehistoric quarries were *Homo sapiens* or modern humans, albeit living very different lives from the ones that we are used to. Pierre Vermeersch and his colleagues have noted: 'It appears from our research that the raw materials sought by Palaeolithic man for the manufacture of artifacts were chert cobbles with a mean diameter of about 10 cm.'[2] These cobbles, which are exotic in origin,[3] were deposited in the Nile Valley from ancient tributaries upstream of Qena and are found in ancient terraces above the River Nile, most of which are located below 50 metres. Chert is generally considered to be a less pure form of flint, and the chert and flint nodules that provided the Stone Age communities of Egypt (and elsewhere) with a ready-made and easily worked source of raw material for their stone tools are similar in appearance and texture (although flint is darker and finer-grained than chert). This helps to explain why archaeologists quite often use the words 'flint' and 'chert' interchangeably.

Middle Palaeolithic communities did not simply open up these chert extraction sites at random and obviously recognized parts of the landscape that were suitable in this respect, showing that they had 'A good understanding of the local geomorphology [landscape features] and geology'[4] of the Nile Valley. Many of the extracted cobbles found at these sites also have just a single flake removed from their outer surface or 'cortex', revealing how prehistoric flint knappers were testing the quality of their raw material. Experienced knappers would be able to recognize the better-quality cobbles by the sound they made when struck with a hard hammer stone, resulting in the removal of a single flake.

Taramsa-1

The most notable of these Egyptian Middle Palaeolithic quarries is the large and impressive site of Taramsa-1, located on an isolated low hill (Taramsa Hill, c.15m high) on the left bank of the Nile, about 1.5 miles south-east of the famous Dendera Temple complex (one of the best-preserved monuments from ancient Egypt). Taramsa-1 dates to the Late Middle Palaeolithic and the Belgian archaeologists discovered that numerous trenches and pits had been dug into the extensive deposit (c.4m thick) of chert cobbles that caps the hill, testifying to the many quarrying episodes that took place here throughout the Middle Palaeolithic. These trenches and pits reach depths of up to 2m but are generally about 0.5m deep and cover an area of around 1000m².

Much waste material or debitage associated with the production of stone tools using the Levallois technique was found during the excavations on the hilltop. Many of the finished artefacts made at these sites must have been 'exported' to nearby settlements, although unfortunately these living sites are likely to have been buried beneath the alluvia or mud laid down by more recent Nile floods. Nevertheless, caches of Levallois flakes or blanks for stone tools have also been found at Taramsa-1, 'at some distance from the spots where they were produced, clearly having been selected away and stored for future use.'[5] Furthermore, several 'stockpiles' of chert nodules were found near areas of the site that had clearly been locations associated with stone-tool production.

An important aspect of the lithic assemblage at Taramsa-1 is that 'it shows evidence of technological experimentation…resulting in a volumetric blade technology using the Levallois method.'[6] In other words, it is at Taramsa-1 that we see the beginnings of the new stone-tool technology of the Upper Palaeolithic, which was based around the production of narrow blades or 'blanks' on which various stone tools were made.

As well as providing fascinating evidence relating to the quarrying and production of stone tools during the Middle Palaeolithic, the burial of the earliest 'Egyptian' yet found was discovered at Taramasa-1 by Pierre Vermeersch and his colleagues. This rare and hugely important find came to light in March 1994 when a human skull and a few bones were spotted in a dump of waste material lying against the wall of an ancient extraction pit. It was apparent that the skull and bones were brittle and also in danger of being destroyed by cobbles from the wall of the pit, which had started to collapse. It was therefore prudently decided to carry out an immediate excavation, which subsequently uncovered the partially and poorly-preserved skeleton of

The Taramsa-1 child burial. (*Professor Pierre Vermeersch, Belgian Middle Egypt Prehistoric Project of Leuven University*)

a young boy or girl (probably aged 8 to 10), who – rather poignantly – was placed in a seated position on the floor of the pit, leaning backwards against a bed of sand with his/her face looking up to the sky. What caused the death of the child is unknown, but even for the standards of the time when most people did not live much beyond thirty years, he or she died well before their time.

The skeleton was examined by a leading expert in the study of human evolution, Professor Chris Stringer, who confirmed that the boy or girl was an anatomically modern *Homo sapiens* and it has been noted that 'the child has a relatively large face with [facial and cranial] anatomy similar to the modern humans from Qafzeh and Skhul.'[7] Located in northern Israel, these hugely important cave sites yielded an unrivalled collection of Middle Palaeolithic human fossils roughly dating to c.90,000–120,000 years ago, with the remains of ten early modern or 'archaic' humans unearthed at Skhul and five at Qafzeh in the earlier twentieth century. An intriguing discovery made at Qafzeh was the double burial of a young woman and child, with the child's skeleton laid at the feet of the woman's, suggesting a close familial relationship (mother and child?) between the two individuals. It has been noted that the ancient human remains found at Qafzeh and Skhul 'appear to represent a range extension of east African modern humans into southwestern Asia during a warm phase of [the Middle Palaeolithic].'[8]

Exactly when the young boy or girl uncovered at Taramsa-1 was buried seems to be a matter of debate. Originally, Pierre Vermeersch and his colleagues proposed a date of c.55,000 BCE in the Late Middle Palaeolithic, but following a more recent dating of samples from the site taken from material 'immediately relevant to the burial situation'[9] they now favour an earlier date of c.75,000 years ago. However, it has been argued that it is more likely that the child was buried some 24,000 years ago,[10] which, if correct, would mean that the Taramsa-1 burial was carried out in the Late Upper Palaeolithic.

As has also been pointed out, 'The Taramsa skeleton is evidently relevant to the issue of the origin and "Out of Africa 2" by anatomically modern *Homo sapiens*.'[11] Basically, the Out of Africa 2 theory posits that there were two significant waves of modern human migration from northern Africa to Europe and Asia: 'Two distinct movements have been recognized within the Out-of-Africa-2 model, one occurring between c. 130 and 80 ka [thousand years ago], the other taking place after 50 ka.'[12]

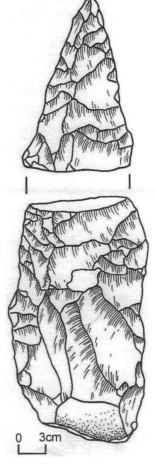

Another important quarrying and production site from Late Middle Palaeolithic Egypt is Nazlet Safaha, which lies about 30 miles downstream of Taramsa-1. At Nazlet Safaha, prehistoric workers extracted chert cobbles from 'Several distinct exploitation sites',[13] with the pits and trenches similar in size to those found at Taramsa-1, although they cover a much larger area measuring about 3000 m². It has been noted that 'The total area exploited at Nazlet Safaha and Taramsa 1 can be prudently estimated at 20,000m² [and that] 5,000,000 [cobbles] have been extracted from...these two sites alone.'[14] In fact, in total many millions of chert cobbles must have been extracted from all the Late Middle Palaeolithic quarries identified by the Belgian Middle Egypt Prehistoric Project. This lends support to the idea that in the Late Middle Palaeolithic, the area of the Nile Valley in which these sites are found was more densely populated than might otherwise be assumed.

0   3cm

Lanceolate point from Taramsa-8. (*Redrawn after Van Peer et al., 2008*)

It is also worth mentioning that at the chert extraction site of Taramsa-8 (located about 1 mile south of Tarmasa-1), evidence was found to suggest that 'complex tools were being produced at workshops, probably to be exported to living sites, which are still not found.'[15] This evidence took the form of a superbly made but broken 'lanceolate' point that was found in an extraction ditch along with the stone flakes from its production (another lanceolate fragment and a bifacial axe were also found in the ditch). Microwear analysis of this large stone projectile was carried out using a stereoscopic microscope. This revealed that it had originally been hafted (presumably in a wooden shaft), but had subsequently fractured in two when a knapper was completing its final shaping, leading to the lanceolate point being thrown into the ditch by its presumably frustrated maker. As pointed out, this evidence of hafting may indicate that not only stone tools but also hafts were produced in the workshops at the Egyptian Middle Palaeolithic chert quarries.[16]

Nazlet Khater-4

Excavated in the 1980s by the Belgian Middle Egypt Prehistoric Project, the Upper Palaeolithic chert extraction site of Nazlet Khater-4 is of undoubted importance: not only are sites dating to this period very rare in Egypt, but it has also provided some of the oldest archaeological evidence for underground mining in the world. In fact, the only evidence for underground mining which pre-dates that from Nazlet Khater-4 is that recovered from 'Lion Cavern' at the Ngwenya Iron Mine in Swaziland. Excavations carried out here in the mid-twentieth century revealed that Upper Palaeolithic communities had targeted a seam of 'specularite-rich haematite' (red ochre or bloodstone), and it was estimated that about 33 tons were removed by Middle Palaeolithic miners.[17]

Nazlet Khater-4 is situated in Middle Egypt near the rural village from which it takes its name, not far from a jutting limestone cliff c.300m in height which forms a rather spectacular backdrop to the site. Upper Palaeolithic people dug a complex and quite sophisticated network of ditches, vertical shafts and low, horizontal underground galleries in order to reach a deposit of chert cobbles (c.0.5m thick). The ditches measured c.1m wide by c.1m deep and the shafts were dug down to a depth of 2m, some of which had been widened at the bottom to form bell-shaped pits. The horizontal galleries start from the trench walls or the bottom of pits and in some cases extend as far as 10m underground, with many linked together by subterranean passages. The galleries would have been cramped, hot and oppressive places in which to work, and they may also have been dangerous, with the fragments of wood found in some galleries perhaps the remains of wooden support posts that had been put in place in order to prevent their collapse. Whatever the case, the excavations revealed that some of the gallery roofs had collapsed, perhaps during the Upper Palaeolithic mining operations at the site, although it is probably more likely that these collapses occurred a long time after the abandonment of the mining complex.

Scratch marks from the picks used to extract chert cobbles still survive on the walls of some shafts and galleries at Nazlet Khater-4, and a few picks were actually found still in place in some of the galleries and shafts. The horns of gazelle and hartebeest were used as picks, the ends of which are worn, testifying to their use as cobble extraction tools. Also discovered were around thirty large hammerstones that were probably used for loosening the chert cobbles in the walls of the ditches; most were made from limestone cobbles, but chert was also used for some examples. Other archaeological evidence from Nazlet Khater-4 includes the remains of six hearths containing fragments of charcoal, with one hearth containing burned branches, waste material from stone-working, a couple of small bifacial stone axes or 'adzes' used as hammers in chert extraction, and the shells of edible freshwater mussels brought to the site from the River Nile. This evidence suggests that Upper Palaeolithic people may have been living at Nazlet Khater-4 while working there, at least on a short-term basis. The Upper Palaeolithic date of Nazlet Khater-4 was confirmed by the radiocarbon dating of charcoal

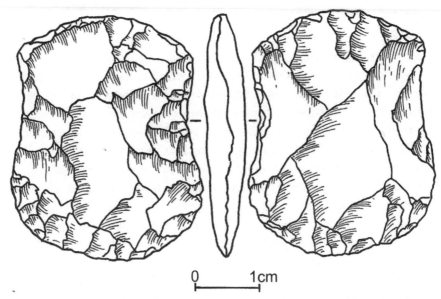

0   1cm

Small bifacial flint axe from Nazlet Khater-4. (*Redrawn after Vermeersch, 2010*)

fragments taken from the hearths and other parts of the site. The dates obtained indicate that Nazlet Khater-4 was in use for a long period of time, with mining activities beginning at the site around 40,000 years ago in the Early Upper Palaeolithic and only ending some 5,000 years later.

The Nazlet Khater Burials

In early 1980, the Belgian Middle Egypt Prehistoric Project was excavating a Middle Palaeolithic chert extraction site on 'Boulder Hill',[18] near the village of Nazlet Khater, when they unexpectedly came across two skeletons placed in crude graves comprising natural desiccation cracks that had formed in the dried-out, ancient clay deposits covering the hill.

The first grave contained a skeleton lying on its back in two adjoining pits dug into the desiccation crack, and 'The body orientated NW-SE, had been laid on its back in a contracted position, legs joined together but upright. Arms were flexed towards the skull.'[19] The people responsible for the burial had also placed limestone boulders in the grave fill, above the ribcage and the head area. Unfortunately, the skeleton was so badly preserved that its 'bones disintegrated when blown upon'.[20] All that could be ascertained from a later study of the skeletal remains by physical anthropologist Veerle Van Rossum was that they belonged to an adult of indeterminate age or sex. Charcoal fragments and a piece of ostrich eggshell were found in the grave, and a patch of burned earth was also noted just below the ribs of the skeleton. Pierre Vermeersch has remarked: 'I am tempted to consider the ostrich eggshell as a grave good because it…is probably not intrusive from above. The interpretation of the burned earth and the charcoal is more difficult to evaluate. Has it something to do with a certain burial practice?'[21] The archaeologists also made the sad discovery of some tiny rib bones and vertebrae, either from a foetus or newborn baby. One of the charcoal fragments found in the grave was dated by accelerator mass spectrometry (AMS for short), with the result suggesting that its occupants had been laid to rest on Boulder Hill c.39,000 BCE in the Early Upper Palaeolithic.

The second burial, which only lay about 30m to the south, had also been placed in a slightly modified narrow desiccation crack, with limestone boulders again placed in the grave fill as if to protect the body; a very large boulder that lay nearby may have marked the position of the grave (Plate 3). In contrast to the other burial, the skeleton was well-preserved and belonged to a young adult male. It was also virtually complete, only lacking the foot bones and those from the bottom parts of the tibia and fibula, making 'it the oldest almost complete…modern human skeleton in northern Africa.'[22]

The young man had been buried in the grave lying on his back at full length, with his left arm bent so that his hand rested on his pelvis. On the floor of the grave, next to the right-hand side of the skull, somebody had placed a small bifacial stone axe very similar to those found at Nazlet Khater-4 and, as noted, 'It is clearly to be considered a grave good.'[23]

Although at the time the Belgian archaeologists were unable to obtain a date from the skeleton of 'Nazlet Khater Man', they reasonably concluded that he was also buried in the Early Upper Palaeolithic, around the same time as his less well-preserved counterpart in the other grave on Boulder Hill. Not only were both individuals laid to rest lying on their backs in similar graves, both grave fills also consisted of loose aeolian sand and local limestone boulders. That Nazlet Khater Man was also an inhabitant of Early Upper Palaeolithic Egypt was later confirmed when Electron Spin Resonance (ESR) dating on fragments of his tooth enamel provided a date range of c.40,000–34,000 years ago. Therefore, as with the other burial from Boulder Hill, this date is consistent with the dates obtained for the chert mining activity at Nazlet Khater-4, 'which ranged from 40–35 ka, and confirms the association between the two sites.'[24] The fact that Nazlet Khater-4 only lies about 400m south-east of Boulder Hill lends support to this association, as does the stone axe buried with Nazlet Khater Man which, as previously mentioned, closely resembles those found at the nearby chert mine. Thus, as Pierre Vermeersch has remarked, 'It therefore seems very likely that the Nazlet Khater burials are related to the Upper Palaeolithic population...which practised chert mining at Nazlet Khater-4.'[25]

Interestingly, detailed analysis of Nazlet Khater Man's skeleton by French physical anthropologist Isabelle Crevecoeur brought to light interesting evidence on his bones to suggest that he was involved in 'intensive mining activities'.[26] For example, there were lesions on the cervical vertebrae, revealing that he had arthritis in his neck and there were also 'rotator cuff lesions' on his left humerus or upper arm bone. Lesions such as these have been recorded in Neolithic or more recent populations involved 'in specific activities like mining extractions [and] might be related to heavy load carrying with forehead straps.'[27] There were other skeletal signs pointing towards Nazlet Khater's involvement in mining activities, such as the slight deformation or bony lesion identified on one of his right metacarpals (finger bones), perhaps caused by the repeated impact on his hand while using an extraction tool such as a stone axe to loosen and remove chert cobbles. Metacarpal lesions such as these have been identified on the skeletons of more recent miners, such as the ones who worked at the Brandes-en-Oisans

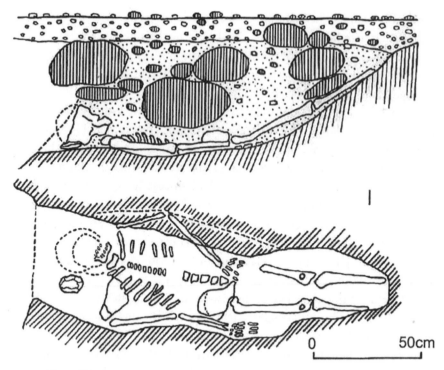

Plan of Nazlet Khater Man's burial. (*Redrawn after Vermeersch et al., 1984*)

Medieval lead and silver mine in the French Alps between the twelfth and fourteenth centuries AD.

Isabelle Crevecoeur thus concluded from her analysis that the 'palaeopathologies' seen on the skeleton of Nazlet Khater Man pointed to 'a coercive lifestyle that subjected this individual to heavy mechanical stress.'[28] In his earlier analysis of Nazlet Khater Man's skeleton, Andor Thoma also noted that one of his upper leg bones (the femoral diaphysis) displayed a strong curvature that might have been a 'response to heavy burdens that the individual had had to carry since childhood.'[29] Whether Nazlet Khater Man was forced against his will to work in an Upper Palaeolithic chert mine can never be known. However, it is not impossible, and as Thoma further suggested, this young man from Egypt's distant past may have been a slave worked to death in a chert mine.[30]

Bir Tarfawi

Located in the far south of Egypt's Western Desert, Bir Tarfawi is a large 'deflational basin'[31] measuring some 9 miles north-south and 2 miles east-west, with the archaeological work carried out here in 1973–74 and 1985–87 by the Combined Prehistoric Expedition[32] yielding much important evidence relating to life in Middle Palaeolithic Egypt. Indeed, it has been stated that 'the Middle Palaeolithic record at Bir Tarfawi is unparalleled. The number and state of preservation of many of the sites provide a unique opportunity for the study of Middle Palaeolithic society [in Egypt].'[33] Today, Bir Tarfawi is located in one of the harshest and hottest places on the planet, but things would have been very different here in the Middle Palaeolithic as a sequence of four lake-episodes (dated from about 160,000 to 60,000 years ago) was identified during the archaeological investigation of Bir Tarfawi. These lakes testify to wet or 'humid' periods with significant amounts of rainfall in the Middle Palaeolithic and would have been set in 'a kind of dry savanna with…shrubs and trees.'[34]

The Combined Prehistoric Expedition's investigation of the rich Palaeolithic archaeology of Bir Tarfawi brought to light 'a complex pattern of specialized site-types'[35] that had specific functions. Site E-86-1, for example, was one of several similar sites found around a silt-pan that represented a dried-up seasonal pool. There was one thin 'cultural horizon' or layer of artefacts at the site, which comprised many Levallois cores and flakes and a limited number of stone tools. It seems that the site was a temporary workshop where stone tools were produced over a brief period, with the raw material coming from outcrops of quartzitic sandstone about 2 miles away. Living sites were also identified on the ancient remnants of the beaches that had once fringed the lake edges, with some representing single occupations and others multiple reoccupations of the same site.

The most notable site at Bir Tarfawi is BT-14, of which it has been said '[its] extensive faunal remains…plus its great size and the presence of internal artifact clusters within the site distinguish it as one of the most important Palaeolithic finds in Egypt.'[36] The excavations here unearthed some 1,700 stone tools (of the Aterian industry) and an abundance of very well-preserved animal bones from species such as rhinoceros, giraffe, warthog, buffalo, jackal, hyena, extinct Pleistocene camel, gazelle and even porcupine. BT-14 was clearly used as a place where animal carcasses were processed for their meat by Middle Palaeolithic communities and an early excavation report describes the place as a 'huge Aterian kill site with numerous bones scattered over an area measuring a few thousand square metres.'[37] Also recovered from site BT-14 were ostrich eggshells, grinding stones probably used for processing plant foods, and stone 'anvils' that may have been used for smashing animal bones by Middle Palaeolithic people.

Most of the animal bones found at Bir Tarfawi came from dorcas and dama gazelle, and as Achilles Gautier has noted:

> This situation can be interpreted in two ways. Middle Palaeolithic man at Bir Tarfawi may have been a hunter bagging mainly gazelles and including only now and then larger [animals] in his hunter's bag. However, he may also have been a successful hunter but of gazelles and smaller creatures such as porcupine, occasionally scavenging on the carcasses of the bigger game.... In the latter case, the few finds of jackal and hyena may be the remnants of scavenging carnivores man had to kill when he stole the prey of these or other carnivores.[38]

Another Middle Palaeolithic butchery site (BS-14) was discovered in 1973 by the Combined Prehistoric Expedition in the Bir Sahara depression, which only lies some 9 miles to the east of Bir Tarfawi. The remnants of two separate lakes were identified, around which were found numerous animal bones similar to those recovered from Bir Tarfawi, as well as an abundance of snail shells and some ostrich eggshells.

Bahariya Oasis

In 2003–2004 a joint archaeological survey[39] was undertaken at Bahariya Oasis, a large depression in the Western Desert, about 230 miles west of Cairo. An area measuring c.19 × 13 miles was surveyed and brought to light a considerable amount of archaeological evidence relating to the lives of the hunter-gatherer communities who lived here during the Middle Palaeolithic. Five isolated Acheulean handaxes were also found scattered widely apart in the landscape during the survey, revealing earlier occupation of the area by *Homo erectus* during the Lower Palaeolithic.

Near the Umm el-Okhbain and Mannsaf 'playas', which represent the remains of ancient lakes long since dried up, concentrations of Middle Palaeolithic tools were discovered. These tools testify to 'cumulative settlement' (i.e. repeated occupations) near the edges of the lakes, and various artefacts such as Mousterian points, side-scrapers, burins, retouched blades and finely-made 'leaf-points' were found.

On the peaks of Gebel el-Showish (a dominant mountain ridge in the area that reaches about c.280m in height), the survey team found several 'mountain-top workshops' where Levallois stone tools had been made. Dense accumulations of stone-working debris were found scattered around the outcrops of quartzite and chert that had provided the raw material for these tools. Another workshop was recorded on the top of 'Black Mountain',

Landscape in Bahariya Oasis. (*Ahmedehab1, Creative Commons*)

another ridge located about 4 miles north-east of Gebel el-Showish, and a scatter of stone-working debris found on the southern edge of the 'White Mountain' limestone escarpment was interpreted as a possible 'strategic hunting post'.

Somewhat curiously, no evidence was found at the lower-lying Middle Palaeolithic settlements 'of a direct import of products down from the [mountain workshops]',[40] so where the stone tools made at these elevated production sites ended up remains unknown.

Sodmein Cave

In contrast to its western counterpart, signs of Stone Age life are scanty in the Eastern Desert, but there is the important site of Sodmein Cave situated in the Red Sea Mountains c.25 miles from the town of Quseir al-Qadim on the Red Sea coast. Excavations were carried out in the cave by the Belgian Middle Egypt Prehistoric Project in the 1990s and archaeological evidence left behind by both Middle and Upper Palaeolithic groups was discovered (evidence of Neolithic inhabitation was also found in the cave).

Sodmein Cave is large but quite shallow, and stands at the bottom of an impressive limestone cliff with five Middle Palaeolithic levels and two Upper Palaeolithic levels (ranging in date from c.120,000–250,000 years ago) uncovered here, although the various groups who had lived in the cave had not done so for very long:

> Prehistoric man very often visited and revisited the cave site. However, from the extent of the occupation debris, we may deduce that his stay at the cave was of very short duration, even only for overnight. The cave was probably a halt place for people that, for some unknown reason, had to travel along the Red Sea coast.[41]

The remains of several fireplaces were also discovered in the cave, with the earliest Middle Palaeolithic example yielding the burned bones of animals such as elephant, buffalo and crocodile indicating that the landscape was very different than the one that exists in the locality of the cave today and that there must have been an open source of water somewhere in the area. The presence of these bones points towards successful 'big game hunts' by Middle Palaeolithic hunting parties.

Two 'Emireh points' were also identified in the latest, uppermost Middle Palaeolithic level (MP 1) at Sodmein Cave. These stone projectiles are a characteristic feature of the Late Middle/Early Upper Palaeolithic Emiran industry of the Levant,[42] and are named after the cave-site of Emireh in eastern Galilee, Israel, where it was discovered. These two artefacts may well indicate the arrival of immigrants in Egypt, but if so, where they came from is uncertain as archaeologists have proposed three places of origin for the Emiran industry: the southern Levant where it was first recognized, north-east Africa and the Arabian Peninsula. However, it has also been argued that 'the specimens [from Sodmein Cave] do not fit the definition of Emireh points' and instead should be classified as Levallois points.[43]

Microwear analysis on one of these Emireh/Levallois points and other Middle Palaeolithic projectile points found in the cave revealed impact damage on their ends. Levallois lithics that had been used as the tips of thrusting spears were also identified as a result of this analysis, along with a woodworking tool and a butchering knife. A few other stone tools (e.g. burins) were recovered during the excavations in the cave, along with many cores, blades and flakes relating to Upper and Middle Palaeolithic stone-tool production.

An Aterian Hunting Site on the Gilf Kebir Plateau?

The Gilf Kebir ('Great Barrier') plateau is a huge sandstone landmass (rising to 300m in height and covering an area of around 3,000 square miles) located in the far south-west of Egypt's Western Desert that is best known for its remarkable prehistoric rock-art sites (more of which in the next chapter).[44] However, many other Stone Age sites have been discovered in the harsh but spectacular landscapes of the Gilf Kebir such as the small but intriguing one that Jean-Loïc Le Quellec and his colleagues came across during their archaeological surveys of the plateau between 2004 and 2011.

The site is located on the edge of the plateau, at a height of about 1,025m in the southern part of the Gilf Kebir, and offers wide-ranging views out over the desert; as Le Quellec has noted, it 'would have provided a superb vantage point for hunters scouting animal herds in the valley below.'[45] A small cluster of Aterian artefacts was found at the site comprising two denticulates, the basal fragments of four broken tanged points, a leaf-shaped point and an almost complete tanged point with impact damage on its tip. This Aterian assemblage lay on the northern side of seven small heaps of sandstone roughly aligned in a straight line, which may have supported long-since decayed wooden poles of a structure of some sort, with an accumulation of stone-working debris found on the southern one. Le Quellec came up with an interesting interpretation of this intriguing evidence:

> According to the small extension of the lithic scatter on Site No. 2 (less than 100 sq m) and considering the organisation of [the] lithic industry on both sides of the stone line there, this location can be considered to be a specialized site.... Here...all the tanged tools are broken except one point showing [evidence of impact damage], and their disposition behind a line of wooden poles which might have been used to stretch a hunting net, strongly suggests the possibility of a hunting site.[46]

The evidence found at the site by Le Quellec and his colleagues does lend support to this idea, but what species of wild animal may have been hunted so high up in the southern Gilf Kebir by people of the Aterian culture remains unknown.

Chapter Three

The Oldest Art in Egypt

O f all the countless reminders of Stone Age life that survive in Egypt, there can be little doubt that the rock art[1] found at numerous sites along the Nile valley and in the Western and Eastern Deserts ranks among the most enigmatic. This ancient imagery often possesses a rather haunting quality: pictorial messages from the distant past made by people who have long since gone, but to whom we feel connected because of the innate human desire to create art. It does seems highly unlikely, however, that Egyptian rock art was simply 'art for art's sake' and that Stone Age people came to gaze at in the same way that we do when we look at artworks in galleries and museums. What motivated the various peoples of the Egyptian Stone Age to produce this rock art, and what it means, can obviously never be known for sure. However, as will be seen, some interesting suggestions have been put forward in this regard by those scholars who study this somewhat undervalued but hugely intriguing aspect of Egypt's prehistoric past.

The 'Ice Age' Art of Qurta

In 1962–63, archaeologists of the Canadian Prehistoric Expedition discovered prehistoric rock art depicting wild cattle and other animals near the village of Qurta on the northern edge of the Kom Ombo Plain in Upper Egypt. As mentioned in the Introduction, the Canadian expedition discovered and excavated several Late Palaeolithic settlements of the Ballanan-Silsilian culture in this region and some of these lay near the rock art site, with one example only located about some 150m away. This suggested that the rock art could possibly have been created by the Late Palaeolithic communities who lived in these settlements. However, it was felt more likely that it was later in date than the Late Palaeolithic, and after its discovery by the archaeologists of the Canadian Prehistoric Expedition, the Qurta rock art was basically forgotten about for the next forty years or so, becoming little more than an interesting side note in the margins of Egyptian prehistory.

In October-November 2005, however, the Qurta rock art was rediscovered by an archaeological mission from the Belgian Royal Museums of Art and History, and in February-March 2007, they returned to begin a more intensive survey of the sandstone cliffs where the art was located. The Belgian archaeologists subsequently discovered three separate rock art sites (Qurta I, II & III) located high up on the cliffs at c.40m above the Nile floodplain, with at least 180 engraved images or 'petroglyphs' discovered during the survey. Most of the petroglyphs depict wild cattle or aurochs (Plate 4), but birds (waterfowl), hippopotami, fish, gazelle and hartebeest are also included in the Qurta rock art repertoire, as well as some highly-stylized human figures or 'anthropomorphs', and a few abstract, non-figurative symbols. Also worthy of mention is the strange, unidentifiable animal depicted at the Qurta II rock art site, which has a head of indefinite form, a lumpy body with two hind legs and a short tail. Whether this is just a badly executed rock drawing of a real animal or a depiction of some 'Otherworldly' creature is unclear, but the latter is probably more likely.

As has been pointed out, none of the animals depicted at Qurta show evidence of domestication and there is little doubt that the cattle 'should be identified as *Bos primigenius* or aurochs (wild cattle).'[2] Close analysis of the rock art images by the Belgian archaeologists revealed that they had been

General view of the sandstone cliffs at Qurta, location of one of the most important assemblages of prehistoric Egyptian rock art. (*Professor Wouter Claes, Belgian Mission to Qurta, Royal Museums of Art & History, Brussels*)

hammered ('pecked') or incised into the rock with stone tools of some sort. Some of the rock art images were integrated with natural features and, for example, at Qurta II, a Stone Age artist had cleverly used a vertical crack to suggest/depict the back part of a large aurochs. A curious feature of some of the aurochs and hippopotami images is that numerous, haphazard shallow incisions or scratches were made in the rock immediately over where their heads and necks are depicted. Exactly why prehistoric people felt the need to do this is beyond our understanding, but it seems probable that these marks held some symbolic meaning and were not just randomly made.

The Belgian archaeologists initially felt that the Qurta rock art was indeed Late Palaeolithic in date, although at the time they had no evidence to support this theory. However, during their 2008 field campaign it was discovered that some of the rock art panels at the Qurta II site were partially covered by sandstone debris that had detached from the rock face, and also wind-blown 'aeolian' sand, which was rather fortuitous as the latter is 'ideally suited for optically stimulated luminescence (OSL) dating'.[3] Subsequent OSL dating of this sand by scientists at Ghent University, Belgium, showed that it began to accumulate at the base of the rock art panel at least c.15,000 years ago. This date, however, only provides a minimum age for the rock art and 'It is clear that the buried drawings at QII were already considerably weathered before they became covered by sediment [and] it seems likely therefore that the rock art is considerably older than the minimum ages obtained by means of OSL.'[4] Just how much older is hard to say for sure, but it has been estimated that the Qurta rock dates to c.17,000–15,000 BCE.

With regard to the possible meaning of the Qurta rock art, Dirk Huyge has pointed out, the cliffs upon which it was created 'offer a splendid view of the hunting and fishing grounds of the period.' Huyge has therefore wondered whether we can 'associate the rock art with a kind of practical magic associated with hunting [and] that the originators of the art tried in this way to dominate nature...by supernatural means?'[5] The 'hunting magic' theory became popular in the early twentieth century among scholars studying the 'parietal' (cave) art of Upper Palaeolithic or 'Ice Age' Europe, which has been dated to c.35,000–10,000 BCE. This theory has lost ground in more recent times and is no longer 'fashionable' among scholars of Ice Age art. Whatever the true symbolism of the rock art at Qurta, the fact remains that the place where it is located would have provided a good vantage point for Late Palaeolithic hunters. Furthermore, animal bones found by the Canadian archaeologists at the Late Palaeolithic settlement sites close to Qurta revealed that 'not only aurochs and hartebeest, but also hippopotamus, gazelle, fowl and fish figured on the menu',[6] all of which are depicted at the Qurta rock art sites.

The Qurta Rock Art: A European Connection?

An intriguing feature of the Qurta rock art is that stylistically it resembles the cave art of Upper Palaeolithic Europe. The people who created this European cave art left many stunning images for us to marvel at, such as those seen at the world-famous Chauvet and Lascaux caves in France and the equally renowned Cave of Altamira, Spain. In this respect it has been noted: 'As regards style and a number of iconographical particularities...the Qurta rock art shows remarkable affinities with the Late Magdalenian rock art of Europe.'[7] One of the most striking of these 'iconographical particularities' is that several of the Qurta aurochs are depicted with their rear legs folded back against the body in an unnatural position. This unusual feature can also be seen in the depictions of aurochs at other European cave art sites, with the most notable example provided by the 'jumping/falling cow' seen in the 'Axial Gallery' at Lascaux; some of the aurochs painted in the 'Apse' area of the cave are also depicted with their rear legs folded back. Furthermore, it has been noted that several of the aurochs at Qurta

> seem to be shown in dynamic poses, their backs curved and their legs bent as if in motion.... The raised position of the tails in some examples may be indicative of running. Some [aurochs] may be rendered frolicking, wheeling and fleeing, rolling in dust or mud onto the side, or may even be shown dead (which in some cases, may explain the unnaturally bent legs). All of these various postures have close counterparts in Franco-Cantabrian Palaeolithic art [found in caves in southern France and Spain].[8]

When examining the parallels seen in the rock art of Qurta and that of Ice Age Europe, the 'headless females' that appear alongside the animal imagery at Qurta should also definitely be considered as 'these can be closely compared to stereotyped stylized depictions of the female form found all across the European Magdalenian world.'[9] These stylized female figures of the so-called 'Gönnersdorf style' occur not only in the decorated caves of the European Upper Palaeolithic but also feature in the 'portable' art of this time. For instance, many engraved schist plaquettes featuring these figures were found at the famous cave site from which they take their name (with

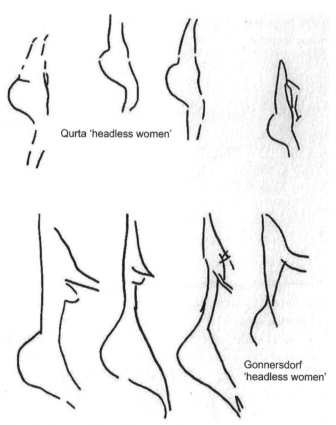

Drawings of 'headless humans' from Qurta and Gönnersdorf. (*Redrawn after Huyge, 2015*)

one example showing four females and what may be a small child), and they also occur on the cave walls at Gönnersdorf. Seven 'definite' examples of Gönnersdorf-type figures can be seen at the rock art panel of Qurta III, where two aurochs (one of which measures an impressive 1.86m in length, making it the largest aurochs drawing at Qurta) and a hippopotamus are also depicted. All the figures face right, appear to be organized in two rows and lack arms, head and feet.

The marked similarities seen between the Qurta rock art and the Ice Age art of Upper Palaeolithic Europe may be nothing more than a prehistoric coincidence rather than revealing connections between Late Palaeolithic groups in North Africa and Europe. On the other hand, 'If we consider... that the sea level of the Mediterranean during the last Ice Age was more than a hundred metres lower than at present, it is not impossible that Palaeolithic man was able to make intercontinental contact and to exchange artistic ideas and symbolism.'[10]

The Wadi Abu Subeira Rock Art

Qurta does not stand alone as the only place in Egypt to provide us with important examples of the 'artworks' of Late Palaeolithic hunter-gatherers, as archaeological surveys carried out by archaeologists from the Egyptian Supreme Council of Antiquities in the Wadi Abu Subeira between 2005 and 2013 uncovered several other rock art sites from this period. As at Qurta, all the animals depicted at these sites 'match the known faunal assemblage in the Upper Egyptian Late Palaeolithic.'[11] Furthermore, as at Qurta, the rock art was 'executed in a naturalistic "Franco-Cantabrian Lascaux-like" style'[12] at Wadi Subeira, and was created either by hammering or engraving. The Wadi Abu Subeira is located about 8 miles north of Aswan in Upper Egypt and at c.35 miles long, is one of the longest wadis or dry valleys in the Eastern Desert. As Per Storemyr has noted, in the Late Palaeolithic:

> The broad Wadi Abu Subeira may have been a small 'fjord', reaching several kilometres into the Eastern Desert: a great habitat for wildlife in the otherwise hyperarid environment and a great place for humans to stay – to fish and hunt – and to access the interior of the desert and perhaps the Red Sea…over the millennia erosion along the slopes of the wadi has probably destroyed many pictures, and most are now found on boulders and slabs. However, some are still in situ…. The rock art is comparable to the better-known occurrence at Qurta by Kom Ombo.[13]

The largest rock art site at Wadi Abu Subeira is Site CAS-6, situated about 1.3 miles from the wadi entrance on a rocky sandstone escarpment measuring c.20–25m in height. More than 100 petroglyphs have been found along a c.1.3-mile stretch of the escarpment, with most of the rock art located in a secondary position on boulders that have tumbled down onto a natural terrace from the top of the escarpment where they were originally located. Smaller numbers of in situ rock art panels survive on the vertical faces of and on top of the escarpment. Aurochs, several species of fish and birds, hippopotamus, hartebeest, gazelle, wild dog and a possible wild ass are depicted at CAS-6 and one image shows a young aurochs being suckled by its mother.

It may be interesting to note that the German ethnographer and archaeologist Leo Frobenius is recorded as having found 'a range of artefacts of Late Palaeolithic character and a microlithic core from greenish stone',[14] probably of the Sebilian industry, in close proximity to CAS-6. Of course, this does not mean that Sebilian 'people' created the rock art found here, but at least it does indicate that Late Palaeolithic groups were present in the area.

The second-largest assemblage of Late Palaeolithic petroglyphs in the Wadi Abu Subeira is found at Site CAS-13, another rocky escarpment located on the northern side of the wadi about 1.5 miles east of Site CAS-6. More than twenty rock art panels have been identified at CAS-13, some on boulders lying on a natural terrace about midway to the top of the escarpment, others in situ on its top or tumbled from here onto its slopes. Evidence for Middle Palaeolithic stone-tool production was also found on the terrace, along with grinding stone 'rough-outs' (unfinished) probably dating to the Roman era. The most notable rock art panel from CAS-13 is the one discovered on a large sandstone slab (c.2.5m by 2.3m) that lay on the escarpment slope. Four aurochs drawings feature on its surface, as well as a life-size depiction of a Nubian ibex, of which it has been said: 'The latter can be considered as one of the masterpieces of the Egyptian [Palaeolithic] art tradition.'[15] Four aurochs images were found on tumbled boulders on the slope and also a fish drawing, while on top of the escarpment, where most of the rock art is still in situ on flat boulders, there are eight panels featuring further depictions of aurochs, fish and one hippopotamus.

Two intriguing stone alignments were also discovered about 300m to the east of CAS-13, similar to examples found on the West Bank of the Nile at

Drawing of the aurochs and ibex rock art panel at site CAS-13, Wadi Abu Subeira. (*Redrawn after Kelany, 2014*)

Gharb Aswan, another area containing a significant concentration of Stone Age rock art that we will return to below. The purpose and date of these stone rows is unknown, although it has been stated that these 'can best be interpreted as a game drive'.[16]

Further examples of Late Palaeolithic rock art have been found in the Wadi Abu Subeira at sites such as CAS-14 and CAS-20B. At the first of these two sites, a partly buried rock art panel on a tumbled boulder shows a fish superimposed over the head of a hippo, while two other loose boulders bear fish images. Evidence of ancient quarrying was also found at CAS-14 in the form of a broken grinding stone rough-out, as well as tool marks relating to the splitting of a stone block, with 'The high degree of weathering as well as the dark patina of these features [suggesting] a very ancient date for these quarrying activities.'[17] At least nine rock art panels were identified at CAS-20B, some of which feature enigmatic circular 'peck marks' only, with others featuring what may be hartebeest. One panel depicts what may possibly be two human figures with protruding buttocks, although, if so, they are quite different in style from the headless female anthropomorphs seen at Qurta.

The Late Palaeolithic rock art discovered by the Egyptian archaeologists at the small wadi of el-Aqba el-Saghira, some 2 miles from Wadi Abu Subeira, is also worth mentioning. Although much of the rock art at this site has sadly been destroyed by modern clay quarrying, sandstone slabs featuring pecked dots and engraved lines were discovered as well as a small, partially destroyed rock art panel on a broken sandstone slab (c.70cm by 60cm). This featured a probable hippo, a bovid of some sort (aurochs?) and a bird similar to those seen at Qurta; an intriguing and unidentified animal with a long, curled-up tail can be seen just below the bird and Adel Kelany has wondered 'Could it possibly be the representation of a monkey?'[18]

'Fish Traps' and a Prehistoric 'Masterpiece': Rock Art at el-Hosh

The abundant prehistoric rock art found on the sandstone cliffs and hills near the village of el-Hosh on the West Bank of the Nile in Upper Egypt was first noted in the late nineteenth century by the Reverend Greville Chester and the more famous William Flinders Petrie, 'Father of Scientific Archaeology'.[19] In the 1930s the German explorer Hans Winkler, who 'laid a sound foundation for scientific research on the rock art of Egypt',[20] carried out a survey of Upper Egyptian rock art and included some of the rock art from el-Hosh in a subsequent publication. However, it was not until

Aurochs engravings at el-Hosh. (*Wouter Claes*)

November 1998, when a team from the Royal Museums of Art and History (RMAH), Brussels, returned to el-Hosh that a more in-depth and thorough study of the rock art was begun.

The 1998 survey was conducted along a c.6-mile stretch of the Nile and 'a multitude of rock art sites was located containing thousands of petroglyphs.'[21] The Belgian archaeologists focused on three areas: Gebelet Yussef, Abu Tanqura Bahari and Abu Tanqura Qibli, with the majority of the rock art found here dating to the Late Predynastic and early pharaonic periods c.4000–2650 BCE and including images that are typical of the Egyptian rock art of this time such as boats and wild and domesticated animals. However, rock art that seemed out of place among that from the Late Predynastic and early pharaonic periods was also found, with curious, curvilinear, mushroom-shaped designs the main characteristic and most striking feature of this unusual art (Plate 5). These designs frequently occur in clusters, although there are a few isolated examples, and in most cases they are 'accompanied by a range of abstract and figurative motifs, including circles, ladder-shaped drawings, human figures…footprints, crocodiles (highly-stylized and seen from above) and harpoon-like objects.'[22] A plausible theory is that the 'El-Hosh curvilinear designs may be representations of fish traps as their outlines bear remarkable similarities to the ground plan of a universally known fish-trapping device, namely the labyrinth fish fence.'[23] In fact, at

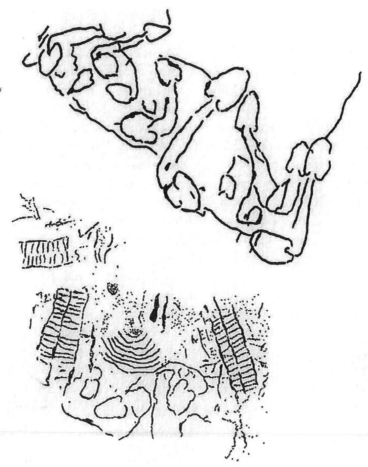

'Fish-trap' designs and ladder motifs from el-Hosh. (*Redrawn after Huyge, 2005*)

Ain Sukhna, on Egypt's Red Sea coast, fish traps are still in use that in plan closely resemble the mushroom-shaped designs at el-Hosh.

As to the date of the 'fish trap' designs and the other carved motifs with which they are associated, it was initially assumed by the Belgian archaeologists that they were created in the sixth or fifth millennium BCE, or perhaps even a couple of thousands of years earlier in the Epipalaeoithic period. Subsequent radiocarbon dates obtained from samples of organic material contained within some of the curvilinear motifs and on the surrounding rocks at the Gebelet Yussef site indicated that these intriguing petroglyphs were created before c.6000 BCE, sometime in the Epipalaeolithic. It has been suggested that the el-Hosh Epipalaeolithic rock art 'may be attributable to the Elkabian [culture], dated to about 7000–7600 BCE and known from the sites of Elkab in the Nile Valley and Tree Shelter in the Red Sea Hills of the Eastern Desert.'[24]

It could be possible, as Dirk Huyge has suggested, that in the Epipalaeolithic the area around el-Hosh was a place where people congregated, coming here 'to perform concerted fishing activities and, quite possibly, associated ceremonies and rituals, including the creation of rock art.'[25] Huyge has also remarked, 'I think it may be tentatively suggested that these drawings relate to special ritual techniques that had to be observed in order to increase the efficiency of fishing gear and to secure a "miraculous draught of fishes".'[26]

In March-April 2004, the archaeological team from the RMAH resumed their investigations at el-Hosh, discovering several new rock art panels, with one found in the cliff face at Abu Tanqura Bahari featuring several aurochs and two probable headless human figures or anthropomorphs. The Belgian archaeologists considered this rock art to be either Neolithic or Late Palaeolithic in date, and also noted the similarity of the aurochs images at Abu Tanqura Bahari to those discovered at Qurta by the Canadian expedition in the early 1960s. The subsequent dating of the Qurta rock art to the Late Palaeolithic and the discovery that headless human figures also feature among its petroglyphic repertoire strongly suggest that the rock art found in 2004 at Abu Tanqura Bahari likewise dates to the Late Palaeolithic.

Limited excavations were also undertaken in 2004 in the vicinity of the Gebelet Yussef rock art site to see if any archaeological evidence could be found of the Stone Age people who had carved the fish trap petroglyphs and their associated imagery. Unfortunately, none that could be linked to this Epipalaeolithic rock art came to light, although an intact grave from the Naqada II period was discovered. This contained a well-preserved skeleton lying in a contracted position and several pottery vessels, which included a finely-decorated vase featuring human figures, boats and birds (ostriches or flamingos).

Due to the discovery and investigation of the Late Palaeolithic rock art at Qurta, the next time the Belgian archaeologists resumed their work at el-Hosh was in February-March 2010. Along with further examples of fish-trap designs and their associated motifs, they discovered an isolated geometric design on top of the Abu

Drawing of the el-Hosh Epipalaeolithic 'masterpiece'. (*Redrawn after Huyge & Storemyr, 2012*)

Tanqura Bahari plateau that 'fits perfectly within the Epipalaeolithic rock art repertoire'[27] at el-Hosh. This design, which is only 35cm long and 18cm wide, has been pecked out on a sandstone slab and basically consists of a double ladder-shaped motif crowned by three wavy lines, on top of which are concentric semi-circles and horizontal lines. This design is unparalleled at el-Hosh, and indeed in Egyptian rock art in general, and has been described as a unique 'masterpiece' of prehistoric art.[28] We will never uncover the true motivation behind the creation of this striking Stone Age image, but it has been suggested that it may perhaps represent an elaborate headdress or mask, or alternatively a stylized topographical image.[29]

Late Palaeolithic Rock Art in Sinai?

In 2000, the Egyptian naturalist Gabriel Mikhail was led by a local Bedouin to a remote rock shelter located about 50 miles south of the Mediterranean coast in the central limestone plateau of the Sinai Peninsula. The shelter contained ancient rock art and the few photographs Mikhail took showed 'some remarkable animals engraved in what appeared to be raised relief, in a style totally different from the known petroglyphs of the Eastern and Western Deserts of Egypt.'[30]

In January 2001, Hungarian rock art specialist and desert explorer András Zboray visited the rock shelter to make a more detailed study and record of the numerous petroglyphs found here. These are situated on the back wall of the shelter, widely spaced out in groups, and Zboray identified depictions of a wide range of animals in the rock art: ibex, ostrich, oryx, gazelle, antelope, Asian or African wild ass and an extinct species of wild camel (*Camelus thomasi*). Interestingly, he also identified two petroglyphs depicting headless female figures, which are similar to the Late Palaeolithic ones seen at Qurta, although unlike those, the ones found by Zboray have both pronounced buttocks and breasts.

Whether the rock art found at this secluded Sinai rock shelter was created by Late Palaeolithic people remains unknown, as it has not been scientifically dated. However, as Zboray notes, there is 'a dense scatter of flint debitage and a few occasional finished artefacts' in the vicinity of the wadi, with these stone tools 'displaying fine pressure-flaking retouch, a feature common to advanced blade industries from the late Palaeolithic well into the Neolithic.'[31] The fact that no pottery has been found in the wadi perhaps indicates that the images carved in the walls of the rock shelter are pre-Neolithic in date, but whenever they were created, 'The appearance of the petroglyphs in the shelter, both in style and in weathering, suggests an age of great antiquity.'[32]

The Gharb Aswan Rock Art

Gharb Aswan, on the West Bank of the Nile opposite the city of Aswan in Upper Egypt, is an area of desert hinterland best-known for its collection of ancient Egyptian tombs (the 'Tombs of the Nobles') and the ancient Coptic monastery of Saint Simeon's (built in the seventh century AD), which although now ruinous, still stands majestically overlooking the River Nile. As mentioned above, there are also intriguing stone alignments found at Gharb Aswan, which have been interpreted as probable game drives. These stone rows are found in abundance at Gharb Aswan, criss-crossing the landscape and totalling c.13 miles in length; it has been suggested that these alignments were 'probably mainly intended for trapping gazelle'.[33] The date of these alignments is unknown, but some have been destroyed by the later quarrying activity that took place at Gharb Aswan during the New Kingdom (1550–1069 BCE) in ancient Egypt, providing what archaeologists call a *terminus ante quem* for these stone rows (i.e. they must have been built before the New Kingdom).

More importantly, however, Gharb Aswan is also home to an assemblage of prehistoric rock art featuring various geometric and figurative motifs, which archaeologists think were probably created by the Epipalaeolithic hunter-gatherer communities who lived along this stretch of the Nile Valley. It is at 'Ripple Rock' and 'The Terrace', which are located on an elevated part of the landscape known as 'Cobble Ridge', that the most conspicuous examples of this rock art are found. Measuring several hundred metres long and comprising quartz cobbles (that may have been used as raw material for Stone Age tools) and metamorphic and igneous rocks, Cobble Ridge has been described as 'A unique place in the local topography'[34] which, after the nearby Gebel es-Sawan hill (c.200m high), is the highest point in the local landscape. On the western side of Cobble Ridge is a solitary, thin sandstone slab (c.2.5m long by 1.5m wide) known as 'Ripple Rock', with a main central design featuring long lines connected to concentric curved lines and maze-like patterns; two concentric circles, two crocodiles and two unidentified animal figures can also be seen. Several other smaller rock art panels lie close to Ripple Rock and feature such things as crocodiles, a possible warthog, parallel dotted lines, ovals, footprints, unidentified animals and possible human figures.

The Terrace rock art panel (c.6m × 4m) is located on a sandstone terrace at the southern end of Cobble Ridge and features motifs such as concentric circles with radiating lines and nested arcs. There is also a rock art panel nearby featuring a curious human-like figure with a small head (on top of which there is a suggestion of a knotted hairstyle), a pear-shaped, elongated body and thin arms and legs that end in circular blobs. The figure appears to be a male and is accompanied by a four-legged animal with a tail (possibly a dog) that is much larger in comparison. Nearby is another rock art panel featuring three other human-like figures, one of which appears to have enormous ears. Of course, we have no way of knowing what these human-like figures actually represent, although it is perhaps more likely that that they depict mythological or supernatural figures rather than real people.

Probable Epipalaeolithic rock art can be found elsewhere at Gharb Aswan and, for example, there is the intriguing 'Crocodile Beach' site near Cobble Ridge. Although the petroglyphs found here have been badly eroded, it is still possible to

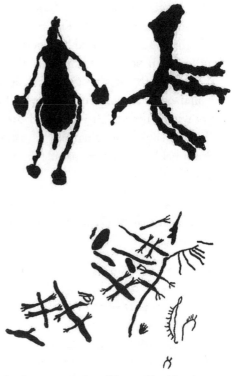

Rock art motifs from 'Terrace Rock' and 'Crocodile Rock', Gharb Aswan. (*Redrawn after Storemyr, 2009*)

discern various motifs and a group of crocodiles, which are located 'beside a broad crack in the bedrock – as if they have emerged from the river, now lying on the beach.'[35] There is also the rock art found on the impressive 'Commander's Rock', a huge, isolated sandstone boulder that measures about 4m long and 3m high and sits in a natural amphitheatre in the desert landscape. One side of the boulder is covered with a complex geometric arrangement of circles and lines, and a few crocodiles can also be seen. The largest of the circles are clearly grouped together near the base of the boulder and the lines are placed along a ridge that runs across its middle.

Interestingly, the rock art sites of Ripple Rock, The Terrace, Crocodile Beach and Commander's Rock are all located at high points in the landscape, with the former three located on or near Cobble Ridge. It seems unlikely that this is mere coincidence, and that prehistoric people randomly selected Cobble Ridge and its environs as an area suitable for locating rock art; therefore, as Per Storemyr has said, 'We are left to speculate on the meaning of this "special" place.'[36] He has also drawn attention to the complex geometric design found carved into a rockface at Wadi Umm Salam in the Eastern Desert. The concentric and radiating lines that form the design are superimposed by a petroglyph of a Predynastic boat of the fourth millennium BCE, revealing that the former pre-dates the latter. Although the date of this design is unclear, it would not look out of place among the Epilalaeolithic rock art of Egypt. Whatever the date of this design, Storemyr has wittily noted: '[It is] located by a "special" place – right in front of the "Jacuzzi site", a deep natural whirlpool in a small gorge by the main wadi. Presumably, prehistoric people did not mark this place only as a good one for dipping their toes.'[37]

The Wadi Sura Decorated Caves: The 'Cave of Beasts' and 'Cave of Swimmers'

The most famous rock art sites in Egypt are the 'Cave of Swimmers' and the 'Cave of Beasts' in the Wadi Sura ('painted valley') region. The Wadi Sura forms part of the spectacular Gilf Kebir plateau in the south-western corner of the Western Desert, near the Libyan border. When the evocative and enigmatic rock art painted on the walls of these two 'caves'[38] was created is not known for sure, but archaeologists have roughly dated it to c.6500–4400 BCE.[39] However, it has also been argued that the various painted motifs more probably date to between c.4300–3300 BCE, 'which was the time of the most intensive inhabitation in the area of the Gilf Kebir.'[40] Rock art resembling that found in the Caves of Swimmers and Beasts is found at other sites in the Wadi Sura region, with the painted images found here and in the two caves known as the 'Wadi Sura style'.

From 2009 to 2011, archaeological evidence relating to the people who created the Wadi Sura rock art was brought to light by a combined mission from the University of Cologne, the Cologne University of Applied Sciences and the *Deutsches Archäologisches Institut*, Cairo (the Wadi Sura Project). Included among this evidence were numerous sherds from Khartoum-style pottery vessels as well as lithic artefacts such as microlithic 'transverse' arrowheads and large quantities of goat dung, with the pottery and lithics typical of the Western Desert 'Neolithic'.[41] Much of the Wadi Sura-style rock art is found at rock shelters and at many of these, hooks can be seen cut into their overhangs, which were 'obviously used to put up equipment, such as baskets, water skins, or ceramic pots in nets, as is known from more recent ethnographic parallels.'[42] A small but fascinating find from one of these decorated rock shelters was a pottery sherd that still bore traces of red

View over the Wadi Sura from the top of the Gilf Kebir Plateau. (*Clemens Schmillen, Creative Commons*)

ochre on its surface having been used as a 'palette' by a prehistoric artist, with lumps of red ochre also found at some sites.

The Cave of Swimmers was discovered in 1933 by the Hungarian explorer Lázló de Almásy, the main subject of Michael Ondaatje's best-selling book *The English Patient* and the subsequent big-screen adaptation of the book by Anthony Minghella, which was a box office success in the late 1990s. The cave (not the real one) makes an appearance in Minghella's 1996 film, and in no small part this helped this remarkable rock art site to become a popular destination for the more adventurous 'off-road' tourists who visit Egypt. Sadly, it seems that some of these tourists have irreversibly damaged its paintings (which are not in a particularly good state of preservation anyway) by chipping bits of them from the walls as souvenirs and by pouring water on the images to enhance them for photography; graffiti has even been left on the walls of the cave by some mindless idiots.

Located at the base of a tall sandstone outcrop, the Cave of Swimmers site takes its name from the paintings of small human figures (sixteen in total) or anthropomorphs who appear to be swimming or floating in a line on its wall, all but one of whom are shown facing right, heading towards a depiction of a headless creature or 'beast', with the first figure touching one of its legs. In his *Récentes explorations dans le Désert Libyque* (1932–36), Lázló de Almásy wrote: 'I was impressed by a fresco depicting swimmers.... How curious to see images of swimmers in the heart of the Libyan desert in a spot where today there is no water for hundreds of kilometres around.'[43]

De Almásy also speculated that the 'swimmers' could be connected to a ritual of some sort that aimed to gain the favour of water deities at a time when the Western Desert was starting to become dangerously arid. Interestingly, geomorphological investigations suggest that there may have been pools in front of the cave at the time when these figures were painted.[44]

Other scholars have suggested that the 'swimmers' may be prehistoric people or 'shamans' moving through the 'Otherworld' in a trance-like state: 'Are these bodies in levitation or in adoration, painted by artists who themselves were in trance, illustrating the different states of consciousness undergone in the course of initiation?'[45] The idea that Stone Age rock art was often created by people or religious specialists of some sort who had entered altered states of consciousness by some means (e.g. hallucinogens or rhythmic drumming) is popular, but has also been rejected by several scholars.

Including the 'swimmers', there are around 100 human figures depicted in the cave, which form the main component of its rock art repertoire. The figures vary in size and are shown in different postures and, for example, one scene appears to show people jumping or being thrown into the air by a group of standing figures, perhaps representing a ritual, athletic dance of some sort. Such dances have been recorded among various African tribes, such as the Masai (the 'Lion's Dance') of East Africa or the Guere people of West Africa. In one part of the cave an isolated human figure (c.12cm high)

Swimming or floating figures in the 'Cave of Swimmers'. (*Roland Unger, Creative Commons*)

has been painted in red, and as noted, this probable male has 'stretched-out arms and widely spread legs. The impression is that it captures a person in the moment of intensive running.'[46] The figure holds what looks like a hafted stone axe in its right hand and also appears to be wearing a tall headdress of some sort, with these details perhaps indicating that this is a depiction of a prehistoric chieftain or some other such powerful figure. Miroslav Bárta has suggested that there could be a relationship between this unique figure and the ancient Egyptian *Sed* festival of renewal and regeneration, during which pharaohs performed a ritual run between boundary markers that probably symbolized the borders of Egypt, with scenes showing this performance not uncommon in ancient Egyptian iconography.[47] Therefore, it is perhaps possible, as Bárta proposes, that the roots of the ancient Egyptian *Sed* festival may lie among the Neolithic communities of the Gilf Kebir region, although there are several archaeologists who would disagree with his theory.

In addition to the numerous human figures, several types of animals are depicted in the Cave of Swimmers, including giraffe, gazelle, ostrich and two domesticated cows. There are also several 'negative' handprints or stencils, which are often superimposed by the other images, revealing that they are the oldest paintings in the cave, although just how old is unknown.[48] These prints were made when people placed their outstretched hands against the cave wall and subsequently blew paint around them with a hollow instrument of some sort, with these intriguing prehistoric 'autographs' providing us with a fragile but highly evocative reminder of the people who lived in the Wadi Sura region several millennia ago. Why these people felt the need to leave their handprints in the cave remains in the realms of speculation. However, it seems likely that this was a ritual practice connected to religious beliefs, and perhaps they were trying to communicate or make contact with the supernatural beings they believed 'lived in another world, located behind the "veil" of the rock wall'.[49] In many ancient and more recent 'primitive' societies, caves and rock shelters were (and still are) viewed as sacred, liminal places associated with deities or ancestral spirits, forming a portal or threshold between the world of the living and the 'Otherworld' where immortal supernatural forces dwelt.

Lázló de Almásy also discovered another decorated rock shelter just 40m to the south of the Cave of Swimmers, although the paintings in the 'Cave of Archers', as it is known, are far fewer in number and in even worse condition than those of its neighbour, being much more faded and indistinct. This smaller site takes its name from the depiction of about twenty long-legged, narrow-waisted, tall human figures, some of whom hold bows and arrows,

The Cave of Swimmers (left) and the Cave of Archers. (*Roland Unger, Creative Commons*)

on a small section of the cave wall; one archer can be seen firing his bow, and in front of the figures, to the right, a herd of cattle is also depicted. The main pigment used for the rock art in the two caves was red ochre, although yellow ochre was also used as well as kaolin (a type of china clay), all of which were available in the local area.

The Cave of Beasts

It was only in May 2002 that the Italian businessman Massimo Foggini and his son Jacopo discovered the 'Cave of Beasts' which, as has been pointed out, 'is one of the most important prehistoric rock art sites in northern Africa.'[50] In fact, containing some 8,000 painted and engraved images, the Cave of Beasts is one of the most richly decorated rock art sites in the world and is also one of the most notable sites of Stone Age Egypt.

The Cave of Beasts (also known as 'Foggini Cave') is situated at the top of a sand dune and overlooks a depression or playa representing the remains of a dried-up palaeo-lake. Its complex rock art is distributed over an area of wall measuring c.18m wide by about 8m high, with painted motifs far greater in number than engraved ones (some 300 in total), which somewhat curiously, for the most part, are located in the upper part of the rock art panel. Human figures and handprint stencils are the most numerous (and among the earliest) images in the cave (accounting for some 5,000 motifs in total) and there are also hundreds of animal figures with species such as gazelle, antelope, ostrich and giraffe depicted. There is also an engraved image of what appears to be an elephant, which has been depicted with a very long and thin trunk reaching to its feet, with its legs likewise very long and narrow and looking more like those of a giraffe; a nice engraving of a giraffe is actually superimposed on the elephant's body. Two more giraffe engravings reveal a sense of playfulness on the part of the artist who drew them, as they are cleverly depicted with outstretched necks and legs jumping over a natural cavity in the wall of the cave. Several engraved foot and handprints also decorate the cave wall, as well as objects such as bows and arrows, and numerous indefinable motifs can also be seen.[51] The painted human figures strike various poses, and 'A striking posture frequently depicted...shows humans standing in a semi-squat position, with legs wide apart and the thighs more or less parallel to the ground.'[52] As noted, there are more than 170 of these squatting figures and they appear over most parts of the cave's decorated rock face and are definitely involved in some sort of specific activity, perhaps ritual dancing?[53]

There are also some interesting Stone Age 'vignettes' to be seen in the Cave of Beasts: for example, one shows two archers with bows drawn, who appear to be stalking a probable lion that has been painted in white. In another lively and almost cartoonish scene, we see two stick-like human figures with outstretched arms who are chasing a probable antelope or gazelle that is leaving its tracks in its wake. On a darker note, there is a fascinating scene showing an archery battle between two opposing groups, one of which is composed of more or less naturalistic depictions of human figures, while the other comprises 'filiform' figures who are much thinner and taller than their opponents. As has been pointed out, 'Apart from obviously stressing the "otherness" of the two confronting groups, the filiform configuration may well have been used as a way of representing some foreign, strange, extrinsic forces, whether human or, perhaps, even divine or supernatural.'[54] Further hints of conflict and violence can be seen in other scenes, such as the intriguing one showing what appears to be a struggling man being forcibly led away by another, with the 'captive' perhaps also shown bleeding from a wound in his back. There is also a scene depicting a small group of human figures standing close together, who may perhaps represent bound captives with the prisoners perhaps being 'offered' to a god or chieftain who is depicted in front of them. Such scenes are perhaps related to the conquest of one tribe over another, as has been suggested,[55] although we can of course never know whether the events depicted in them are real or mythological, a problem that often bedevils scholars trying to interpret prehistoric rock art.

Interestingly, among the hundreds of hand stencils that have been identified in the Cave of Beasts, there are thirteen examples that are much smaller than the majority, with several scholars assuming that these tiny handprints belong to babies or small children. However, Emmanuelle Honoré and her colleagues have come up with an intriguing and alternative theory, arguing that these hand-stencils are non-human and were most probably made by the forefeet of either a *Varunus griseus griseus* (desert monitor lizard) or a young crocodile.[56] As they have suggested, these stencils could well be an expression of religious beliefs related to nature.[57]

Also depicted in the Cave of Beasts – and giving this renowned site its name – are several headless beasts similar to the one seen in the Cave of Swimmers and there could, in fact, be as many as sixty-four depictions of these 'non-natural beings' painted in the cave (Plate 6).[58] Rock art experts Frank Förster and Rudolph Kuper have noted the characteristics of the mysterious 'monsters' found in the Cave of Beasts: 'Apparently the beast is a hybrid of different animals, usually showing a long, raised tail comparable to that of a lion, but nevertheless depicted in most cases with two or three legs only, and always missing the head.'[59] As Förster and Kuper have further remarked:

> Surely these beasts do not represent real animals, but something imaginary. Often they are surrounded by small human figures, and occasionally touched by them. The most striking are those scenes where humans appear to be swallowed (or disgorged?) by a beast where instead of the creature's head only a hollow or slit has been indicated by the artist. We also sometimes meet the 'swimmers' from Wadi Sura I [Cave of Swimmers] in clear association, arranged in a long row one behind the other.[60]

Some scholars have suggested that links can be made between the rock art of the Cave of Beasts and the religious cosmology of later pharaonic civilization in the Nile Valley. For example, Jean-Loïc Le Quellec believes that the headless beasts and 'swimmers' are a 'visualisation of the afterlife which may be compared with ancient Egyptian perceptions of the dead's journey through the netherworld'. In his opinion, 'the "swimmers" resemble the deceased floating in the primeval ocean, or Nun, as known from the "Coffin Texts" and other guides to the hereafter.'[61] Le Quellec has further suggested that the beasts may be embryonic versions of the evil spirits and demons of the ancient Egyptian underworld, which had to be caught with nets in order to stop them swallowing the dead (some of the beasts are depicted with what look like straps or nets on their bodies), even suggesting that they can be compared to the demonic goddess Ammit, the 'Devourer of the Dead', who appears in the famous ancient Egyptian 'Book of the Dead'.[62]

Following in Le Quellec's theoretical footsteps, Miroslav Bárta has argued that 'It is above all the Cave of Beasts that shows explicitly that the local populations of herders were the authors of several mythological concepts that later became key elements of ancient Egyptian culture and concept of the world.'[63] In support of his theory, Bárta has drawn attention to specific scenes in the cave, such as the one showing a large figure holding a hafted stone axe or club of some sort, who has an upside-down human figure just to his left: 'We may state that this is a representation of one of the oldest known chieftains, a prototype of the ancient Egyptian king who [was] traditionally portrayed as a warrior smiting with his mace the heads of enemies of the country.'[64] Immediately below the 'chieftain' and his 'fallen enemy' are two rows of opposing human figures that lie either side of a natural fissure in the rock face. The upper one depicts ten figures with their arms raised above their heads, while the lower one shows twenty-three smaller individuals who are turned upside down, with one arm raised above their heads and the other against their sides. Bárta has said of these human figures: 'Are these members of two different, large families that met during a confrontation? Based on ancient Egyptian tradition we might also say that the upper row represents members of the victorious chieftain's band whereas the lower

Scene possibly depicting the conquest of one tribe over another from the 'Cave of Beasts'; note the painted hand-stencils below. (*Clemens Schmillen, Creative Commons*)

register renders defeated and killed enemies.'[65] Bárta has also interpreted another scene in the cave as showing a sky goddess – who he suggests may be linked to the Milky Way because she is painted in white – being supported by an earth god rendered in red, and has compared these figures to the well-known ancient Egyptian deities Nut and Geb.

Some scholars have argued, however, that it is unlikely, as experts such as Jean-Loïc Le Quellec and Miroslav Bárta have suggested that certain scenes in the Cave of Swimmers and the Cave of Beasts suggest that several of the major religious and ideological themes underlying ancient Egyptian civilization originated in the remote Gilf Kebir plateau. Support for this argument seems to be provided by the fact that the bulk of this rock art has been dated to c.6500–4400 BCE, whereas ancient Egyptian civilization did not emerge in the Egyptian Nile Valley until around 3100 BCE; furthermore, the Gilf Kebir lies about 600 miles west of the Egyptian Nile Valley. Nevertheless, the onset of extremely arid conditions in the Gilf Kebir in the fifth millennium BCE, which signalled the end of the wetter conditions in the Eastern Sahara that had turned the Western Desert 'green', probably drove Neolithic cattle-herders from this region towards the Nile Valley. Whether or not these people brought with them their 'mental universe' and contributed to the formation of one of the greatest ancient civilizations the world has ever seen will doubtless remain a matter of academic debate.[66]

Djara Cave

With its cavernous interior and magnificent stalactite formations, this 'dripstone' cave, which is located on the Egyptian Limestone Plateau about 400 miles north-east of Wadi Sura, roughly midway between Asyut and Farafra Oasis, is one of the natural wonders of Egypt's Western Desert. Of more interest to us, however, is that Djara Cave also houses a rich repertoire of Stone Age rock art that was created by prehistoric artists using the engraving or the pecking technique, or a combination of the two.

The German explorer Gerald Rohlfs was the first to record Djara Cave in his 1875 travelogue *Drei Monate in der Libyschen Wüste* (*Three Months in the Libyan Desert*) after having visited it in 1873, although he made no mention of the cave's rock art. The cave then became forgotten until it was rediscovered in 1989 by desert explorer Carlo Bergmann, who became the first person to describe its rock art, also reporting that prehistoric stone tools lay scattered near its entrance. However, it was not until some ten years later in 1999 and 2000 that Egyptian and German archaeologists of the

ACACIA project[67] visited Djara Cave to make a thorough record of its rock art, with at least 133 rather crudely-drawn figures subsequently identified.

The cave is entered through a small and narrow entrance and comprises three distinct areas featuring rock art, with the first of these, directly behind the entrance, known as the 'Hall of the Gazelles' (c.11m × 7m and about 3m high), which slopes down to a lower level of about the same size (but with a higher roof) known as the 'Gallery of the Engravings'. After this second level, the final and most spectacular part of the cave is reached and is known as the 'Large Hall' (roughly measuring 30m long by 30m wide and about 6m high).

Nine separate rock art panels have been identified at various locations within the cave, with the most notable found in the Hall of the Gazelles where there is an impressive stalagmite (c.4m high and c.1.5m wide) towering from the centre of its sandy floor, which is covered with numerous engraved and pecked images. Interestingly, almost 65 per cent of all the rock art found in Djara Cave is located on this stalagmite, suggesting perhaps that it had a special significance of some sort to the prehistoric people who decorated its surface. Around 85 per cent of the images in the cave depict wild animals, with scimitar-horned oryxes, addax antelopes, dorcas/dama gazelles and ostriches identified, along with several cloven-hoofed animals of an indeterminable species. Also included among the rock art are several

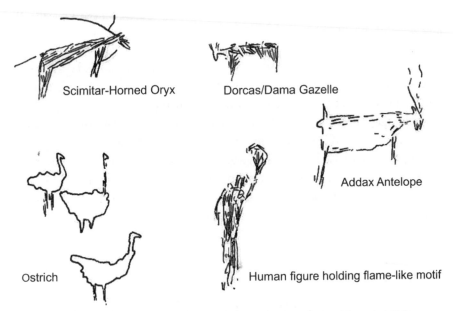

Scimitar-Horned Oryx

Dorcas/Dama Gazelle

Addax Antelope

Ostrich

Human figure holding flame-like motif

Animal and human motifs from Djara Cave. (*Redrawn after Claassen, 2009*)

human figures, some of whom are shown with raised arms holding flame-shaped motifs, perhaps representing torches. These motifs also appear on their own, along with other indefinable rock art that includes zigzag lines, grid patterns and groups of vertical and erratic lines.

An archaeological excavation was also undertaken in the Gallery of the Engravings, with a 10–15cm layer of ash and charcoal uncovered, representing the remains of fires lit by prehistoric people in this part of the cave. Two samples of charcoal from this layer were radiocarbon-dated to c.7000 and c.6200 BCE respectively, and a fragment of domesticated sheep or goat's tooth also recovered provided a date of c.5000 BCE. As noted,[68] these three radiocarbon dates indicate that fires were repeatedly lit over a long period of time in the Gallery of the Engravings. Archaeobotanical analysis of the charcoal pieces, which were incredibly well-preserved, revealed that trees of the genus *Acacia* and *Tamarix*, and various species of plants (e.g. *Zilla spinosa* and *Anastatica hierochuntica*) had been growing in the vicinity of the cave at the time when the fires were lit. Also found was the shell of a freshwater mussel, which may have been used as a handy container for transporting hot embers, and a stone tool (a burin) and core, which interestingly had both been wedged very tightly between the cleft of a stalactite and two stalagmites respectively. These artefacts could have some sort of ritual significance, or alternatively may have been placed in these spots so that they could be found more easily in the darkness of the cave. It may be interesting to note that similar discoveries have been made in some of the famous decorated caves of Upper Palaeolithic Europe and, for instance, at Lascaux, three flint blades covered in red ochre were found thrust into a small niche in the part of the cave known as the 'Meander'. At Enlène Cave, also in France, prehistoric people had deliberately inserted hundreds of small pieces of bone into cracks in the cave wall and it is hard to believe that they served any practical purpose.

Although archaeologists have been unable to directly date the rock art of Djara Cave, the ACACIA project recorded well over 200 prehistoric sites during surveys carried out in the local landscape (an area of c.6m²) between 1998 and 2002. Most of these sites represent seasonal encampments and date to between c.6500 and 5200 BCE, thus providing circumstantial evidence that it was during this period that Stone Age communities created Djara Cave's rock art.

Wadi el-Obeiyid Cave

The remarkable rock art of Wadi el-Obeiyid Cave was discovered in 1995 by the University of Rome Archaeological Mission to Farafra Oasis, which is situated in the central part of the Western Desert, roughly halfway between the Nile Valley and the Libyan border. The cave is located 50m above the floor of a wadi in the base of a sheer and rather spectacular limestone outcrop in the Tarawan Formation, which gleams white under the fierce desert sun. The opening to the cave is unusually square in shape with rather straight sides, perhaps pointing to its artificial enlargement, and the cave itself comprises three roughly circular chambers with dome-like roofs and totals about 13m in length, increasing in height from 1.5m at the front of the cave to 6m in the rear chamber. Both painted and engraved rock art is displayed at various heights on the walls of the three chambers, or the Front, Middle and Back Galleries as they have been prosaically labelled by archaeologists.

The rock art in the Front Gallery includes five animal figures, which include two probable oryx, a goat with twisted horns and a possible *mouflon* (wild sheep), plus a probable handprint painted in the 'negativo' technique like those seen in the Cave of Swimmers and Cave of Beasts. Below these

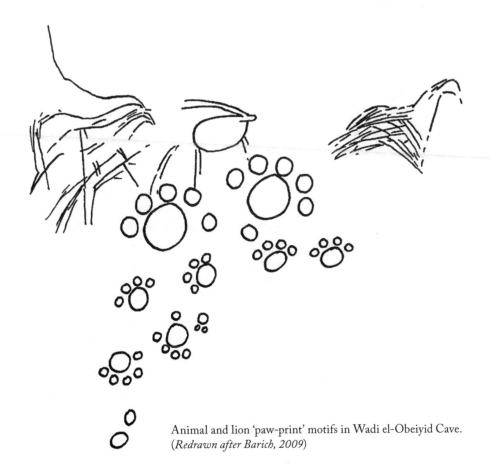

Animal and lion 'paw-print' motifs in Wadi el-Obeiyid Cave. (*Redrawn after Barich, 2009*)

animal figures is a group of motifs that consist of one shallow circular concavity with four or five smaller ones arranged in an arc immediately above. It is quite possible, as several archaeologists have suggested, that these intriguing carved motifs represent lion pawprints and Julien d'Huy and Jean-Loïc Le Quellec have said of them: 'We…think that these sacred engravings represent the passage of a [big] cat which is without doubt mythical and not natural.'[69]

In the Middle Gallery there is another oryx figure, two more handprints and a group of painted geometric signs that are cut through by a random series of incised vertical lines. Also appearing in the Middle Gallery is a very curious engraving that has been identified as a highly-stylized depiction of a boat,[70] although alternative suggestions have been put as to what it might represent. For example, Jean-Loïc Le Quellec and Dirk Huyge have noted that the 'boat' 'has been re-interpreted – even less convincingly – as a metaphor of rain, and some vague comparisons with South African data have led to suppositions that rain rituals were performed in Wadi el-Obeiyid Cave.'[71] It has also been suggested that this mysterious motif could represent an animal enclosure.

The most numerous images in the Back Gallery are handprints (at least fifteen) of various sizes, some of which appear high up on the walls near the c.6m-high ceiling, indicating that ladders must have been used when they were created. Interestingly, near one handprint there are two carved-out hollows and, as suggested, these may originally have supported poles that allowed prehistoric painters to decorate the upper reaches of the Back Gallery.[72] In addition to the handprints in the Back Gallery, there is a painted stencil of a forearm and a clenched fist, an engraving of an oryx or gazelle associated with ovoid 'female' signs, another 'boat' engraving and, at the northern end of the gallery, some further examples of the 'lion's pawprint' motif.

As is often the case with Egyptian Stone Age rock art (and that found elsewhere), no direct dates have been obtained for that which adorns the three galleries or chambers at Wadi el-Obeiyid Cave. However, during Barbara Barich's recent excavation of the Front Gallery, charcoal was recovered from the oldest level of a wind-blown sand deposit and was radiocarbon-dated to c.5870 BCE.[73] This date corresponds to the occupation of the nearby 'Hidden Valley Village', an important Neolithic settlement that was inhabited for more than 1,000 years from c.6200 to 5000 BCE. As Barich has thus stated: 'We can therefore suggest that the cave was visited for ritual purposes by the social group living in the village.'[74] Evidence of this ritual activity may be provided by the large hearth comprising two shafts that had been deeply dug into the floor near the rear wall of the Back Gallery, with the thick black coating of soot on its walls indicating that it 'was presumably used in ancient times'.[75] The mummified corpse of a probable young gazelle was also found lying on top of the hearth when the cave was discovered by the archaeologists from the University of Rome, although when and how the animal died is unclear.

Rock Art in the Dakhla and Kharga Oases

Numerous rock art sites survive in the oases of Dakhla and Kharga in the Western Desert, which are located roughly 150 and 250 miles south-east of Farafra Oasis respectively. Although some of the thousands of images found at these sites date to the pharaonic period, archaeologists have also identified numerous examples that were created by Stone Age communities, roughly between the seventh and fourth millennium BCE from the Neolithic to the Late Predynastic Period. It is also quite possible that some of the prehistoric petroglyphs found in these two Egyptian oases were created before the Neolithic and date back to the Epipalaeolithic or maybe even the Late Palaeolithic.

The bulk of the rock art sites are located in the western part of Kharga Oasis on striking sandstone desert hills or outcrops known as 'inselbergs' and, as has been noted by Salima Ikram, these 'do not seem to have been chosen for any obvious religious reasons, but rather for practical ones. There is a paucity of rocks in the [oasis], particularly ones with surfaces suitable for engraving.'[76] Ikram and her colleagues from the American University in Cairo's North Kharga Oasis Survey (NKOS) have made a valuable contribution to the study of Egyptian rock art by documenting many previously unrecorded rock art sites in the oasis.

One of the most notable of these sites is Aa's Rock, a substantial inselberg measuring more than a mile long and 60m at its highest point, with the playas found nearby suggesting that people and animals could have lived in this area either on a long-term or seasonal basis. Included among the numerous images depicted in the rock art panels covering Aa's Rock are various animals including giraffe, cattle, dogs, birds and oryx, plus geometric designs and human figures. The most commonly depicted animal in the Kharga Oasis rock art is the oryx and, as noted, 'Oryx would have been eaten, and its other body parts (horns, hide, etc.), could have been used in the manufacture of other items such as clothing, bags, handles and weapons.'[77] It has also been said of the numerous oryx images that can be seen at virtually all of the rock art sites in Kharga Oasis:

It is difficult to see these depictions as anything other than some form of sympathetic magic, or a record of the savannah-like environment that must have been common at that time. Sympathetic magic – fertility of the herds and hunting – might be seen as a precursor of the ancient Egyptian desire to control the wild environment.[78]

The most striking rock art panel at Aa's Rock depicts a group of giraffes, human figures and elephants and these figures are thought to have been created in the fourth millennium BCE. Interestingly, some of the giraffes are shown with leads being held by human figures (probably men) and perhaps depict, as scholars such as Lech Krzyżaniak have suggested, animals that had been captured when young and then tamed in an attempt to domesticate them.[79] Dirk Huyge has put forward an alternative and more 'spiritual' explanation for these leashed giraffe motifs, suggesting that

the giraffe had a role as an intermediary between the earthly and heavenly spheres. Its particular responsibility was to act as a bearer or vehicle of the sun god. By performing this duty on a daily basis, the giraffe made it possible for this cosmic deity to bring his voyage along the heavenly vault to a favourable conclusion.[80]

Conversely, some scholars have suggested that these giraffes were kept by prehistoric communities because these striking animals were believed to be 'rain makers/predictors [and also] fertility symbols'.[81] Some of the giraffes are also depicted as though they are seated, with their legs sticking out, perhaps reflecting hunting practices (i.e. the severing of the animal's Achilles tendon) or simply an arbitrary choice on the part of the artist responsible for creating these images.[82]

Also included in the ancient images that cover Aa's Rock is an unusual panel scene depicting a flock of long-legged birds, probably storks or flamingos, perhaps coming in to land on a lake. As there are no real parallels for this unusual scene, the date of its creation is uncertain, although it may have been created in the Late Predynastic Period or perhaps even earlier. There is also an engraving of a human handprint (at the time of writing the only example yet found in Kharga Oasis) and a simple but rather elegant and unusual motif comprising a single spiralling line, which is located high up on the northern face of Aa's Rock. This motif may perhaps represent some type of enclosure or run that was used for trapping wild animals such as gazelle, but whatever the case, it is thought likely on the basis of its position, abstract nature and degree of patination that it was created prior to c.4500 BCE, raising the possibility that the motif dates to the Epipaleolithic.

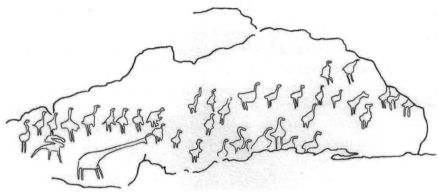

Rock art panel at Aa's Rock depicting storks or flamingos. (*Redrawn after Ikram, 2009*)

Another notable rock art site in Kharga Oasis is Split Rock, which is situated about 8 miles north of Aa's Rock and takes its name from the ancient break that can be seen at the northern end of this c.750m-long inselberg. In addition to animals such as giraffe, oryx, gazelle, Barbary sheep and cattle, several 'fat lady' figures (although some scholars have questioned their identification as females) can also be seen at Split Rock. These figures can be found at other rock art sites in the oasis and are thought to have been engraved on the rock face by local Neolithic communities in the sixth or fifth millennium BCE. The meaning of these intriguing motifs has long been a matter of scholarly debate, but they are often seen as depictions of female deities or goddesses associated with fertility, although an alternative and interesting suggestion is that they represent female sorceresses. Some of the 'fat ladies' found elsewhere at Kharga are paired with male, 'thin men' motifs resembling stick figures, one of which can be seen above a depiction of a probable Late Predynastic boat at Split Rock.

Lying to the west of Split Rock is Prehistoric Wadi where, in addition to the usual animals such as giraffe, oryx and 'fat ladies', there is an intriguing rock art panel depicting a human figure (probably male) with widespread arms.[83] Immediately to the figure's right, a group of sinuous lines can be seen, while to the left, a small group of oryx is depicted. The meandering lines may represent snakes or perhaps even a crude Stone Age map showing intersecting wadis and it may be possible, that taken as a whole, this rock art panel depicts a location where a person can find – or has found – oryx.[84]

Whether or not snakes are depicted in Prehistoric Wadi, there are several undoubted depictions of these ancient reptiles engraved on the walls of the adjoining Snake Wadi: 'There is no doubt that these undulating lines with pronounced heads represent serpents [that in some cases] are long, sinuous and well-fed.'[85] The main rock art panel in Snake Wadi is found carved into the wall of a shallow rock shelter near its entrance. Here, several human figures of varying size can be seen and they appear to be organized in two groups, one above the other. Some of the figures in the higher group appear to be carrying objects; while the group below have their arms spread wide and are perhaps dancing or alternatively maybe performing a religious ceremony of some sort. Two elephants and some oryx are also depicted, and there are more enigmatic engravings in the form of dotted lines, with a structure of some sort that has a possible entrance or doorway in its middle shown above the upper group of figures.

Interestingly, grinding stones and Neolithic stone tools have been found in the vicinity of the main rock art panel at Snake Wadi, perhaps providing us with more than a hint in which period of the Egyptian Stone Age its rock art was created.

Of all the many rock art images from Kharga Oasis, the most unusual are those found engraved on the sandstone wall of a shallow wadi not far from Split Rock. The curious motifs that comprise this rock art are situated on a concave rockface that – perhaps significantly – faces east and is illuminated by the rising sun. Salima Ikram has provided a useful description of this rock art:

> The main panel bears a group of carvings depicting a variety of objects: several that are comb-like, some random lines and ovals, one that is star-like, and many that are spider-like…. The spider-like creatures consist of an oval depression…equivalent to the abdomen or opisthosma, with eight deeply-incised protrusions, some flexed and some straight, indicating legs; smaller, much shallower oval depressions in at least two cases indicate the 'head' (cephalothorax or prosoma).[86]

The southern part of the panel (a piece of rock about 2m square) has broken off and now lies on the ground, with spider-like motifs similar to those seen on the main panel deeply carved into its surface, although their 'legs' are not flexed and balanced on either side of the 'body' as they are in the former. No definitive date has been obtained for the possible spider and other motifs, but based on the patination covering them, 'They seem to date to a very old phase of rock art'[87] and are thus at least Neolithic in date, if not earlier.

Salima Ikram is of the opinion that spiders are indeed depicted on the main panel and that it is also possible that if not spiders, some indeterminable insect may possibly be shown on the broken-off panel, but if so, it is unclear what species it may be. She has also remarked that 'Perhaps the spiders had a symbolic, totemic or aopotropaic [able to avert evil] value for the people who carved their image…derived from their characteristics or appearance. It is possible that the images are linked to the sun in some way.'[88]

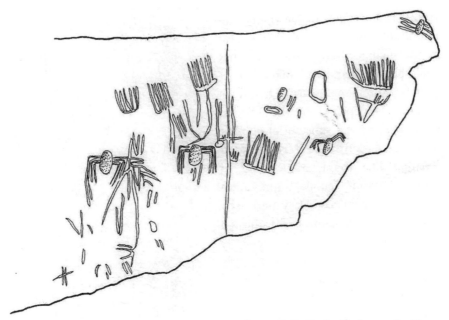

Rock art panel with comb-like and 'spider' motifs near Split Rock. (*Redrawn after Ikram, 2015*)

We will never know whether this interesting idea is true, but spiders do play a role in the mythologies of several 'primitive' and ancient cultures around the world. Interestingly, as Ikram also points out, a species of spider known as *Argiope lobate* (of the Araneidae family of spiders) lives in both Egypt's Western and Eastern Deserts and can be seen 'sunbathing' in the middle of their orb-like webs, surviving under the noonday sun.[89] Perhaps then, people did carve images of *Argiope lobate* spiders in Spider Wadi because the ability of these small creatures to survive the ferocious heat of the desert sun made them 'worthy of reverence or totemic allegiance'.[90]

Dakhla Oasis Rock Art

As in Kharga Oasis – and Egyptian prehistoric rock art in general – it is animal petroglyphs that are predominately found in the rock art of Dakhla Oasis, with a wide range of animal species such as giraffe, antelope, oryx, cattle, dog, hare, birds, elephant and crocodile depicted. Giraffes are the animal most commonly seen, some of these shown with leashes around their necks, and there is also a scene of a giraffe hunt, with the hunter armed with a bow and accompanied by his dogs. As Paweł Polkowski and his colleagues have pointed out, hunting wild animals provided Egyptian Stone

Age communities not only with an important source of protein but also goods such as hides and pelts that could be traded and exchanged.[91]

In addition to the many hundreds of animals depicted in the Dakhla rock art there is a substantial number of 'fat lady' motifs like those found at Kharga. The characteristic traits of these fascinating 'female' figures are 'a schematic upper body barely marked by a head, stick-like trunk and truncated arms, and a strongly, even excessively emphasized lower body, often richly decorated.'[92] This decoration shows things such as hairdos, bracelets, body art and dress ornaments, and some figures also have noticeable breasts and bulging bellies, perhaps representing pregnancy. At Dakhla

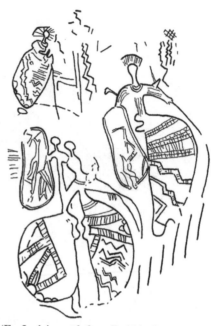

'Fat Lady' motifs from Dakhla Oasis. (*Redrawn after Huyge, 2003*)

these figures are often found alongside depictions of animals, particularly giraffes (some of which are also shown with pronounced stomachs, again suggesting pregnancy), and interestingly, many were 'engraved on exposed, evidently carefully chosen vertical rock faces which could be observed from afar, almost always high up and only rarely in the lower parts of the hills.'[93] Most striking of all are the isolated examples found carved into flat rock faces on hill summits, some of which are intriguingly located inside artificial shallow hollows or 'querns', which archaeologists think may have been made by people grinding grain or, alternatively, minerals used for body paint. It has been remarked in respect of the 'fat ladies' of Dakhla:

> The exposed and frequently isolated location of panels with 'female' representations argues in favour of their intentional placement and their uncommon importance for the community which made them. The location on a hill summit could have had some link with rain as a source of potable water. The same can be said of the engravings inside the querns, where grain as a source of food could be associated with life and survival. A justified presumption, considering the rather oppressive natural environment in which their potential authors lived.[94]

Other Egyptian Rock Art Sites

There are other notable examples of Egyptian rock art worth mentioning here, such as that found in the desert immediately to the north-west of Luxor by the Theban Desert Road Survey, which was founded in 1992 by American Egyptologists John and Deborah Darnell. A huge wealth of remarkable rock art has been brought to light by the survey, among which is a fascinating rock art panel, likely dating to the Late Predynastic, that features an 'elaborate tableaux of strange human figures, nicknamed "aliens" by their discoverers.'[95] These figures have broad, wedge-shaped bodies and thin, stick-like arms and legs, with some wearing headdresses of some sort and what may be animal tails; various animals such as giraffes, ibexes, hippopotami, antelopes and dogs are also depicted alongside the 'aliens'. John Darnell has noted that this fascinating scene (known as the 'Hunters Tableau') shows 'desert huntsmen...with their hounds and desert game. They wear animal tails, probably those of Cape hunting dogs[96] and caps, probably of leather, adorned with ostrich feathers.'[97]

Perhaps the most important (and earliest) rock art site discovered by the Theban Desert Road Survey is the 'Cave of the Hands', which takes its name from the numerous handprints painted in red that cover the ceiling of the cave located here. Most of these are of the more 'negative' type, formed by the blowing or spraying of paint around an outstretched hand, but there are also some 'positive' examples made by hands that had been dipped in pigment. Also painted on the cave's ceiling in red is a large human figure who wears a fancy headdress and appears to be running. Just to the left of the cave, there are two crevices featuring depictions of human figures, some of which are 'oddly stylized and altered, some elongated, others with enormous hands'.[98]

Rock Art of the Eastern Desert

The Eastern Desert has an abundance of Stone Age rock art sites, although these have not attracted as much archaeological attention as their western counterparts across the Nile. Nevertheless, several surveys have been undertaken in the Eastern Desert by various researchers, and many impressive and important rock art sites containing thousands of prehistoric petroglyphs have been brought to light as a result.

For example, there are the sites discovered to the East of Edfu in the Wadi Baramiya by Austrian researcher Gerald Fuchs in the 1980s. Fuchs discovered at least fifty rock art sites containing several thousand engravings from the Late Predynastic which depict a striking array of boats, animals and human figures. The largest and most elaborate of these sites is Site ET-A/WB 4, which extends over 100m on the south-eastern face of the wadi. The most spectacular image in this huge rock art panel is a curved boat measuring almost 2m in length, which has a seventy-strong schematically depicted crew, who are shown as vertical strokes. Immediately above is a similar but much smaller boat with a curved prow and stern containing twenty-one crew, two of which are much larger than the others and are located near the stern. The figure closest to the stern is obviously male and stands up with his long arms outstretched, almost as if he is exhorting the crew, while his companion in front appears to be standing with hands on hips. A couple of human figures and various animals such as antelope, wild asses and a bull are shown above and below the two boats.

In 2000, the Eastern Desert Survey, led by British Egyptologist Toby Wilkinson, made another major rock art discovery, with more than thirty new sites recorded in an area of the Eastern Desert between the Wadi Hammamat and the Wadi Baramiya. Much of the rock art found at these sites is contemporary, with and similar in style to that brought to light by Gerald Fuchs in the Wadi Baramiya, although some motifs were probably created before c.4000 BCE. Included among the rock art found in this 'Sistine Chapel of predynastic Egypt'[99] are many depictions of boats, animals and human figures, some of whom wear plumes in their hair and feather headdresses, and there is also a nice example showing seven dancing women holding hands and who seem to wear skirts of some sort.

Although they are only found in the Sinai Peninsula, there are also Egyptian rock art sites that feature neither painted nor engraved images but rather what archaeologists refer to as 'geoglyphs' (i.e. a design formed on the ground with stones or other materials). Several of these geoglyph sites were discovered by the Israeli archaeologist Uzi Avner in the east-central part of Sinai near the Egyptian-Israeli border during the archaeological surveys and excavations he carried out here, and in the Negev between 1977 and 1982. Avner found several sites in the Khashm et-Tarif area, which 'consist of "animal mosaics", circular groupings of zoomorphic figures (sheep?) made of many small, upright rocks set on edge and embedded in the soil.'[100] The significance of these highly intriguing stone zoomorphs is unknown, but they are found in close association with what have been identified as prehistoric cult structures or 'sanctuaries' that have been roughly dated to c.5500–3000 BCE.

While I was writing this book in 2020, two new important rock art sites were reported as having been found within months of each other in the southern part of the Sinai Peninsula. The first site to be discovered is a shallow rock shelter (about 22m wide, 4m high and 3m deep) situated about 20 miles north of the famous medieval monastery of Saint Catherine, and its walls and ceiling are covered in an array of images painted in red pigment that includes animals, people and several positive handprints. Egypt's Ministry of Antiquities think that the oldest paintings in the cave are depictions of animals that look like donkeys or mules, and that they were painted sometime between 10,000 and

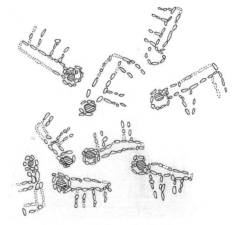

Animal 'geoglyphs' from the Sinai Peninsula. (*Redrawn after Avner*)

5,500 BCE, with images of women and animals seen in another part of the cave dated by the ministry to circa fifth-fourth millennium BCE.

The second site discovered is a rather spectacular cave located in the mountainous area of Wadi el-Zuma in northern Sinai. The cave measures c.20m high and c.15m deep and contains numerous engravings – mostly along the inner walls – depicting various species of animals such as ostrich, cattle, leopard and mule, some of which have been created using an unusual 'bas-relief' style (i.e. rather than being engraved or inscribed, they are slightly raised). The archaeologists from the Ministry of Antiquities who discovered the cave also found the remains of an ancient settlement containing two circular buildings, although at the time of writing these structures have not been dated. Hesham Hussein, lead archaeologist of the team investigating the cave and Sinai's director of antiquities, is of the opinion that at least some of the engravings date to the Naqada Period. It could perhaps be possible that even earlier images will be identified when the cave is studied more thoroughly. Whatever the true date of the obviously ancient imagery seen in this impressive cave-site, it seems likely that other caves decorated with mysterious Stone Age rock art will be discovered in Egypt in the future.

Chapter Four

Neolithic Settlements in the Western Desert

M any 'Neolithic'[1] settlements can be found in the Western Desert and although these lonely and little-visited sites now lie silent, long bereft of their inhabitants, they represent fascinating 'time capsules' from a hugely important period in Egypt's Stone Age past, which marked the beginning of the end of the hunter-gatherer way of life that had persisted for thousands of millennia. The Neolithic settlements of the Nabta Playa Basin can undoubtedly be counted among the most significant of these sites, with this area of the Western Desert representing 'one of the key locations in the research of early Holocene settlement in north-eastern Africa.'[2]

Nabta Playa

The Nabta Playa Basin is a large depression or playa located about 60 miles west of the Nile Valley on the south-eastern edge of the Western Desert near the modern Sudanese border (c.19 miles to the south). The Combined Prehistoric Expedition (CEP),[3] which has been carrying out valuable archaeological research in this corner of the Western Desert since the 1970s, has investigated hundreds of Neolithic encampments and settlements (dating from c.8800 to 4500 BCE) around the shores of a former palaeo-lake that formed here as a result of summer rains during the Holocene Wet Phase. Fred Wendorf and his long-time collaborator and friend Romuald Schild, who co-directed the important excavations at Nabta Playa in the 1970s and 1990s, noted that the microlithic stone tools found at the earliest Neolithic sites of the 'El Adam' phase (c.8,800–7,800 BCE) 'are closely similar to those found in the Arkinian [industry] in the Nile Valley that is about the same age or slightly older.'[4] The Arkinian industry is known from a handful of sites around the second cataract of the River Nile, in northern Sudan, and it is therefore quite possible – if not probable – that immigrants from this region established the first Neolithic settlements at Nabta Playa. Also found at the Nabta Playa El Adam sites were end-scrapers made on stone tools left here by earlier Middle Palaeolithic groups who had lived in the area along with grinding stones, small numbers of 'Khartoum-style' pottery sherds, hundreds of hare and gazelle bones and a smaller number of bones from other animals such as turtle, small rodents and birds. A small number of cattle bones and teeth were also recovered from the El Adam sites by the CEP and, as noted, Fred Wendorf and Romuald Schild 'identified the Nabta cattle remains as a domesticated descendant of the wild *Bos primigenius* [aurochs].'[5] Wendorf and Schild have said of the El Adam communities at Nabta Playa:

> [They] were cattle pastoralists who brought their herds into the desert after the summer rains, coming into the desert from some as yet unidentified area where wild cattle were present and where the initial steps towards domestication first occurred…. This may have been the Nile Valley, between the First and Second Cataracts [northern Sudan/ Lower Nubia], because wild cattle had been present in that area…as were people with lithic industries closely similar to those in the earliest Holocene sites in the Western Desert.[6]

As Kathryn Bard has noted, the Early Neolithic communities in the Western Desert 'may have been kept for milk and blood, rather than primarily for meat, as is still practised by cattle pastoralists in East Africa.'[7]

The idea that the cattle remains from Nabta Playa were from domesticated animals remains a controversial issue, but Wendorf and Schild's main – and perhaps strongest – argument in support of their theory is that at Early Neolithic Nabta Playa, cattle could not have survived without human assistance as there was not enough water here:

> Other evidence favouring the hypothesis that the Saharan cattle were domestic is seen in the restricted environment of the Western Desert during the early Holocene, particularly the absence of permanent water. Without permanent water it is highly unlikely that *Bos* could exist there except under human control. Cattle need to drink almost every day and would not have been able to move from basin to basin as the water in those basins dried up, and as the dry season intensified, they would not have been able to return to the Nile Valley, or to move further south where permanent water was present.[8]

Further possible support in favour of this theory may be provided by in-depth linguistic studies undertaken in north-east Africa. It has been claimed that these studies have shown how words connected with cattle-herding date back to before the emergence of agriculture, therefore placing their origin in the Early Holocene c.9000 BCE, when prehistoric groups from the Nile Valley repopulated the Western Desert.[9]

There are several scholars, however, who are not prepared to accept that the cattle bones found at the Nabta Playa, Early Neolithic, El Adam sites came from domesticated *Bos primigenius* or wild aurochs. Michael Brass, for example, has argued that

> ...any *Bos* under the control of humans would also require adequate grass cover and the water to sustain this nourishment. The desert playas would have held large amounts of water after the rains. Grass cover adequate to sustain domesticated *Bos* would also be capable of sustaining wild *Bos*. It should further be noted that hundreds of gazelle and hare bones have been found in the El Adam layers at Nabta Playa – gazelles are medium-sized animals and hares prefer short grasses. All in all, there is no reason to conclude that the environmental conditions were such that wild *Bos* could not have survived.[10]

Site E-75-6

One of the most notable and largest of the Nabta Playa sites investigated by the CEP is Site E-75-6, which saw several successive episodes of occupation dating back to the El Adam period, with the most notable occurring during the Early Neolithic 'El Nabta' phase around 9,000 years ago. Site E-75-6 was located on the fossilized remnants of a dune in the lower part of the Nabta Playa Basin and was not completely excavated by the archaeologists of the CEP. However, the remains of at least fifteen Stone Age dwellings were uncovered, which comprised two types: long, oval structures measuring about 6m long and 2.5m wide, and circular structures measuring 3–4m in diameter. These dwellings were arranged in three or four rows, probably corresponding to the shifting shoreline of the prehistoric lake: 'All of them appear to have been simple brush or mat covered huts, with several shallow, saucer-like floors separated by thin lenses of silt.'[11] These separate silt lenses indicated that people abandoned the huts each year at the height of the summer rains and then returned in the autumn/winter dry season when the floodwaters had subsided.

Abundant evidence of a wide range of wild plant foods was recovered from the hut floors, among which species such as wild sorghum, *Ziziphus* fruits, edible tubers, the *Capparis* shrub (which yields caper fruits) and the herb *Schouwia* were identified. The remains of one to five hearths were found on the floor of each hut, as well as several small, shallow, hemispherical pits or 'potholes' containing ash, charcoal and the charred remains of plant foods. Outside the huts, three wells were dug by the inhabitants of site E-75-6, so that subsurface water could be accessed in the dry season, with the deepest one sunk 2.5m below the surface; one or more large bell-shaped pits that would have been used for storing plant foods also lay next to each of the huts.

Sites E-06-1 and E-08-2

The CEP has continued its archaeological investigations at Nabta Playa in more recent years, and in 2006, 'Exploration of a new site, E-06-1... produced extraordinary results.'[12] Site E-06-1 has been dated to the early El Adam settlement phase, and this superbly preserved seasonal encampment, which has been dated to c.8400–8000 BCE, yielded a wealth of fascinating archaeological material relating to its long-vanished inhabitants. It has been said of this remarkable reminder of late Stone Age life in Egypt's Western Desert:

> The perfectly preserved stratigraphic setting of the site, numerous hearths and traces of dwellings, rich cultural material including pottery, radiocarbon dates and the presence of several large bovid remains, presumably of early domestic cattle, render Site E-06-1 an exception on the map of settlements of El Adam communities. It opens new perspectives for the study of Early Holocene colonization of the Western Desert by the first hunter-gatherer cattle-keepers.[13]

Of course, there are some scholars who would question the presumption that 'early domestic cattle' were being kept by 'hunter-gatherer cattle-keepers' at Site E-06-1.

The remains of eleven roughly oval-shaped structures measuring c.2–3m in diameter were unearthed (with more probably waiting to be discovered at the site), and these were probably simple brush huts similar to those seen at Site E-75-6. Numerous artefacts were discovered at Site E-06-1, most of which were found in association with the remains of open-air hearths outside the huts; inside the huts the remains of hearths and small pits for storing vessels were identified. Included among the artefactual assemblage were many hundreds of microliths and smaller numbers of end-scrapers; typical tools of the El Adam phase. Small numbers of larger 'macrolithic' tools were also found at the site comprising polishers and 'calibrators', with the former small sandstone slabs 'used for polishing objects made of stone, horn, bone [ostrich] eggshell or wood.... The surface bears traces of characteristic scratches or polishing, as well as the remains of raw material.'[14] Most of the polishers survived as fragments and only one complete example was found; several hammerstones and grinding stones were also excavated at the site. The calibrators were made from fine-grained sandstone and the parallel grooves seen on these objects are thought to have been used to smooth off and polish the edges of perforated ostrich eggshell beads that were linked together to be used as jewellery. As has been noted, the form and dimensions of the hundreds of ostrich eggshell beads found at Site E-06-1 'fit the calibrators' working surfaces'.[15]

As at all the El Adam phase Early Neolithic settlements in the Western Desert, pottery was scarce at Site E-06-1, with only eight sherds from bowls of various sizes recovered. Nevertheless, this small ceramic assemblage and the pottery found at other El Adam settlements is important because it represents one of the oldest-known examples of pottery production in the world. Research has shown that this quite sophisticated pottery was made from locally sourced clay found at the edge of the palaeo-lake around which the Early Neolithic settlements at Nabta Playa clustered.

Before they were fired, the El Adam potters decorated their bowls either with combs that had a few rectangular or round-tipped teeth (perhaps made from fragments of ostrich eggshell), or pottery discs or rollers with serrated edges, with the former pressed into the wet clay of the vessels and the latter rolled across it. The discs were made of sherds from broken bowls and measure c. 4.5–6cm in diameter with the tops of the prongs or teeth on their serrated edge square or oval; the centre of each disc is perforated with a small hole and small sticks must have been passed through these to facilitate their rolling. Close examination of El Adam pottery shows that individual vessels frequently display several impressed lines that run parallel to each other and are evenly spaced, suggesting that several of these toothed discs were used in conjunction to decorate bowls. Examination of the larger sherds found at Site E-06-1 reveals that the vessels they came from were decorated in this way.

Osteological analysis of faunal remains from Site E-06-1 revealed a range of animal species typical of the Nabta Playa El Adam settlements: dorcas gazelle, Cape hare, dama gazelle and cattle, although most of the bones belonged to the former two species. Numerous fragments of ostrich eggshell were also recovered,

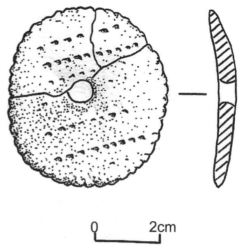

Pottery disc used to decorate El Adam bowls. (*Redrawn after Jórdeczka et al., 2011*)

1. Lower Palaeolithic Acheulean handaxe found near the city of Naqada. (*Dr Osama Shukir Muhammed Ahmin, Creative Commons/ Petrie Museum of Egyptian Archaeology, Acc. No. U.C.13577*)

2. A typical Levallois point found near Luxor, Upper Egypt. (*Metropolitan Museum of Art, gift of C.T. Currely, 1906, Creative Commons, Public Domain*)

3. The burial of Nazlet Khater Man. (*Professor Pierre Vermeersch, Belgian Middle Egypt Prehistoric Project of Leuven University*)

4. Late Palaeolithic engravings of aurochs at Quarta (*Bos primigenius*). (*Wouter Claes, Belgian Mission to Qurta, Royal Museum of Art & History, Brussels*)

5. Rock art panel at el-Hosh, featuring 'fish-trap' designs and wild animal motifs. (*Wouter Claes*)

6. Scene showing a group of human figures and three headless creatures or 'beasts' in the 'Cave of Beasts'. (*Clemens Schmillen, Creative Commons*)

7. The Nabta Playa 'Calendar Circle', reconstructed at Aswan Museum. (*Raymbetz, Creative Commons*)

8. The Nabta Playa 'Ring Hill' monument, with the grave pit clearly visible inside the stone ring. (*Professor J. McKim Malville*)

9. The Nabta Playa megalithic 'cow' sculpture. (*Professor J. McKim Malville*)

10. 'Tulip' beaker found at the Gebel Ramlah Neolithic cemeteries, Western Desert. (*Professor Joel D. Irish*)

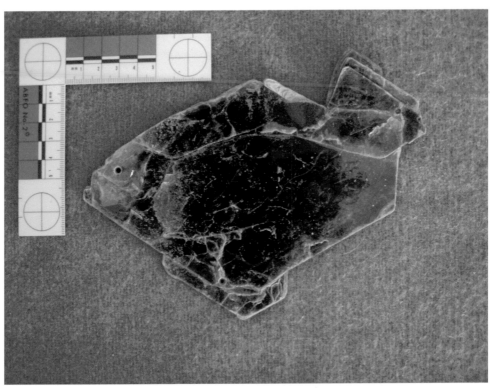

11. Sculpture of a fish made on a piece of mica slate, from Gebel Ramlah. (*Professor Joel D. Irish*)

12. The reconstructed burial of Gebelein Man in the British Museum. (*Jack, 1956, Creative Commons*)

13. Enigmatic clay head found at Merimde Beni Salama. (*kairoinfo4u, Creative Commons*)

14. Ivory female figurine of the Badarian culture, the Louvre Museum. (*Rama, Creative Commons*)

15. Black-topped, red ware vase of the Naqada culture. (*Keramion, Creative Commons*)

16. Carved stone jar of the Naqada culture, made from breccia. (*Brooklyn Museum, Charles Edwin Wilbour Fund, Creative Commons-BY*)

17. The superb Gebel el-Arak Knife, Naqada culture. (*Einsamer Schütze/Rama, Creative Commons*)

18. The 'Bird Lady' of Brooklyn Museum, a clay figurine of the Naqada culture. (*Brooklyn Museum, Charles Edwin Wilbour Fund, Creative Commons-BY*)

19. The famous Narmer Palette, found at Hierakonpolis in the late nineteenth century. (*Creative Commons, Public Domain*)

20. Frederick Green's copy of the painted scenes from the famous Tomb 100, Hierakonpolis. (*Creative Commons, Public Domain*)

with whole shells probably used as water containers (perhaps also used to contain blood and milk) decorated with various motifs; also providing the raw material for the hundreds of perforated beads found at the site that must have been used for personal adornment.

Site E-06-1 also yielded seeds from *Tamarix* trees, *Citrullus colocynthis* (bitter apple), *Echinochloa colona* (more commonly known as jungle rice or deccan grass) and in one of the remains of the hearths unearthed at the site thirty-five seeds of *Poaceae* grasses were found, providing insights into the contemporary environment.

In 2008/2009, the CEP excavated another El Adam seasonal encampment at Nabta Playa, which only lay some 40m to the east of Site E-06-1. Although this site (E-08-2) was not as well preserved as its neighbour to the west and lacked structural remains, it yielded a rich artefactual assemblage. As well as many hundreds of typical stone tools, around 300 ostrich eggshell beads were found (around half of which were not fully finished) and six fragments of shell that had been 'decorated with typical El Adam motifs, all representing a high standard of craftsmanship.'[16] The ostrich eggshell fragments displayed incised circles and 'lenticular' (shaped like a convex lens) motif; it has been noted that 'Decorated vessels made from ostrich eggshells are a characteristic product of the El Adam population, constituting an example of an important tradition and one that is also important in terms of cultural identification.'[17] As has also been pointed out, 'the possibility that the eggs themselves constituted a significant contribution to the diet should not be overlooked. Weighing on average 1.4kg....a single ostrich egg could have provided nutritious food for six to seven people.'[18]

Other finds from the site included a calibrator similar to the one found at Site E-06-1, two sandstone slabs bearing obvious signs of burning, which are thought to have been used for baking, and several grinding stones and quern stones that would have been used to process wild plant foods. Also found among the various artefacts recovered from the site was a piece of flint shaped somewhat like the head of a horned cow, which displays signs of working and polishing. The meaning of this curious object is lost in the distant past, but it has been suggested that it perhaps functioned as an amulet of some sort.[19]

Middle Neolithic (c.6100–5600 BCE) sites at Nabta Playa feature circular stone dwellings that are semi-subterranean, with their floors sunk c.30–40cm below the surface; their walls comprised vertical stone slabs and sloping entranceways provided access to the interiors, with hearths usually located in the centre of the floors. Some of the Middle Neolithic dwellings at Nabta Playa were probably similar in appearance to the jacal huts (small, wooden-framed structures with wattle and daub walls) built by native peoples in places such as south-west America and Mexico. Numerous, large bell-shaped storage pits and grinding stones have been found at most of these Middle Neolithic sites, testifying to the exploitation of wild plant foods. The faunal remains include the bones of various wild animals and, significantly, also those of domesticated goats and sheep, marking 'an important new addition to the food economy of the Middle Neolithic'[20] at Nabta Playa. A very large Middle Neolithic site (E-75-8) was also discovered on a high dune overlooking the dried-up lake,

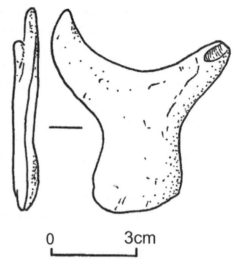

0   3cm

Flint 'cow amulet' from Site E-08-2, Nabta Playa. (*Redrawn after Jórdeczka et al., 2015*)

and although this lacked any structural remains, the remains of numerous hearths and an 'unusually deep trash accumulation (2m)',[21] which included a large number of cattle bones, were discovered. This evidence suggested that Site E-75-8 was an 'aggregation locality' where many people gathered together and it has been remarked that 'it is useful to note that among many African pastoralists today, cattle are frequently sacrificed and consumed at important ceremonial occasions to celebrate the birth or death of an important personage and at betrothals and marriages.'[22] People returned to perhaps participate in community ceremonies at Site E-75-8 in the Late Neolithic, after Nabta Playa was reoccupied following an arid period at the end of the Middle Neolithic which lasted 100 years or so.

Late Neolithic (c.5500–4000 BCE) Nabta Playa habitation sites are larger and contain numerous shallow, stone-lined oval hearths, although evidence of dwelling is lacking. Stemmed, bifacially flaked arrowheads are also a common feature of these sites, perhaps indicating that tensions were rising between Late Neolithic communities in the region. Another feature of the Late Neolithic at Nabta Playa is the appearance of a new type of 'black-topped' pottery that replaced the long-lived Khartoum ceramic tradition that had persisted for many hundreds of years. As has been noted, 'Black-topped pottery is made by hand...and is characterised by a distinctive black lip. It is a marker of many [Neolithic] cultures present at sites in the Western Desert.'[23] Exactly why black-topped pottery replaced the older Khartoum tradition at Nabta Playa and elsewhere is unclear, but it may have had something to with the onset of the extremely arid conditions that characterize the Western Desert today. With the increasing desertification of their environment, different Neolithic groups would have been forced to gather around diminishing water resources. In turn, this aggregation may have 'forced the formation of new groups in which technological change was an outgrowth of a melding of cultures. When new cultures are formed, new pottery styles can be either an amalgam of previous styles or a formation of totally new types that reflect the needs of the newly-formed system.'[24]

Gebel Ramlah

Archaeologists of the Combined Prehistoric Expedition have also carried out recent excavations at Gebel Ramlah (only c.13 miles north-west of Nabta Playa), discovering plentiful evidence of Neolithic settlement around the edges of a palaeo-lake that once existed here. Included among the many remnants of Neolithic life that they discovered were the remains of small, stone-tool workshops and areas associated with the processing of grain and red ochre. Objects such as V-shaped, comb-decorated pottery beakers, a fragment of a bone harpoon, a rectangular stone palette and grinding stones were found, along with ancient hearths surrounded by sherds from smashed pottery vessels and containing burned animal bones. Other notable discoveries were a large stone that had been used for the tethering of livestock, and an intact necklace comprising about 200 ostrich eggshell beads and a central, triangular pendant made from animal bone. A handful of isolated graves was also discovered on the edge of the settlement areas, and one contained the skeleton of a c.5-year-old child (dating to the early Middle Neolithic c.5900 BCE), who had been buried without grave goods. In another grave, the skeleton of a young man aged about 30 was unearthed; the only item found in his grave was a small, bifacial, barbed and tanged flint arrowhead, which lay near his sacrum bone (located at the bottom of the spinal column).

Hidden Valley Village

As mentioned in the previous chapter, a Neolithic settlement known as 'Hidden Valley Village' lies close to the rock art site of Wadi el-Obeiyid Cave in Farafra Oasis, and some of its inhabitants must have created the striking and enigmatic images that have survived on its walls for many millennia. In terms of aesthetic appeal and mystery, the archaeology of Hidden Valley Village cannot compete with the rock art that decorates Wadi el-Obeiyid

Farafra Oasis landscape. (*Roland Unger, Creative Commons*)

Cave. However, a series of excavations undertaken at the settlement by archaeologists from the Sapienza University of Rome have shed considerable light on the various Neolithic communities who lived here between c.6200 and 5000 BCE.

The people of Hidden Valley Village settled along the shoreline of an ancient lake that lay in the deepest part of a desert basin located on the northern edge of Wadi el-Obeiyid and the Italian archaeological mission uncovered the collapsed remains of several circular or oval huts that were lined with limestone slabs. What these Stone Age dwellings looked like in their original form is unknown, although it seems likely that their roofs, and perhaps also their upper courses, were made of organic materials such as brushwood and animal hide. Whatever their original appearance, 'these stone structures [were] occupation spaces for nuclear families that have left traces of their presence as numerous hearths full of ash, charcoal, stone tools, faunal remains and carbonized organic materials.'[25] Although this evidence does not prove permanent year-round occupation of Hidden Valley Village, it does strongly imply that the Neolithic groups who lived here did so on a more permanent basis than their predecessors of the earlier Neolithic who lived in ephemeral seasonal camps.

The faunal remains recovered from Hidden Valley Village included the bones of gazelle and Barbary sheep as well as those of domesticated sheep and goats, which along with domesticated cereal crops are generally believed to have been introduced into Egypt by small groups of immigrants from south-west Asia (the Levant). Herds of livestock would have been driven across the Sinai Peninsula, or perhaps even brought in boats that sailed along the southern Mediterranean coastline from the Levant. Genetic DNA research supports the idea that Levantine migrants brought domesticated crops and animals to Egypt, although as noted, 'It has to be considered that the subsequent development of cereal cultivating and livestock-keeping in Egypt was achieved to a large extent by indigenous people from Egypt who adopted them from the immigrants.'[26]

Many carbonized plant remains were found in the Hidden Valley Village dwellings and included *Asphodelus* (a species of asphodel plant) and large quantities of grain from wild grasses such as *Echinocloa*, *Panicum* and *Setaria*, which were recovered from the hearths and cooking holes found on the house floors. Wild sorghum grass comprises c.40 per cent of the plant remains found at the site (sorghum was also common at Nabta Playa), and 'may have been preferred by human groups for its bigger grains and better nutritional qualities'.[27]

Various types of stone tools such as scrapers and bifacial knives and axes were found at or in the immediate vicinity of the village, with numerous arrowheads also recovered during the surveys and excavations carried out by the archaeologists from the University of Rome between 1990 and 2005. Some of the arrowheads were quite substantial in size and it has been suggested that these were designed for killing humans rather than wild animals, as they would not have been effective in the hunting of the small and medium-sized game that lived in the surrounding environment at the time.[28] Other finds from the settlement included numerous ostrich eggshell containers, grinding stones, nodules of red and yellow ochre and ostrich eggshell beads comprising both unfinished and complete examples. The ochre was probably used as a prehistoric cosmetic and maybe even in the decoration of nearby Wadi el-Obeiyid Cave; traces of red ochre were also found inside the perforations of some ostrich eggshell beads, suggesting 'the use of coloured string to hang these ornaments'.[29] Traces of red ochre were also found on the inner surfaces of some of the fragments from broken ostrich eggshell containers, perhaps indicating that when complete, they had been used to store pigments, a practice that has been ethnographically documented among African bushmen.[30]

A handful of more unusual and intriguing finds were unearthed in Hidden Valley Village, such as the 'broad limestone slab decorated with small incised depressions'[31] found on the floor of one of the huts, and the 'very roughly made clay figurine which may depict either a human being or a bird'[32] that was recovered from between stone slabs surrounding a hearth. Three tools

Flint arrowheads
from Hidden
Valley Village.
(*Redrawn after
Lucarini, 2014*)

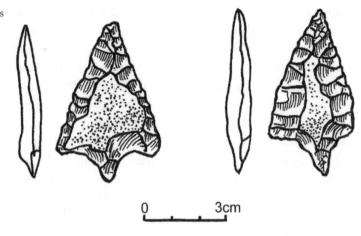

0   3cm

made from animal bone were also unearthed during the excavations, two
of which were long and narrow needle-like objects measuring c.13cm by
c.0.5cm and c.16cm by c.0.5cm respectively; the third tool was broader but
shorter, measuring c.7cm long and c.12cm wide.

Undoubtedly, the rarest find from the village was the upper part of a
left human femur or thigh bone, which may have been ritually deposited,
although it is probably more likely that the bone was moved to the hut in
which it was found by natural causes. Either way, as has been remarked,
'Although this find did not provide sufficient information to determine the
human group to which it belonged, it was of enormous importance as it was
the first (and only) human remain hitherto brought to light in the entire
Farafra [Oasis] area.'[33]

Sheikh el-Obeiyid Village

In 2006, the Italian mission from the University of Rome selected a new
area for archaeological investigation, the Sheikh el-Obeiyid Plateau (located
about 12 miles west of Hidden Valley Village), subsequently discovering
a previously unknown large Neolithic settlement 'containing the most
elaborate dwellings known so far'.[34] The settlement or 'village' had been
built by Neolithic pastoralists in a commanding position on the northern
plateau of Farafra Oasis, from where it originally overlooked a large lake (Bir
el-Obeiyid Playa) that lay about 130m below. Twenty-five circular or oval
stone huts, arranged in four clusters, were discovered and range in size from
3m to 7m in diameter, with their walls either consisting of overlapping rows
of large limestone slabs set upright in the ground, or small slabs lain on top

of each other or on the bedrock from which they were quarried. The huts are located on the edge of a terrace and, as a result, the Neolithic settlement would have been exposed to strong winds from the south, although it would have provided 'a good living alternative'[35] to the marshy environment of the lake immediately below during the wet season.

Layers of ash and charcoal and various artefacts were found within the huts, confirming that they had functioned as Neolithic dwellings, with several radiocarbon dates obtained from charcoal recovered from one of the huts indicating that the village was built around 8,000 years ago, c.6000–5700 BCE. Various types of stone tools such as scrapers, bifacial knives and 'borers' were unearthed during the excavation of the site, along with grinding stones and an abundance of ostrich eggshell fragments, with an area associated with the manufacture of ostrich eggshell beads also identified outside one of the huts. A large hearth (4m in diameter) was located at the edge of the terrace on which the village was positioned and 'Considering its position, it is likely that it was used as a night land marker',[36] perhaps by people returning home from a day's hunting-and-gathering trip to the lake and its environs.

About 140m behind the village, there is a small cave in the main limestone escarpment of the Sheikh el-Obeiyid area, which is topped by a striking 'tower karst' (rocky limestone hills with near vertical sides), known locally as Shakhs el-Obeiyid. The cave yielded Neolithic stone tools as well as various objects (i.e. pottery sherds, wooden tools, and leather and pumpkin water containers) probably left by more recent pastoralists moving between the northern oases of Farafra, Bahariya and Siwa. Plentiful archaeological evidence left by 'less recent' Neolithic pastoralists was found around the edges of the playa below the settlement and in the connecting 'piedmont basins' (small side valleys where pools would have formed). This evidence consisted of hundreds of temporary campsites which yielded thousands of stone tools and ostrich eggshell fragments, and smaller numbers of grinding stones and pottery sherds.

Two cairns made of small, overlapping limestone slab structures were also found at either edge of the Sheikh el-Obeiyid settlement. The excavation of these cairns revealed that they covered intriguing structures consisting of two opposing walls constructed from limestone slabs set upright on the bedrock, which in turn are covered by horizontal ones, and they look like miniature versions of the impressive megalithic long dolmens built by the Neolithic communities of Western Europe. The internal 'corridors' of these structures were devoid of any bones, human or animal, and were also empty of any man-made artefacts. Their purpose therefore remains a mystery, but 'these structures might be considered as primitive cenotaphs or symbolic graves'[37] that functioned as territorial markers defining the boundaries of the settlement.

Neolithic Settlements in the Fayum and Dakhla Oases

Abundant evidence for Neolithic settlement has also been found by archaeologists in the Western Desert oases of Dakhla and the Fayum, with the former located about 60 miles south-west of Cairo and the latter in the middle of the Western Desert some 190 miles west of the city of Luxor. The earliest evidence of cereal agriculture has been found in the settlements of the Fayum A culture, whose communities also raised domesticated animals. Based on current evidence, the Fayum A culture is the first 'fully-fledged' Neolithic society in Egypt, and this combination of crop-growing and the rearing of domesticated animals represented a significant step towards the establishment of the ancient Egyptian state.'

The people of the Fayum A culture (c.5450–4400 BCE) lived around Lake Moeris (Birket Qarun), which originally was a vast saltwater lake, and their settlements were discovered in the 1920s by Gertrude Caton Thompson and Elinor Wight Gardner (who also identified a 'Fayum B' culture, which was thought to represent an impoverished later phase of the Fayum A culture but it is now known to represent the Epipalaeolithic period in the Fayum). Caton Thompson and Gardner investigated two significant areas of Neolithic settlement to the north of Lake Moeris, carrying out excavations at two elongated mounds or 'koms' (Arabic for hill) that they labelled W and K, uncovering a wealth of cultural material in the process (Kom W was the larger of the two sites). As William C. Hayes tells us:

> For their settlements the Fayum-A people selected sites in the lee of the low sandrock 'buttes' which ring the north shore of the lake, usually near an inlet or other indentation in the shoreline, where the fishing would have been good, and never very far from the level stretches of old lake bed upon which they grew their modest crops of wheat and barley. Of their flimsy huts or shelters...nothing now remains; but the village sites are marked by sunken hearths, or fireholes, ranging in number up to between two and three hundred for a single settlement (Kom K) and having occasionally coarse pottery cooking vessels, containing the bones of fish and animals, still in position in them.[38]

During their archaeological investigation of the two settlement areas, Thompson and Gardner discovered numerous grain storage pits (about 1m in diameter) or 'silos', many of which were covered with mats or straw and lined with 'coiled' basketry. The storage pits cluster in groups, suggesting that agriculture was practised by the whole community and, in one area, more than 100 silos were found. Some of the pits or silos even still contained preserved grains of emmer wheat and barley and, as has been noted, 'So well preserved was some of the grain that investigators at the British Museum tried (unsuccessfully) to germinate it.'[39] A superbly preserved sickle, which still had its flint blades attached to its handle (made from tamarisk wood) was even found in the bottom of one of the pits and would have once been used for harvesting grain or barley.

Many hundreds of other objects testifying to the daily lives of the Neolithic communities who once lived around the shores of Lake Moeris were recovered from Koms W and K: limestone querns, stone axes, flint sickle blades, some of which still bore the characteristic sheen or polish acquired from cutting wheat or barley stalks, bone harpoon-heads and needles, pierced Red Sea shells used as jewellery, freshwater mussel shells probably used as convenient spoons, a shell bracelet made for an infant (it was less than 5cm in diameter), stone palettes used for grinding ochre, amazonite beads imported from the Eastern Desert or Libya, 'pebbles apparently collected because of their odd forms',[40] miniature stone axes and fossilized shark's teeth worn as pendants, ostrich eggshell beads, limestone spindle whorls used in spinning flax (a piece of linen was even found near one of the silos), and superbly made 'winged' or hollow-based arrowheads. In respect of these distinctive projectiles, it has been stated that 'there is little doubt that this type of weapon was invented for hunting hippopotami.'[41] Support for this idea is provided by the example of a concave-based arrowhead found between the ribs of a hippopotamus skeleton unearthed by Caton Thompson and Gardner at another Neolithic site in the Fayum. It has been suggested that the Neolithic inhabitants of the Fayum felt it necessary to hunt these dangerous animals because their cereal crops were threatened with destruction from hippopotami, which leave the water at night to eat grasses on land: 'Cultivation plots on lakeshores could easily be raided by hippopotami.'[42] There were also hundreds of pottery sherds from simple plain red or black burnished cups, bowls and pots that had flat or rounded bases, and large rectangular dishes featuring moulded 'peaks' or 'ears' at each corner, which may have functioned as rudimentary handles.

Several hippopotami bones were found by Caton Thompson and Gardner during their excavations, alongside the bones of other large mammals such as elephants and crocodiles, with fish bones and freshwater mussel shells testifying to the importance of the nearby Lake Moeris as a provider of food.

In fact, archaeozoological studies have revealed that fishing was a major subsistence activity in the Fayum during the Neolithic, as was the case in the preceding Epipalaeolithic. Nevertheless, 'it is the presence of the bones of domesticated goats, sheep, cattle and pigs that shows that the progression of the Fayum culture into one was Neolithic.'[43]

The lack of substantial dwellings at sites of the Fayum A culture is often seen as evidence that its Neolithic communities were not sedentary and followed a nomadic, pastoral lifestyle, living in seasonal encampments. It has been suggested, however, that at Kom W at least, 'It is probable that Neolithic farmers...were not merely sowing seeds in naturally empty areas such as receding lakeshores where fertile soils were readily available, but also actively making cultivation plots by felling trees in shrubland.'[44] Therefore, it has been argued that

> given threats from predators [e.g. hippopotami and elephants], Neolithic farmers based at Kom W would not have been able to leave their cultivation plots unattended at any time while the cereals were growing. In short it is hard to believe that there was any moment in the year when Kom W became completely abandoned as its entire community left for another place in an annual subsistence schedule.[45]

Dakhla Oasis Sites

Two Neolithic 'cultural units' have been identified in Dakhla Oasis by archaeologists: the Bashendi (c.6500–c.4000 BCE) and the later Sheikh Muftah, c.4000–c.3000 BCE, which also survived into the early pharaonic Old Kingdom period (2686–2160 BCE), as shown by the discovery of Sheikh Muftah artefacts in archaeological contexts dating to the fifth and sixth dynasties of the Old Kingdom.[46] However, as has been noted, 'while [Sheikh Muftah communities] were in contact with the Nile Valley and elsewhere, there is little indication that they participated in the growing prosperity and social complexity of Predynastic and later Egypt.'

The most impressive settlement of the Bashendi culture is the sprawling Site 270, which in fact is the largest habitation site in north-east Africa and could perhaps be classed as a true Stone Age village. The settlement dates to the earlier phase of the Bashendi culture (Bashendi A, c.6420–5700 BCE) and covers an area measuring c.300m by 150m, containing 200 circular and rectangular huts built from stone slabs, which are grouped together into perhaps six clusters, with some of the rectangular dwellings measuring up to 12m in length. Whether the hut clusters represent 'social groupings or the shifting of the settlement through time is not clear',[47] although the former is thought to be more likely.

Various artefacts such as bifacial flint knives, numerous stone arrowheads (135 in total), ostrich eggshell beads, marine shells and a few pottery sherds have been recovered from the site. The bones of domesticated goats and possibly cattle were also found, and the various radiocarbon dates obtained from Site 270 range between 6200–5400 BCE and give an average date of 5800 BCE. The contemporary but much smaller sites, 306 and 307, are located nearby and may be 'special purpose sites'.[48] Eight structures were found at the former, along with a substantial amount of grinding equipment that included fifteen stone slabs and almost fifty smaller hand-stones that would have been used for the processing of wild plant foods. Analysis of botanical remains found at Bashendi A sites has revealed that wild sorghum and wild millet were important staples.

Eleven closely-grouped hut circles were discovered at Site 307, along with an unusual amount of pottery. Although this ceramic evidence only consisted of some twenty sherds from at least three vessels, far less pottery was found at Site 270. Bashendi A pottery comprises vessels of the widespread Khartoum tradition and in Late Bashendi A sites, simple thin-walled vessels that are mostly undecorated (a small number have black rims) make an appearance.

About 400m from Site 270, Site 269 was discovered. This is a large stone ring or oval (48m by 35m in diameter), that has a wall built of horizontal sandstone slabs rises to a height of around 1m (although it was originally higher) and measures 3m to 10m wide. Artefacts found near or within the interior of Site 269 'suggest rough contemporaneity with site 270'[49] and it is quite possible – if not probable – that this somewhat intriguing stone enclosure (which may possibly have been an animal pen) was built by the people who lived at Site 270.

During the later phase of the Bashendi culture (Bashendi B, c.5650–3950 BCE), it is evident that 'The settlement pattern changes dramatically as the slab-built settlement sites are abandoned. Localities now are typically open-air sites consisting of clusters of hearth mounds and associated cultural debris,'[50] representing the living sites of mobile herders who moved around Dakhla Oasis. Domesticated cattle and goat bones are found alongside those of game animals such as gazelle and hartebeest at Bashendi B sites, as well as large grinding slabs attesting to the processing of wild plant foods. Among the artefacts found at Bashendi B sites are small, polished stone axes, bifacial knives and arrowheads, pendants and bracelets made from shell, small polished stone palettes, and beads and toggles made from amazonite, carnelian and limestone.

Also found on Bashendi B sites are the simple pottery vessels that first appear in Late Bashendi A, with some archaeologists suggesting that this ceramic tradition originated in the Levant, although others have argued that it is more likely to be African in origin. Whatever the case, the distinctive

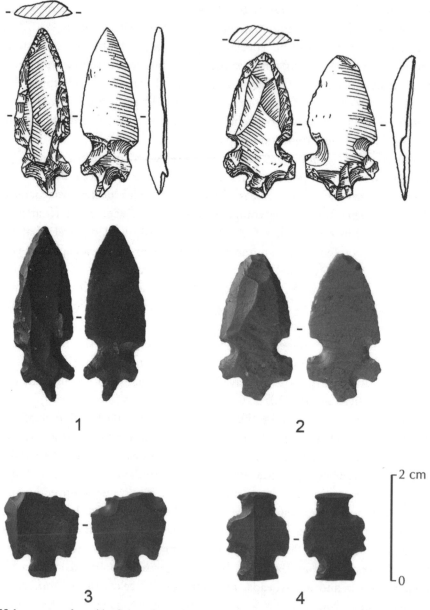

Helwan points from Abu Salem, Saudi Arabia. (*Image courtesy of Crassard et al. 2013, Creative Commons*)

stone arrowheads known as 'Helwan points', which have been found in small numbers at some Bashendi A sites and other Neolithic sites in both Egypt and Saudi Arabia, were Levantine in origin. These unique, side-notched arrowheads are named after Helwan in Egypt where they were first identified, but they are a common artefact of the Pre-Pottery Neolithic (PPN) culture (c.10,000–7000 BCE) of the Levant. These distinctive projectile points probably arrived in Egypt through trade and exchange between prehistoric communities, although it is not impossible that they were brought by actual immigrants from the Levant.

The Sheikh Muftah sites are similar in appearance to those of Bashendi B, consisting of low earthen mounds covered by fire-cracked rock (hearth mounds) and fire pits sometimes containing ash, burned animal bones, pottery sherds and lithics, although evidence of structures is scarce. The animal bones found at these sites are more fragmented than those found at the ones of the earlier Bashendi culture, perhaps indicating that meat was cooked in pots. Although much of the pottery found on Sheikh Muftah was locally made, some vessels were imported from contemporary communities living in the Nile Valley. A typical but notable example of a Sheikh Muftah site is Location 136, which lies in the south-east corner of Dakhla Oasis. Numerous hearth mounds and fire pits were found on this extensive site, which measures around 3,000m², and a wealth of artefacts that included some 8,000 pottery sherds, more than 500 stone tools (e.g. arrowheads, scrapers, sickles), and small numbers of grinding slabs and hand-stones for processing wild plant foods. Domesticated cattle and goat bones dominated the faunal assemblage, although wild animal bones (e.g. gazelle and hare) were also found.

Like their late Bashendi predecessors, Sheikh Muftah communities appear to have been nomadic pastoralists who lived a mobile lifestyle living in temporary campsites as they moved from place to place in Dakhla Oasis, with all their known sites found close to ancient water sources. Scientific analysis of rare skeletal material (from six individuals) found at two sites in the oasis indicates that the people of these communities lived 'a somewhat "hardscrabble" existence'[51] as it revealed evidence of malnutrition and heavy workloads that put serious stresses and strains on their bodies. In fact, it seems likely that life was not always easy for many of Egypt's Stone Age communities, although some of us may still look back on the simple lives they lived in the natural environment with envious eyes.

Chapter Five

Desert Megaliths and Burials

N abta Playa is not only home to some of the most important evidence of Neolithic settlement in Egypt, but is also the location of a remarkable ceremonial complex containing a unique collection of fascinating monuments built by groups of nomadic cattle pastoralists who lived in seasonal encampments along the shore of the lake during the Late Neolithic between c.5500–3400 BCE. It has been said of these Late Neolithic Egyptians: 'These nomads skipped sedentism with its associated agriculture, permanent villages and political hierarchy, and entered the Late Neolithic with their own repertory of concepts involving astronomy, design of sacred structures, and ritual.'[1]

The earliest monuments in the Nabta Playa ceremonial complex were built by the Ru'at El Baqar people (the 'Cattle Herders') and were discovered in the early 1990s by the Combined Prehistoric Expedition. The CPE found at least ten stone mounds or cairns built from sandstone boulders, situated along the western bank of a large wadi (known as the 'Valley of the Sacrifices') that enters the Nabta Playa basin on its northern side. Seven of these cairns were excavated, and it was discovered that they contained cattle burials. Below the largest and perhaps oldest of these stone tumuli, in a clay-lined pit with a wooden roof, the poorly-preserved but complete skeleton of a young cow was found, which had been lain on its left side with its head to the south, with radiocarbon dates obtained from a piece of tamarisk in the roof indicating that the animal was buried around 5400 BCE. No burial pits were found below the other six burial mounds, but butchered cattle bones were found scattered among their stones. This evidence speaks of a Late Neolithic cattle cult in the Western Desert, and it has been remarked that 'the Valley of the Sacrifices brought water to the playa and would have been an appropriate place to ask the gods for rain by performing human and cattle sacrifices and other rituals.'[2]

It may perhaps be straying too far into the realms of morbid speculation to suggest that people were ritually killed in the Valley of the Sacrifices as offerings to rain-giving gods, but it has been noted that the burial of a young female was found at the base of a sandy mound in the wadi.[3] It has also been recorded that the burial of a 'healthy young male' was found at Nabta Playa, and that curiously, he was missing his skull, which may have been removed to be used as an offering before this individual was buried.[4] A double burial was also found in the Late Neolithic layer of Site E-75-8, with the lower half of one of the skeletons curiously missing.

At the end of the Valley of the Sacrifices, a small stone circle (c.4m in diameter) was discovered on a low sandy knoll, with this intriguing monument somewhat similar to the much larger megalithic ('great stone') circles that were built across Britain and Ireland from the Late Neolithic to the Early Bronze Age. The 'Calendar Circle', as it has been labelled, was in a fragile state when discovered, with several of its small upright slabs collapsed; new stones were also added to the monument by modern visitors, which did not help matters. It was therefore decided to move the circle to the Nubian museum at Aswan, where it has been reconstructed (Plate 7).

Like many of the stone circles of Britain and Ireland, it is suspected that important astronomical alignments were incorporated into the architecture of the Nabta Playa circle:

> The circle...contained four sets of prominent upright slabs, which appear to be gates for viewing. When one is lying in the sand, these portals provide sightlines approximately toward the north and the position of the rising sun on the June solstice. These two alignments may reveal two major astronomical elements in the lives of the nomads. North was important when navigating across the oceans of sand of the Sahara. Even though there was no star at the north celestial pole during this period, the point in the sky around which stars circle would have been a useful navigation tool. The June solstice would have been significant for marking a date near the onset of monsoon rains.[5]

Alternative suggestions regarding the astronomical significance of the Nabta Playa circle are that it was aligned on the heliacal rising[6] of the star Sirius, which 'was an important marker for the ancient Egyptian calendar',[7] or that three of its inner stone slabs were aligned on the three stars comprising Orion's Belt (Alnitak, Alnilam and Mintaka). Of course, astronomical alignments in the Nabta Playa circle can never be proved for sure; neither can the idea that it 'may have been a place for rainmaking rituals'.[8] Nevertheless, it is likely that the stones of the circle were not randomly arranged and were connected to a significant astronomical event (or events) and that people also performed rituals and ceremonies within and around its stones. A radiocarbon date of c.5000 BCE was obtained from a hearth next to the stone circle, giving a 'relative' date for its construction.

It is worth noting that the desert explorer Ralph Bagnold recorded the discovery of another stone circle in 1930, which was situated about 360 miles west of Nabta Playa below the imposing Gilf Kebir Plateau:

> In a small basin in the hills we came next day upon a circle 27 feet in diameter of thin slabs of sandstone, 18 to 24 inches high. Half were lying prone, but the rest were still standing vertical in the sand. There was no doorway or other sign of orientation, and though we searched within and without the circle, no implements could be found. I understand that other similar circles have been found in the neighbourhood of the Gilf Kebir.[9]

The modern desert explorer András Zboray has noted that the circle originally consisted of twenty-nine thin stone slabs similar to those used in the Nabta Playa circle. Zboray also searched the immediate vicinity of the Gilf Kebir circle for any artefacts that could help suggest when it was constructed, but unfortunately his search was fruitless. However, it is possible – if not probable – that the Gilf Kebir stone circle was constructed around the same time as its counterpart that lies over 350 miles to the east at Nabta Playa.

About 500m to the west of the Valley of the Sacrifices is the 'Ring Hill' monument, which comprises a large outer ring or circle of horizontal slabs measuring c.17m in diameter, inside which is one or possibly two smaller stone rings (Plate 8). A circular shaft dug into the bedrock was discovered roughly within the centre of this double or triple ring of stones, offset to the east, and its excavation yielded the skull of a boy about 3 years old and some pottery sherds. Radiocarbon dates obtained from the skull indicated that it was deposited in the shaft c.3700 BCE, towards the end of the Neolithic at Nabta Playa, which was abandoned by cattle pastoralists some 200 years later in the middle of the fourth millennium BCE because by c.3500 BCE, the Western Desert had basically become the inhospitable wilderness that it is today. It could be possible that the child's skull was deposited as an offering to supernatural forces, perhaps raising the dark spectre of human sacrifice again as has been suggested in relation to the skeleton of the young female found in the Valley of the Sacrifices. As its name suggests, the Ring Hill monument is located on top of a low hill and commands wide-ranging views of the desert. It has been suggested that 'The asymmetry of the inner ring and the location of the grave suggest an intentional orientation to the rising sun around the day of equinox.'[10]

Lying to the south of the Valley of the Sacrifices along the western edge of Nabta Playa, the CPE discovered around thirty megalithic monuments

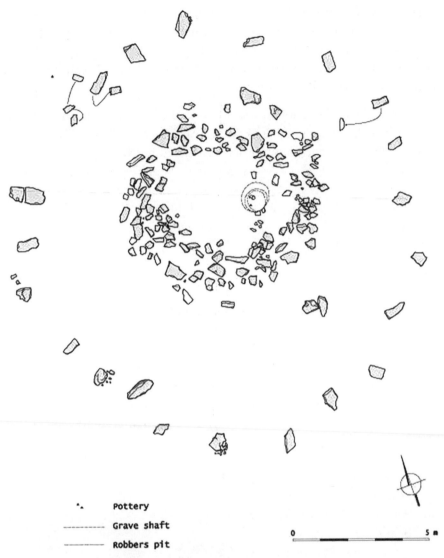

Pottery

---------- Grave shaft

————— Robbers pit

0   5 m

Plan of the 'Ring Hill' monument at Nabta Playa. (*Professor J. McKim Malville*)

or 'Complex Structures' that were built by the Bunat El Ansalm people ('the Megalith Builders') between c.4600 and 3400 BCE. These monuments consist of small groups or clusters of roughly shaped, large standing stones or stelae set upright or on edge, usually arranged in ovals measuring c.6m long by 4m wide, in the centre of which are large rectangular recumbent slabs. The largest example, Complex Structure/Cluster A, consisted of two central recumbents with a roughly pyramid-shaped stone on top, surrounded by huge boulders, some of which had been shaped and weigh up to 1.5 tons.

When they dug below the central megalithic setting of the monument, the CPE archaeologists made one of the most remarkable discoveries from prehistoric Egypt. At a depth of c.1m, a huge and carefully-shaped boulder had been deliberately buried in a pit and, as noted by its excavators Fred Wendorf and Romuald Schild:

> At first [it] was thought to resemble the keel of an upside-down boat... but when placed upright, it looks vaguely like an animal, possibly a cow. The long axis of the sculpture was orientated north-south, and at the north end was a rough fan-like projection, like the head of an animal or person. It is slightly more than 2m long, 1.25m wide and 0.5m thick, and it weighs about 2.5 tons. One side of the stone is convex, the other is flat; both of the upper sides are carefully smoothed, but the two undersides are rough and unshaped.[11]

An interesting suggestion put forward as to the possible meaning of this highly intriguing Neolithic 'sculpture' is that it 'may have been a surrogate sacrificial cow'.[12] Whatever its original significance, this amazing Stone Age monument was subsequently removed to the Aswan Museum for safekeeping, where it can be seen today (Plate 9).

Below this megalithic 'cow', at the base of the pit some c.3m from the surface there was a substantial, mushroom-shaped table rock. This 'had been carefully shaped and worked into a circular outline with smoothed, recurved sides and a flat, smooth surface on top.... It has two projections about 40cm wide, one to the north, and the other to the south-west.'[13] Table rocks have been discovered – either through excavation or by drilling – at some of the other megalithic structures or clusters investigated by the CPE. The function of these structures remains a mystery, but perhaps as Wendorf and Schild have suggested, they were shrines or '"proxy tombs", erected to honour elite members of the group who died elsewhere during their seasonal movements "on the trail".'[14]

Investigations carried out at Nabta Playa in the 1990s by Professor John McKim Malville (a solar physicist and an expert on archaeoastronomy) and colleagues from the Combined Prehistoric

Professor Fred Wendorf and the remarkable Nabta Playa 'Cow' sculpture, not long after its excavation. (*Professor J. McKim Malville*)

Expedition identified five megalithic alignments that radiated outwards from Complex Structure A. These alignments featured small groups of shaped sandstone blocks, and 'Many…if not all, are sculptured with anthropomorphic shoulders, suggesting that they served as stele, perhaps representing the dead.'[15] Radiocarbon dates obtained from the quarry that supplied the sandstone blocks for the megaliths indicates that they were set up c.4500–4200 BCE. About 100m east of the quarry, many unused blocks were found in a storage area, though why they were never used to build megalithic monuments at Nabta Playa remains a mystery.

Archaeologists suspect that the Nabta Playa megalithic alignments had an astronomical significance of some sort. For example, it has been plausibly suggested that the three alignments (A1, A2, A3) to the north-east of Complex Structure A were orientated on the different rising positions of the star Arcturus, 'the brightest star in the northern celestial hemisphere and the fourth brightest star in the night skies.'[16] The two alignments to the south-east of Complex Structure (B1, B2), may also have 'pointed' towards significant stars on the horizon, and it has been proposed that B2 'may have been lined up with stars in the belt of Orion [and that] the set of megaliths, B1, would have lined up with Sirius and [Alpha Centauri], which is the third brightest star in the night sky.'[17] A speculative but interesting suggestion regarding the megaliths found in the Nabta Playa alignments is that they 'may represent departed members of specific clans who perhaps were specialists who used these particular stars for navigation across the desert.'[18]

The Sacred Mountain Tumuli

About 2 miles to the north of the Valley of the Sacrifices is a prominent desert massif that has been labelled the 'Sacred Mountain' or Gebel el-Muqaddas in Arabic. In 2005, a team of Polish archaeologists discovered 'a large sacred area' above a large, sandy basin or 'cirque' that dissected the southern part of the mountain. This area contained a massive hearth, hundreds of cairns made from sandstone boulders, and pavement-like structures comprising low piles of sandstone slabs.[19]

The Polish archaeologists returned in the winter of 2007/2008 to investigate a small section of this area (Site E-06-4), although their excavations yielded little in the way of artefacts. For example, below Tumulus 2, which measured about 4m in diameter and c.0.5m high (although originally it may have been much higher), an oval pit measuring about 1m in diameter and 1.5m deep was discovered, and the only objects found in its fill were two microlithic tools. Excavation of the pit that lay below the roughly circular arrangement of slabs forming Structure 2/1 (c.1.4m in diameter and 0.4m high) unearthed four microlithic tools and two box-like arrangements of thin sandstone slabs. The artefacts found in the excavated pits below the other cairns and 'slab pavement' structures included twelve fragments from the long bone of a gazelle, two more microlithic tools, a fragment of shell from a Nile oyster, nine fragments of gazelle teeth and thirty-five pieces of charcoal from a tamarisk tree. A radiocarbon date of c.7000 BCE was obtained from the latter, placing the Sacred Mountain sites in the Early Neolithic.

Although artefacts may have been scarce at Site E-06-4, the evidence found here suggests that the 'Sacred Mountain' is an apt name for this distinctive desert massif, and that the Early Neolithic inhabitants of Nabta Playa came here to make offerings in specially constructed monuments to the spirits or deities that they believed lived in the mountain. Support for the idea that the mountain was a Neolithic 'holy' place reserved for religious rituals and ceremonies is provided by the fact that no evidence of settlement has been found on the mountain. Other archaeological evidence found by the Polish archaeologists (e.g. the huge hearth mentioned above and a low sandstone hill scattered with butchered animal bones) has been dated to the Middle and Late Neolithic, indicating the continued importance of the Sacred Mountain to the Neolithic inhabitants of Nabta Playa.

Megaliths of Sinai

Although they are little-known outside academia, it is also worth mentioning here the *massebot* monuments found in the eastern half of the Sinai Peninsula. Hundreds of these monuments have been recorded in Sinai (and in the adjoining Negev Desert of Israel), and there are likely to be many more unrecorded examples, given 'that most of the Negev and Sinai have yet to be systematically surveyed'.[20] *Massebot* are unworked and worked standing stones, ranging in height from as little as a few inches to c.2m and were erected as isolated monuments or in groups (*massebah*), with the stones arranged in straight or curved lines and sometimes also in circular settings. Small 'cells' comprising a semi-circular line of fieldstones are often found immediately in front of these standing stones, with the floors of these cells sometimes paved with slabs and usually sunk a little way below the surrounding surface.

Archaeological excavations carried out at several examples have revealed that *massebot* monuments have a long history, having first been erected by people of the Natufian culture c.11,000 BCE,[21] with the latest examples raised between c.3000 and 2000 BCE, although most examples date to between c.7000 and 3000 BCE. As has been noted, later 'biblical and other written sources from a variety of cultures and periods indicate that *massebot* were perceived as abodes for the power and spirit of deities.'[22] Archaeological excavations at these prehistoric standing stones have unearthed items such as bracelets and beads made from Red Sea shells, stone tools (e.g. 'fan' scrapers), grinding stones and pottery sherds.

Perhaps the most notable of the Sinai *massebot* are those found in the Wadi Zalaqa in the south-eastern part of the peninsula. Their stones are orientated north-east, perhaps towards midsummer sunrise or alternatively towards the distinctive peak known as Ras el-Kalb ('the Dog's Head'), which may have been viewed as a sacred part of the landscape. Most *massebot* are thought to have been orientated towards the south-east, the direction of the midwinter sunrise. Two tumuli or stone burial mounds (known as *nawamis*) dating to the fifth millennium BCE were also found nearby, with excavations carried out at four other examples in Sinai yielding the skeletons of two people who had been laid to rest in foetal positions, facing towards the east. *Massebot* can often be found set into the walls of these burial mounds, usually on the eastern side but also sometimes on the southern one instead, and they were also incorporated into what appear to have been simple open-air shrines or sanctuaries (c. the seventh to fifth millennia BCE). These monuments comprise rectangular or circular open 'courtyards' with their low walls of fieldstones only one course high, inside which altars and stone basins can sometimes be found sunk into the floor. Artefacts such as Neolithic flint blades and axes, grinding stones, scrapers, seashell bracelets, fossils and small stones that are distinctively coloured or shaped have been unearthed by archaeologists at these simple structures. Small stone circles (c.1.5m in diameter) are often associated with these shrines or sanctuaries and are arranged in 'chains' comprising several examples which can reach up to c.500m in length; similar stone circles can be found near some of the *massebot*.

The Gebel Ramlah Cemeteries

In 2001 and 2003, archaeologists of the Combined Prehistoric Expedition made a significant contribution to the story of prehistoric Egypt when, at Gebel Ramlah, they excavated the first Neolithic cemeteries to be found in the Western Desert. Their excavations uncovered many richly-furnished graves, the contents of which shed much fascinating light on the lives of the Late Neolithic people who were buried here in the mid-fifth millennium BCE (radiocarbon dates retrieved from two pieces of charcoal and a fragment of long bone have revealed that the cemeteries date to c.4700–4500 BCE). Like the isolated burials mentioned in the previous chapter, the cemeteries were found on the edges of the Neolithic settlement area at Gebel Ramlah.

The remains of almost 70 individuals were recovered from 32 shallow grave-pits in 3 discrete burial areas – E-01-2, E-03-1 and E-03-2 – and 5 infants (0–2 years of age), 10 children (3–12), 2 juveniles (13–17) and 50 adults (ranging in age from c.18 to 40 years or more) were identified. Sixteen of the graves contained a single individual, fifteen contained two or more individuals and one grave (Burial 12) in cemetery E-01-2 contained a fine collection of grave goods but no human remains. It may be possible that Burial 12 was a 'cenotaph' grave: 'Perhaps it was a symbolic grave of a person who, for unknown reasons, could not be buried with the other family members. The graveyard itself can probably be interpreted as a burial ground for an extended family.'[23] Burial 2 in cemetery E-01-2 contained five 'semi-disarticulated' adult skeletons (i.e. their bones were not articulated in their original anatomical order). This 'lack of articulation suggests that no soft tissue (e.g. ligaments) was present on any of the remains at the time of their deposition. It is possible that these individuals died elsewhere and, after some period of time, their bones were brought to the Gebel Ramlah cemetery for interment.'[24] It has been suggested that these individuals may have been Neolithic people who died guarding their animals far away from their village.[25]

Unusual and rather poignant evidence pointing to how the living 'looked after' the dead was also found at the Gebel Ramlah Neolithic cemeteries, with two skulls from two 12 to 14-year-old females found at cemetery E-01-2, revealing 'intentional (and incorrect) tooth replacement in antiquity'.[26] As noted, 'the anterior teeth of [both] females apparently fell out when handled during later burial events. In both cases, an attempt was made by the Neolithic gravediggers to replace these loose teeth; however, several teeth were put into the wrong sockets or placed backwards.'[27] At Cemetery E-03-2, eighteen teeth were also found in the right orbit (eye socket) of an individual, while the nasal aperture of another skull contained a single tooth. In the same cemetery, four bone bracelets were found around a right humerus [upper arm] bone, which had been displaced because of a later burial, with these ornaments 'maintained in their original position by insertion of the individual's own ulna and radius [lower arm bones]'.[28] This evidence for the later manipulation of the bones of the dead by the living 'suggest[s] a deep conviction about the importance of body preservation, i.e., keeping it together, ideally in an undisturbed state. Perhaps this was necessary to secure eternal life, similar to the belief that is so popular throughout all of ancient Egyptian civilization.'[29]

The Neolithic people buried at the Gebel Ramlah cemeteries were laid to rest with an abundant collection of grave goods, and perhaps the most striking are several finely-made and richly-decorated 'tulip' beakers. These rather beautiful pottery vessels are characterized by their flaring rims and globular bases and are decorated with incised geometric motifs such as diamonds, triangles and sinuous lines, with a white pigment also often used to infill this decoration (Plate 10). One of the Gebel Ramlah tulip beakers has two holes just below its rim and 'their placement gives the vessel an anthropomorphic appearance.'[30]

Included among the objects recovered from Gebel Ramlah was evidence of Neolithic cosmetics. This consisted of pieces of red ochre, yellow limonite ore, malachite (copper ore) and stone palettes and grinders for preparing the ore; one palette and grinder still had traces of red ochre on their surfaces. Some of the pieces of ore were found inside small containers made of cow horn, with one double container made from ivory. A small but superb stone bowl made from gneiss may also have been used in the preparation of

Stone bowl made from gneiss found in one of the Gebel Ramlah graves; note the human skull in the bottom right-hand corner of the photograph. (*Professor Joel D. Irish*)

prehistoric 'make-up', but whatever its function, many hours must have been spent in the carving of this bowl.

Interestingly, it was also evident that some of the bodies in the graves had been liberally sprinkled with red ochre, a practice that stretches far back into human history and

> Researchers emphasise the deeply symbolic and diverse meanings of the colour red, mainly expressed in the burial context. The colour red is reminiscent of natural substances sharing the same colour, such as blood. The presence of the colour red in burials is regarded as being connected with the concept of death and with the preservation of the energy of life, providing magical force for the route to the world beyond.[31]

The graves also yielded many items of personal ornamentation, which included bracelets made from ivory and Red Sea shells, many hundreds of tiny limestone, shale and shell beads, larger beads made of various materials such as agate, carnelian and clay, several pendants made from shell and animal teeth, and what are thought to be lip or nose plugs made of carnelian, turquoise or bone. Among the many other artefacts recovered from the Gebel Ramlah cemeteries were spherical polished chert and agate pebbles, needles made of mammal or bird bones, small sandstone containers with lids, flint blades and axes, a bone dagger and an ornamental stone point. Somewhat curiously, thick sheets of non-local mica (a type of slate) were also

Ornamental stone point from Gebel Ramlah. (*Professor Joel D. Irish*)

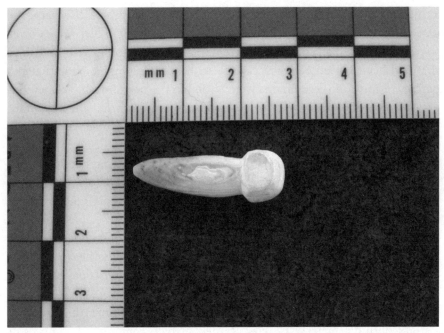

Probable representation of a human tooth carved from a seashell, found at Gebel Ramlah. (*Professor Joel D. Irish*)

found in most of the graves, one of which had been shaped to look like a fish (probably a Nile tilapia), with its eye represented by a small drilled hole; the 'fins' of this rather remarkable Stone Age fish sculpture also feature drilled holes, suggesting that it may have been suspended somewhere (Plate 11). The significance of this unique piece of portable Neolithic 'art' can only be guessed at, but it represents one of the most notable objects ever recovered from Egyptian prehistory and also hints at humorous creativity on the part of its maker.

Perhaps the most curious object recovered from the Gebel Ramlah cemeteries is what seems to be a life-size carving of a human tooth made from a shell that probably originated in the Red Sea. Bioarchaeologist Professor Joel Irish has noted: 'Although not a perfect replica, based on its single conical root and skilfully-rendered spatulate crown, the carving was clearly modelled after a maxillary incisor.'[32] As he has further remarked, although it is probably unlikely, the tooth carving could actually have been a prosthesis: a dental implant 'meant to replace a missing tooth in a living individual'.[33]

In 2009, a Polish archaeological expedition led by Professor Jacek Kabaciński from the Poznań branch of the Institute of Archaeology and

Ethnology Polish Academy of Sciences made a so far unique discovery: the oldest infant cemetery yet known in the Western Desert. Thirty-five graves were recorded, which contained the remains of around forty newborn babies that had been buried between c.4700–4300 BCE, making it likely that the parents of some of these infants were buried in the neighbouring cemeteries excavated in 2001–2003. Three graves containing both female and infant burials were also found in the cemetery, and it is quite possible – if not likely – that the women were either the actual or 'symbolic' mothers of the babies with which they were buried.[34] Grave goods were few and far between, with some graves containing a single shell from the Red Sea and one yielding an ivory bracelet; in all of the graves, however, there were small pieces of red ochre. It has been suggested that newborns played a significant role in Late Neolithic society at Gebel Ramlah and held special status, leading to the creation of a separate cemetery for the infant dead.[35] Whether or not this was the case will never be known for sure, but the cemetery does reveal the fragility of life in Late Neolithic Egypt.

Six years later, Professor Kabaciński and his team unearthed another Late Neolithic cemetery at Gebel Ramlah, which contained the burials of sixty adults. Some intriguing and unusual evidence came to light during the archaeological investigation of the cemetery, such as the deliberate cut marks found on the femur of one of the two skeletons found buried together in Grave 11, or the grave that had been uncommonly lined with stone slabs. In another grave, the archaeologists discovered a male skeleton covered with sherds of broken pottery, stones and lumps of red ochre, which had presumably been scattered on the man's body by the mourners who attended his funeral.

The Wadi Atulla Tomb

Lying about 40 miles from the Red Sea Coast in Egypt's Eastern Desert, the Wadi Atulla tomb has yielded similar cultural material to that recovered from the burials at Gebel Ramlah, with some archaeologists attributing the archaeological evidence found at the two sites to the 'Tasian' culture. It has been remarked that '[the Tasian] culture may be the most distinctive "missing link" in the picture of interaction between desert dwellers and the Nile Valley cultures, which led ultimately to the development of Egyptian civilization.'[36] The Tasian culture was first identified by the English archaeologist Guy Brunton during his excavations in the Qau-Matmar region of Middle Egypt for the British School of Archaeology in Egypt in the 1920s. Brunton also identified a separate Neolithic culture that he labelled the 'Badarian', which we will examine in more detail later. Maarten Horn has noted that 'The introduction of the Tasian culture initially met with mixed reviews but has subsequently gathered general acceptance in its reinterpretation by Renée Friedman as a desert-dwelling group of people that interacted with the Badarian population in the Nile Valley.' However, some scholars have argued that the Tasian culture is an archaeological 'non-entity' and that it is 'simply a part of the Badarian culture',[37] with Horn himself proposing that the Tasian and Badarian cultures should be amalgamated 'into a single "Badarian" archaeological unit'.[38]

Although it was known that the Wadi Atulla tomb, which lies near the top of a high sandstone ridge, had been plundered both in ancient and more modern times (1981 and 1992), in the late 1990s Renée Friedman and her colleagues decided to investigate the site to see if there was anything worth salvaging. They were subsequently rewarded with the discovery of several interesting artefacts that had obviously been deemed worthless by the various tomb robbers who had plundered this ancient burial place over the years. Radiocarbon and AMS dating of material from the tomb produced dates of 4940 and 4455 BCE.

The tomb comprises a deep pit measuring c.4m wide by 4m deep, with several rough niches cut into its walls and, given its size and depth, it is felt that it may originally have been a prehistoric mining pit (talc and serpentine are widespread in the area) that was subsequently reused as a burial place. Most of the archaeological material was retrieved from around the tomb entrance, where it had been unceremoniously dumped by the tomb robbers. Although badly weathered and extremely fragmentary, some human remains had survived and consisted of the temporal bones (from the skull) of at least fourteen individuals, and several teeth from young children, teenagers and adults. More than fifty pottery fragments from at least fifteen vessels were recovered, with four tulip beakers reconstructed from the sherds. Ten beakers (most of which were intact) were previously found at the tomb in 1981 and were photographed by archaeologists in 1983, but sadly they had subsequently disappeared by the time Renée Friedman and her colleagues arrived to investigate this ancient burial site.

Included among the non-ceramic finds were several pieces of malachite and red ochre, a roughly-shaped oval stone palette probably used to grind these ores, fragments from a bivalve shell (probably a Nile oyster), numerous beads made from serpentine, soapstone or shells from the Red Sea, fragments of a mica slab, a finely-worked bifacial flint knife, a bone handle from a tool of some sort and a worked soapstone fragment from a possible human or animal figurine. The 1983 photographs also show two large teardrop-shaped, pierced stone pendants, a large sea-shell and an object that may either be a ground stone axe or a palette. Similar objects were found in the Gebel Ramlah cemeteries and indicate that the people buried here had 'far-reaching contacts with the Eastern Desert and the Red Sea'.[39] The distinctive tulip beakers found at both Gebel Ramlah and Wadi Atulla also point to connections with Nubia, where similar pottery vessels are found in contemporary elite Neolithic burial mounds. Whether or not we classify the people buried at the Gebel Ramlah cemeteries and in the Wadi Atulla tomb as 'Tasians' or 'Badarians', the archaeological discoveries made here 'attest to a wide-ranging desert culture that found neither the deserts nor the river [Nile] an impediment to movement.'[40]

The Wadi Khashab Ceremonial Complex

Also located not far from the Red Sea Coast in Egypt's Eastern Desert is the impressive Wadi Khashab Cemetery or ceremonial complex which, like many recently-discovered archaeological sites in Egypt and elsewhere, was first identified on satellite images, with a ground survey of the site by Steven Sidebotham in 2010 confirming the existence of a burial complex with associated megalithic features. Under the direction of Piotr Osypiński, excavations were subsequently carried out here in 2012 and 2014/2015 and as he has said: 'There is no doubt that the site did not merely fulfil the function of a graveyard for a population inhabiting the area in the fifth millennium BC, but that it was also a ceremonial complex with a number of non-utilitarian functions.'[41]

The main component of the Wadi Khashab ceremonial complex is a roughly circular stone enclosure or ring (c.18m in diameter) composed of horizontal and vertical slabs, inside which is a cemetery containing animal and human burials. Only about half of the cemetery has been excavated by Osypiński and his colleagues, but they have uncovered twenty graves here (which have been plundered, probably at some point in the fourth millennium BCE), most of which contained the fragmentary skeletons of either cattle or sheep. The cattle graves are surrounded by oval stone superstructures measuring c.1.5m to 3m in diameter, the original height of which could not be ascertained, with the smaller sheep graves also surrounded by similar architectural features. It was concluded that originally, the horns of the cattle protruded above the stone mounds that covered their graves and 'that [the] cattle burials of Wadi Khashab were sacrifices made in connection with the ritual related to the human burial...not the graves of animals buried over a prolonged period of time.'[42] The human burial in question was found scattered among the slabs of a square stone pavement adjoining a destroyed circular structure (c.2.5m diameter) in the north-western part of the cemetery and comprised a humerus fragment and rib bones belonging to an adult. In the south-western part of the cemetery, a simple pit grave containing the burial of an infant between 1 and 2 years old was discovered, with the burial dated to c.4200–4000 BCE. The child had been placed in a sitting position, facing south-eastwards, and wore a necklace or snail shells from the Red Sea and a bracelet made of small faience beads.

Just outside the stone enclosure, five toppled standing stones lie on the ground and, when erect in their original positions, they must have been easily spotted from some distance away as they measure c.3m in length. About 50m to the north-east, the remains of a smaller circular enclosure were discovered and many small standing stones encircle this monument, most of which are fallen and lie scattered about on the desert surface, although those that are still erect measure about c.40cm in height. Five stone pavements with diameters of 1m to 2m were found even further to the north-east and although an excavation carried out near one of these structures did not bring to light any artefacts that could date these structures, it seems quite likely that they formed part of the Wadi Khashab ceremonial complex.

Interestingly, all the monuments of the complex are aligned along a north-east/south-west axis, perhaps marking the midsummer sunrise and midwinter sunset respectively. Whether or not this was the desired intention of the people who constructed them, as Piotr Osypiński and Marta Osypińska have remarked:

> The crucial issue to explore is the reason behind the decision by a group of people for whom cattle and sheep-breeding played a major role to erect a megalithic and sacrificial structure almost exactly in the middle of the mountains separating the Nile Valley and the Red Sea coast. Was it an expression indicating the centre of the territory that they occupied, or instead perhaps its limit?[43]

We may not be able to answer this question with certainty, but there can be little doubt that the Wadi Khashab ceremonial complex represents a rather extraordinary reminder of the Neolithic pastoralist communities who inhabited this part of Egypt's Eastern Desert some 6,000 years ago.

Chapter Six

Troubled Times in Prehistoric Egypt

Discoveries made at archaeological sites around the world have revealed that prehistoric hunter-gatherers were not always the peace-loving 'children of nature' envisaged by some people, and that violence and 'warfare' were not unknown among these ancient communities, perhaps also being more common than we might suppose (some scholars argue that 'true' warfare did not emerge until the Neolithic or even later, with the emergence of the first states). For example, there is a grim but remarkable discovery, quite recently made at the site of Nataruk, which lies about 19 miles west of Lake Turkana in Kenya. Here, in 2012, researchers from the University of Cambridge discovered the fossilized remains of a hunter-gatherer group that had been massacred about 10,000 years ago, with many of the skeletons displaying clear signs of violent death such as shattered skulls and stone projectile points lodged in a male skull and in the thoracic (chest) and pelvic cavities of a male skeleton. Many of the skeletons were found face down, with four also discovered in positions suggesting that their hands had been bound when they were killed; one of these skeletons represented a woman in the late stages of pregnancy (whose feet may also have been tied together).

Many other sites containing evidence of violent conflict between prehistoric hunter-gatherers could be mentioned. One of the most famous is Ofnet Cave in Bavaria, where two pits containing 'nests' of decapitated skulls from thirty-four individuals (mostly women and children) were found in 1908. The skulls, which were sprinkled with red ochre and accompanied by many pierced red deer teeth and snail shells, have been dated to the European Late Mesolithic (Middle Stone Age) C.6500–6200 BCE and many display lethal injuries (caused by stone axes), with possible cut marks from scalping also identified on some examples. We cannot be certain, but it is quite possible, if not probable, that they represent the ceremonial burial of booty from a head-hunting expedition as suggested by Nick Thorpe.[1]

Site 117: The Jebel Sahaba 'War Cemetery'

Perhaps the best-known archaeological evidence testifying to the existence of hunter-gatherer warfare or 'lethal, intergroup violence', as some scholars would prefer, was discovered at the site of Jebel Sahaba (dated to c.11,000 BCE), which is now located just over the Egyptian border in northern Sudan or Nubia. Jebel Sahaba is associated with the Late Palaeolithic Qadan culture (c.13,000–9,000 BCE), which seems to have been confined to a region of the Nile Valley roughly spanning the First and Second Cataracts of the river, from Aswan in Upper Egypt to Wadi Halfa in northern Nubia.

Under the direction of the renowned archaeologists Fred Wendorf and Romuald Schild, an international team of researchers carried out excavations at several sites near Wadi Tushka from 1964 to 1966. These excavations were part of a UNESCO-funded campaign set up to record and salvage the hundreds of Egyptian and Nubian archaeological sites that were going to be drowned by the building of the Aswan High Dam (built between 1960 and 1970), and mark the origins of the celebrated Combined Prehistoric Expedition, which continues to work in Egypt to this day. As noted, one of the largest of these sites (Site 8095) provided 'A rare insight into many features of Qadan life in particular and late Palaeolithic life in general.'[2] Site 8095 actually comprised the remains of numerous, small-scale hunting and fishing encampments located along the edge of the River Nile, with 'dense clusters of cultural material'[3] found at these hunter-gatherer campsites. Included among this cultural material were several thousand microlithic tools,[4] many grinding stones, numerous catfish bones[5] and the bones of wild cattle, hartebeest and gazelle. Twenty-one poorly-preserved human burials were also found at Site 8095, although not all were contemporary with the Late Palaeolithic hunter-gatherer campsites. Cattle horns also lay near the heads of some of the graves' occupants and may have been intentionally placed there by funerary parties.

The rarest and most shocking insight into Qadan life, however, was provided by the Jebel Sahaba cemetery. This site first came to light in 1962 during the preliminary survey carried out by the archaeologists of the UNESCO salvage campaign, who found three fragmentary human skeletons in a pit located in a wadi on the east bank of the Nile, about 2 miles north of Wadi Halfa. Site 117, as the Jebel Sahaba cemetery was labelled, was subsequently excavated in 1965–66 by Fred Wendorf and his team, and it is perhaps not being too overly dramatic to say that 'Signs of staggering human brutality greeted [its] excavators.'[6] Around 40 per cent of the sixty or so people[7] buried at Site 117 who were interred in shallow pits covered with sandstone slabs were accompanied by microlithic projectile points from barbed arrows or spears, which were clearly not deposited with the dead as grave goods:

> One of the unusual features of the burials was the direct association of 110 artifacts, almost all in positions which indicate they had penetrated the body either as points or barbs on projectiles [arrows] or spears. They were not grave offerings. Many of the artifacts were found along the vertebral column, but other [favoured] target areas were the chest cavity, lower abdomen, arms and the skull. Several pieces were found inside the skull, and two of these were still embedded in the sphenoid bones [behind the jaw and cheekbone] in positions which indicate that the pieces entered from under the lower jaw.[8]

In fact, it is estimated that 'of the sixty-one men, women and children buried at Jebel Sahaba, at least 45 per cent of them died of inflicted wounds, making this the earliest evidence of inter-communal violence [or warfare] in the archaeological record.'[9] Some of these people had suffered multiple wounds and had clearly been the unfortunate victims of vicious 'overkill'. One of these victims, Burial or Skeleton 44, was a young woman whose bones were associated with twenty-one projectile points, with three of these 'found in front of, inside and behind the mandible',[10] suggesting that an arrow or spear with composite armatures had penetrated her mouth or face. Two male victims of overkill were also found buried together (Skeletons 20 and 21), with their skeletons lying close to each other on their left sides, almost as if the men were embracing, with their faces looking eastwards. Skeleton 21 seems to have been the victim of a particularly vicious attack as nineteen projectile points were found in and among the bones of his skeleton. Fragments from two projectile points were actually found still embedded in the left pelvis of Skeleton 21, and two other points were also discovered inside his skull. His companion appears to have suffered a less violent but still frightening assault, with six projectile points associated with Skeleton 20. As Renée Friedman has noted, modern analysis of the skeletons prior to their display in the Early Egypt Gallery (Room 64) in the British Museum[11] revealed many more projectile points embedded in their bones (e.g. a further two projectile point fragments were found in the right pelvis of Skeleton 21).[12]

Further signs of violence were identified on some of the skeletons found at Jebel Sahaba by Fred Wendorf and his colleagues. These consist of 'parry fractures' on forearm bones, which are injuries that typically occur when people attempt to parry blows from a weapon of some sort, and cut marks.

Interestingly, cut marks were noted on the femurs of nine individuals and this has been interpreted as evidence of the severing of the hamstring in order that people could not escape their attackers.[13] It is also worth bearing in mind that lethal wounds caused by arrows and other weapons would not necessarily show up on skeletons, and so the death toll at Jebel Sahaba might have been even higher than is suggested by the evidence and it could even be possible that we are looking at the massacre of the whole of a Late Palaeolithic community. However, most archaeologists seem to be of the opinion that the victims of violence at Jebel Sahaba lost their lives in a series of raids and ambushes spread out over several generations, although the possibility that all the dead from the cemetery lost their lives at the same time cannot be totally ruled out.

Whatever the truth, the evidence found at Jebel Sahaba reveals that however we choose to label the deadly armed conflicts of non-state, 'primitive' societies, they certainly took place between rival groups of hunter-gatherers in the Nile Valley during the Late Palaeolithic, some 13,000 years ago (it is worth pointing out, however, that another Late Palaeolithic cemetery on the East Bank of the Nile, opposite Jebel Sahaba, was also excavated by Fred Wendorf, but no evidence of lethal violence was found here). As has been pointed out, Fred Wendorf suspected two driving factors behind Late Palaeolithic 'warfare' in the Nile Valley: 'First, the Nile embayments of that era would have been rich but circumscribed environments surrounded by barren desert. Second, there were several groups of people competing for the fish and nut-grass of each embayment, apparently ready to defend them with violence if necessary.'[14] Renée Friedman has also remarked:

> The reason for all of this violence most likely comes down to climate. The Ice Age glaciers covering much of Europe and North America at this time made the climate in Egypt and Sudan cold and arid. The only place to go was to the Nile, but its regime was erratic: depending on the exact dating, the river was either high and wild, or low and sluggish. Either way, there was little viable land on which to live and resources must have been scarce. Competition for food may well have been the reason for the conflict as more groups clustered around the best fishing and gathering grounds and were unwilling or unable to move away.[15]

Further Evidence for Lethal Violence and Warfare

Fred Wendorf and archaeologists of the Combined Prehistoric Expedition also investigated several Late Palaeolithic sites at Wadi Kubbaniya, just north of Aswan, which was the location of an annual lake created by the Nile floods during the time of the 'Kubbaniyans' around 20,000 years ago: 'From June to September the flooding Nile backed up into the canyon's lower course, submerging all but its tallest sand dunes. This flooding created a rich localized environment where catfish and tilapia gathered and water-loving plants like sedges and rushes grew abundantly.'[16] Therefore, it is not surprising that hunter-gatherer groups were drawn to Wadi Kubbaniya and that Wendorf and his colleagues found many traces of their lives during the excavations they carried out at the Kubbaniyan sites in 1978 and from 1981 to 1984. For example, there were numerous microlithic tools and grinding stones, the bones of wild cattle, hartebeest, the remains of edible plants (e.g. nut-grass tubers, club-rush) and, not surprisingly, an abundance of fish bones. In fact, at one site, more than 130,000 catfish bones were recovered, and it could even be the case that it was the sound created by the mouth-and-tail slapping of thousands of spawning catfish in the Late Palaeolithic lake that attracted hunter-gatherer groups to Wadi Kubbaniya.

It seems then, from the evidence found at the Kubbaniyan sites, that life was comfortable, if not good, for the hunter-gatherer groups who set up their temporary encampments around the palaeo-lake at Wadi Kubbaniya. However, the CEP also made a discovery which suggested that sometimes life at Wadi Kubbaniya during the Late Palaeolithic could turn very nasty. This was the discovery of the burial of a young man in his early twenties, who had died about 20,000 years ago. Interestingly, an osteoarchaeological examination of his skeleton revealed that he 'had an asymmetrically developed right arm, suggesting that he had been a strong right-handed spear-thrower'.[17] Ironically, examination of the young man's skeleton indicated that in Late Palaeolithic Egypt, sometimes 'those who lived by the spear could also die by the spear'. It was discovered that 'His death came as the result of a spear-sized projectile that had left two flint barbs between his ribs and lumbar vertebrae.'[18] Furthermore, the young man had a healed 'parry' fracture on his forearm, indicating that he had used his arm to shield his head from an armed enemy, and another projectile was embedded in his upper arm. The bone had only just started to heal around this projectile, showing that this individual man had survived another attack not long before he was brutally killed.

It may be worth mentioning that evidence of death by spearing in Stone Age societies has been found elsewhere. For example, there is the skeleton of a c.4,000-year-old aboriginal man (estimated to be 30 to 40 years of age) discovered fortuitously beneath a bus-stop in northern Sydney during the laying of electricity cables in 2005. He had fragments of microlithic barbs in his vertebrae as well as a traumatic injury on his skull, and also seems to have had more than one attacker: 'The front and rear entry direction of the points embedded in the spine indicates that a minimum of two spears were used, while the impact puncture on the skull suggests a third weapon – either a barbed spear or club.'[19] His body also appears to have been partially burned by the people who killed him.

The circumstances surrounding the violent death of the young man from Wadi Kubbaniya, who appears to have died as the result of a vicious spear-thrust to his back, can of course only be a matter of speculation. He may have been killed in a wider conflict, or alternatively was murdered in an act of revenge, a 'payback killing' for a murder he had himself perhaps committed, or some other serious transgression such as the desecration of a sacred place. Killings such as these have been widely documented in the ethnographic literature (e.g. in some of the late eighteenth-century accounts of the first European settlers in Australia), which have also shown that these killings could often be the spark that ignited serious episodes of armed conflict between clans and tribes. Whatever led to the untimely death of this young man from Egypt's distant past, his skeleton provides further proof that 'Paleolithic life…in the Nile Valley was not entirely rosy.'[20]

Neolithic Warfare in Egypt?

Skeletal evidence pointing towards warfare, or at least deadly interpersonal violence, has also been found at some Egyptian Neolithic sites. For example, skulls displaying blunt-force trauma have been found at the sites of Merimde Beni Salama, El-Omari and Mostagedda; parry fractures have also been documented on the forearms of some of the skeletons discovered at the latter site.

Also worth noting is Gregory Gilbert's suggestion that some Neolithic settlements in Egypt were 'located in naturally defensible sites, often on slightly higher ground at the end of spurs along the desert edge [and that] settlement compounds may have acted as refuges using the natural advantages of the terrain.'[21]

Regarding the possible existence of warfare in Neolithic Egypt, we should perhaps also consider the 'winged' flint arrowheads made by many of its later Neolithic communities. Although these elegant stone projectiles are often considered to have been made for the hunting of large game animals, it is worth bearing in mind that similar arrowheads were designed specifically as weapons of war by several non-state societies such as the Dani of the central highlands of New Guinea or the Native American Wintu of California. Whether or not the winged arrowheads of the Egyptian Neolithic were made specifically for killing animals, they could certainly have been used to also kill people in times of conflict.

As will also be recalled, a barbed and tanged flint arrowhead was found near the spine of the young man buried in a Late Neolithic grave at Gebel Ramlah in the Western Desert. Of course, this arrowhead may simply represent a grave offering, which was perhaps intended to help the deceased to hunt in the next life. This is probably more likely given that there was no sign of an impact fracture on the arrowhead, but is it perhaps possible that rather than being placed in the grave by a mourner, it entered the grave originally lodged in the body of the man who it had killed?

Hollow-based 'winged' arrowhead found in the Fayum by Gertrude Caton Thompson. (*Metropolitan Museum of Art, Gift of the British School of Archaeology 1926, Creative Commons*)

Gebelein Man

Between 1886 and 1893, the well-known early Egyptologist E.A. Wallis Budge (or to give him his full title, Sir Ernest Alfred Thompson Wallis Budge) of the British Museum made regular visits to Egypt, undertaking these trips because he wished 'to form a complete typical collection of mummies and coffins of the various periods of Egyptian History'[22] for the museum. He subsequently sent twenty-seven ancient cadavers back to the British Museum, buying them mainly from dealers without being particularly concerned about where the mummies had originally come from or what means were used to retrieve them. Such practices might seem rather unsavoury to us today, but were standard practice in the early days of Egyptology, with thousands of mummies exported to European museums from Egypt. Budge's acquisitions included two mummies from the Middle Kingdom, four from the Third Intermediate Period and a large number dating to the Late Ptolemaic and Roman periods. However, the most 'striking group of mummies acquired by Budge were the six naturally mummified bodies of the Late Predynastic Period from Gebelein'[23] in Upper Egypt.

As was the norm in the Naqada culture (and in the preceding Neolithic), these individuals were buried in simple circular or oval shallow pit graves dug into the hot desert floor which, as noted, 'was, accidentally, the most effective means of preserving a dead human body used by the Egyptians.'[24] As there was little to keep the sand away from the dead in these pit graves, corpses dried out very quickly because decomposition fluids were absorbed by the sand that filled the pits, which led to the natural preservation of bodies. Many scholars believe that the idea that the body had to be preserved for eternity in order for the soul to survive, which was such an integral part of ancient Egyptian religion, originated with the later chance discovery of these graves.

Included among the six mummies shipped back to London by Budge is an individual who has been labelled Gebelein Man, or 'Ginger' as he was later nicknamed because of the tufts of ginger hair that can still be seen on his skull (although it is no longer considered 'ethical' to use this nickname). Gebelein Man (or 'Gebelein Man A', as he is more strictly known) is one of the most famous 'occupants' of the British Museum, having been almost continuously on display there since his discovery more than 120 years ago (Plate 12), although it was not until some ten years ago that it was realized that his death had probably not been a peaceful one.

In late 2012, Gebelein Man was packed up and transported about 5 miles down the road to the Bupa Cromwell hospital where his body was CT-scanned, allowing archaeologists to look in detail at his body. The CT scans revealed that he was a young man (c.18 to 21 years old) when he died, which was nothing out of the ordinary given that not many people would have lived beyond 40 years of age in the prehistoric period in Egypt, and indeed, in the succeeding pharaonic one. However, the British Museum archaeologists were probably not prepared for the evidence of 'foul play' that was also brought to light by the CT scans: 'A cut in the skin over his left shoulder blade, as well as damage to the underlying muscle, scapula and fourth rib, suggest he died from a stab wound to the back.'[25] It may also be worth noting that a more recent examination of Gebelein Man led to the discovery of two tattoos on his upper right arm which depict two horned animals, probably a Barbary sheep and an aurochs.[26]

The fact that Gebelein Man was stabbed in the back points towards murder and that he was taken unawares by his killer. However, as Renée Friedman has pointed out, 'a radiocarbon age range [3351–3017 BCE] obtained from analysis of his hair corresponds to the date ascribed to the numerous depictions of conflict in the process surrounding the so-called unification and the establishment of the Dynastic Egyptian state at about 3100 BCE.'[27]

Close-up of the mummy of Gebelein Man, with the hair still clearly visible on the skull. (*Fæ, Creative Commons*)

Therefore, it is not impossible that he lost his life in a battle fought between rival Late Predynastic groups.

As Augusto Gayubas has also argued, 'There is evidence of warlike activities in iconographic representations'[28] as early as the Amratian or Naqada 1 period, c.4000–3500 BCE. Stan Hendrickx and Merel Eyckerman are in agreement: 'From the very beginning of the Naqada I period, semantic representations of military victory are attested.'[29] These scenes of military victory appear on a small group of 'Cross-Lined' ware, pottery vessels such as the fine, well-known example (E3002) that can be seen in the Royal Museum for Art and History, Brussels. This scene shows 'two human figures...with arms raised, each of them wearing a headdress and an animal tail, and one of which is holding by their necks, with a rope, a number of small-size figures, probably captives.'[30] It could be suggested that this scene represents a ritual dance of some sort rather than a military victory, but the larger size of the two figures and the smaller tethered individuals points more strongly towards the subjugation of defeated enemies.

Augusto Gayubas has also noted that 'There is more explicit evidence related to war and leadership in later [Naqada culture] contexts',[31] and the most famous can be seen on the Narmer Palette, which was discovered at the major settlement site of Hierakonpolis at the end of the nineteenth century by the English antiquarians James Edward Quibell and Fredrick William Green. The two early archaeologists also discovered Tomb 100, which featured a remarkable array of painted images on one of its walls, some of them hinting at violence and warfare. We will return to look at the Narmer Palette and Tomb 100 in more detail in the final chapter.

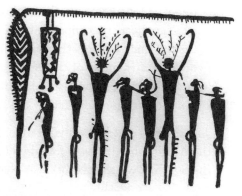

Possible scene of a military victory from a Naqada culture Cross-Lined-ware vessel (E3002), in the Royal Museum for Art and History, Brussels. (*Redrawn after Gayubas, 2015*)

It is also worth noting the broken clay model found by Flinders Petrie at the Naqada culture site of Abadiya. Although rather crude, it clearly shows two individuals standing behind and peeping over a crenellated town wall. It is hard not to see this model as anything other than a depiction of two sentries or lookouts standing on a defensive mud-brick wall surrounding a settlement, and Béatrix Midant-Reynes has remarked:

> It is difficult to know whether these figures are intended to represent giant sentries or whether the wall itself is very low, but this is perhaps not important in terms of the model's overall significance. The

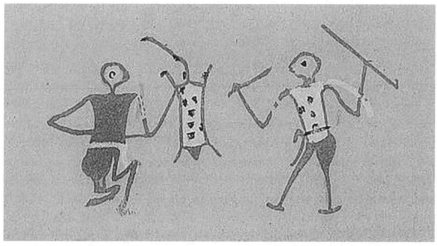

Depiction of two figures engaged in combat, from Tomb 100, Hierakonpolis. (*Creative Commons, Public Domain*)

important elements are the enclosure wall and the two look-out men, which indicate two important aspects of defence, thus recalling not only the tendency towards the clustering of populations from the Amratian period [early phase of the Naqada culture] onwards (a factor which is archaeologically demonstrable) but also a more defensive mentality that is not otherwise indicated by the archaeological remains.[32]

The remains of a substantial wall (c.2m wide), similar to the one depicted in the Abadiya model, were found by Flinders Petrie during his excavations at the South Town site (Nubt) near Naqada.

Skeletal Evidence from Hierakonpolis

During the final days of their 1998 archaeological investigations at Hierakonpolis, Renée Friedman and her team uncovered a double burial (Burial 123 in Cemetery HK43) containing the skeletons of two young men aged 20 to 25, who had been buried side by side in a tightly-flexed position on a large reed mat. One of the young men seems to have had his life cut violently short:

> When Chris Marshall returned to the lab to begin the inventory of the skeletal material, she noticed a mark on the hyoid bone of one of the males (the hyoid is a small bone located on the front, or anterior, part of the throat just below the jaw). She then took a close look at the cervical vertebrae and noticed four more small cut marks. The alignment of the marks and the angle would indicate the likelihood that the throat was slit by a single cut. There was absolutely no detected evidence of healing and there is little doubt that the sharp force trauma to the neck was the cause of death.[33]

Interestingly, it was also discovered that the other young man found in the grave had suffered from a rare malformation of the skull called craniostenosis or 'premature fusion of the sutures of the skull. This early fusion causes the back of the skull to bulge outward with the continued growth of the brain. If viewed from either the top or the back, the skull looks distinctly triangular in shape.'[34] This young man had clearly not had an easy life: as well as having an oddly-shaped head, it was realized that his eyes would have been at different levels in his face, that his jaw was malformed (possibly because of the craniostenosis), that he would not have been able to walk properly because of abnormalities in his legs and knees, and finally that he had several healed fractures on his collarbone and spine.

In Burial 124 the archaeologists found the partial skeleton of a young man who had been decapitated, as revealed by his detached skull and the numerous cut marks identified on his cervical vertebrae. In Burial 120, the skeleton of a woman who had been laid to rest with her arms crossed across her chest was discovered. At first sight, nothing out of the ordinary was noted on her skeleton, but after the earth around her skull had been cleared away, it was realized that a large part of her skull was missing. The skull was subsequently reconstructed after the missing pieces were found elsewhere in the grave, and it was clear that the woman had suffered a massive blow to the back left side of her head that had not healed and thus killed her.

In fact, as Sean Dougherty and Renée Friedman have noted, in total 'At Hierakonpolis, twenty-one individuals (eleven males, two females and eight indeterminable) with vertebrae suggestive of decapitation have been uncovered. In addition, five male individuals are present with cut marks indicative of scalping, a practice thus far undocumented in Egypt.'[35] The most notable of these possible scalping victims was a young male aged 18–21 whose skull displayed almost 200 separate cut marks, with the most severe of these found on the front. Scalping, of course, is most often associated with Native American populations, some of whom took the scalps of enemies defeated in battle.

Of course, this intriguing skeletal evidence from Hierakonpolis could be related to unknown mortuary rituals that involved the mutilation of the body, and perhaps even human sacrifice or the execution of criminals who had carried out some serious wrongdoing such as grave robbery, for example. Nevertheless, it is likely that at least some of the evidence briefly considered above points strongly towards warfare, particularly that found in Naqada culture contexts of the fourth millennium BCE, with many archaeologists of the opinion that armed conflict had some role to play in the forging of the early Egyptian state and the beginning of the pharaonic period. It also seems improbable that deadly conflicts did not flare up at least occasionally among earlier Egyptian prehistoric communities and there could have been many reasons why they 'went to war'. Azar Gat has noted that 'Revenge has probably been the most regular and prominent cause of fighting in anthropological accounts of pre-state societies. Violence was activated to avenge injuries to honour, property, women and kin.'[36] Whatever the reasons, some of the evidence that has been briefly considered here cleverly reveals that there was a dark and dangerous side to humanity in Stone Age Egypt.

Chapter Seven

The First Farmers of Egypt

From 1929 to 1939 the West Nile Delta Expedition, led by the German archaeologist Herman Junker,[1] carried out excavations at what is now recognized as one of the most notable sites of the Egyptian Stone Age: the Early Neolithic settlement of Merimde Beni Salama, which was discovered during the expedition's preliminary survey in the winter of 1927/28. The site is situated about 37 miles north-west of Cairo on the western edge of the Nile Delta, just west of the Rosetta branch of the Nile near the modern village of Beni Salama. Junker subsequently excavated an area covering c.6,400m² at Merimde Beni Salama, with the settlement extending for at least c.200,000m² along the river terrace on which it is situated.

The occupational debris left behind by Merimde Beni Salama's Neolithic inhabitants averages 2.5m in depth and consists of five occupation levels that correspond to the three main cultural stages initially identified by Junker, which have subsequently been dated to c.5000–4300 BCE. From 1976 to 1982, Josef Eiwanger of the German Archaeological Institute of Cairo carried out further excavations at Merimde Beni Salama, mainly to try to make sense of the site's complex stratigraphy, subsequently identifying that the final stage of the settlement (Level III) comprised three occupation levels: III, IV and V. Given the size of Merimde Beni Salama and the depth of its occupational debris, it is not surprising that Junker unearthed a wealth of fascinating archaeological material relating to the lives of the Neolithic families who lived here.

When Merimde Beni Salama was founded some 7,000 years ago, the Rosetta branch of the Nile flowed close by to the east, providing not only a rich source of food but also depositing fertile alluvium during the annual Nile flood, which created land well-suited to the growing of arable crops and the grazing of domesticated animals. Michael Hoffman notes that this important Neolithic settlement 'was originally settled by a people intimately familiar with the mixed herding and crop-raising techniques that had dominated the Middle Eastern and Levantine worlds for 2,000 years.'[2] Included among the archaeological evidence from Level I, or the *Urschicht* ('primary layer'), was a scattering of hearths and postholes representing the remains of light shelters, and a wide variety of objects: decorated pottery bowls adorned with a herringbone pattern, crude flint axes, pottery ladles, ostrich eggshell beads, grinding stones, bone harpoon points, flint knife blades and end-scrapers, fish hooks made from Nile mussel shells, sandstone mortars and pestles (which were found in all levels of the site), and a type of small stone arrowhead resembling the Helwan points used by earlier Neolithic communities in the Levant. The most significant objects found in Level I were an 'anthropomorphic figurine and fragments of bovids represent[ing] the first examples of Egyptian sculpture in the round'.[3]

The bones of wild and domesticated animal species such as sheep, cattle, pig, goat, dog and hippopotamus were also recovered from Level I, as they also were in the later levels, and carbonized grains of domesticated wheat were also found preserved in a hearth, with preserved wheat also found in the granaries of the later settlement stages. Béatrix Midant-Reynes has pointed out that just one hippopotamus 'could supply as much meat as four to five head of cattle or forty to fifty sheep – while its enormous skeleton also provided material for numerous objects, such as harpoons, fish hooks and boring tools.'[4] In the later occupation levels, cattle, pig and fish bones were found in greater numbers. Midant-Reynes has also noted that the archaeological material recovered from Level I 'indicates the presence of a hitherto unknown culture' that may have been in contact with Neolithic communities in the Levant.[5]

In Level II, or the *Mittleren Merimdekultur* ('middle Merimde culture'), evidence of a more intensive phase of settlement was brought to light and was indicated by numerous hearths, pits and postholes. William C. Hayes notes in *Most Ancient Egypt* (1965), one of the best works of the time on the Egyptian Stone Age, that

> Rows of postholes and fragments of the wooden posts themselves show that the villagers of Layer II lived in oval huts of wood-frame and wickerwork construction, perhaps covered with hides [and that] in some instances the roof of the hut had been supported by a stout wooden column at the centre of the dwelling [indicating conical roofs].[6]

Large pottery vessels, presumably for storing water, were found sunk into the floors of some of the huts, along with 'pot basins' which had originally held smaller domestic pottery vessels. Large oval or circular baskets made from rushes or wheat straw used for storing grain were even found preserved on some of the hut floors. Outside the huts, large pits had served as granaries, some of which still bore the remains of the clay-coated baskets that had lined them, and larger but shallow circular pits up to c.4m in diameter and lined with matting may have been used as threshing floors, given that preserved grain was found in and near them.

There were also some obvious differences in the material culture of Level II. For example, in marked contrast to that of the *Urschicht*, it appears that none of the simple pottery vessels made by the inhabitants of the *Mittleren Merimdekultur* were decorated with motifs of any kind, and the distinctive 'winged' or hollow-based arrowheads that are a characteristic feature of the Egyptian Late Neolithic appear for the first time in Level II. It is interesting to note that many of these arrowheads had broken 'wings', indicating that they had been previously used in hunting and perhaps also in warfare. Among the other objects recovered from Level II were more 'classically Neolithic' polished and flaked flint axes, fragments of clay animal figurines (bovids), pendants made from canid teeth, two small axes made from a hippopotamus rib, fragments of alabaster vessels and two pear-shaped mace-heads: one made from alabaster and the other from a rare type of volcanic rock only found in Anatolia and Palestine. Also found in Level II was a bowl that had been deliberately sunk into the ground, inside which there was an intriguing collection of artefacts covered by a reed mat. These comprised five small axes made from schist, a fragment of an ivory bracelet or anklet fashioned from hippopotamus ivory, two conical objects of uncertain function also made from hippopotamus ivory, and a bone figure of an unidentified animal (possibly a hippopotamus). The suspicion is that this object-filled bowl represents an offering of some sort, perhaps made to subterranean spirits or deities, although, of course, as critics of archaeologists are often keen to point out, the unexplained is often explained as evidence of religious rituals!

As pointed out, 'Despite the improvements in house construction and grain storage achieved during the second stage of its history, [Merimde Beni Salama] remained throughout this stage an open settlement of sparsely scattered dwelling-groups, or little "farmsteads",'[7] and it was not until the Level III stage of settlement, or *Jüngeren Merimdekultur* ('younger Merimde culture'), that Merimde Beni Salama took on a 'genuinely village-like appearance'.[8] It was a large village, as it has been estimated that around 5,000 people lived at Merimde Beni Salama during this time, a lot less than the 16,000 initially suggested by the well-known geoarchaeologist Karl Butzer, but still a lot of inhabitants nonetheless. The oval houses of the village were not large, measuring between 1.5m and 3m wide, with semi-subterranean floors sunk into the ground to a depth of around 0.5m and walls made of clods of Nile mud, sometimes tempered with chopped straw; they must have been roofed with plant materials such as rushes and reeds gathered from the nearby Nile. Béatrix Midant-Reynes has remarked:

> Primitive though they may seem, these dwellings were not scattered at random but aligned with one another and lined up in rows, along which streets can be assumed to have passed. Groups of post-holes mark out the ground-plans of huts made from lighter material and horseshoe-shaped shelters opening towards the south-east, which were probably more ephemeral structures serving as workrooms or summer kitchens, protected from the north wind. Finally, a reed enclosure fence, laid out across the ground and very well preserved…strikingly recalls enclosures for livestock in modern Egypt.[9]

Furthermore, William Hayes argued that the alignment of the dwellings in rows forming streets 'almost certainly reflects the existence of some form of local government, headed probably by a town or district chieftain'.[10] Whether or not a 'chieftain' held sway at Merimde Beni Salama, in the later stages of settlement there was 'certainly…a "formal" organization of village life'[11] during the *Jüngeren Merimdekultur.*

Inside the houses, the discovery of grinding stones, sunken water jars, scattered animal bones and hearths attested to domestic activities and, in some examples, access to the interior of the dwelling was provided by a ready-made step consisting of the leg-bone of a hippopotamus. Mud-lined granary pits lay adjacent to the houses and, in some cases, huge pottery jars (c.1m high and 0.5m wide at the shoulder) had also been sunk into the ground to provide storage for grain and other foods.

Many hundreds of artefacts were excavated from the final occupation levels of the village. For example, there were egg-shaped limestone weights probably used in net fishing, clay spindle whorls attesting to spinning and weaving, various items of jewellery such as miniature stone axe-head pendants, pierced shells and stone, bone and ivory beads, a beautifully-made flint spearhead, clay ladles and spoons, and small

Preserved grain from Merimde Beni Salama. (*Metropolitan Museum of Art, gift of Albert Rothbart 1933, Creative Commons, Public Domain*)

pottery vessels with anthropomorphic feet. Also unearthed was a baked clay human figurine, which 'probably represents a woman or goddess, a pair of protuberances rather low on the figure being taken as breasts and a loop of incised dots above and between them as a bead necklace.'[12]

It has also been noted that 'Several female figurines painted in red... come from the site of Merimde Beni Salama [but] sadly...have become lost.'[13] Parallels have been drawn between these figurines and similar ones found at contemporary Neolithic sites in South-West Asia (specifically those in the Jordan Valley) and Sudan.[14] Figurines such as these have often been seen as representations of a Neolithic fertility goddess, which is not implausible given that the continued fecundity of the land was important to early farming communities. Of course, these figurines may be symbols of something else other than fertility, but it does seem likely that they had a religious significance of some sort.

The most enigmatic artefact found in Level III, however, was undoubtedly a small oval head (c.10.5cm high) made from clay, which had two wide gaping holes for eyes, a wide, flat nose and a small, half-open mouth, providing the earliest schematic representation of a face from Egypt yet known (Plate 13). Holes can be seen on the forehead and also on the chin, suggesting that material of some sort was placed in these holes, perhaps to represent hair and a beard. The meaning of this highly intriguing object can only be guessed at, but as has been pointed out, a hole at the base of the head 'raises the possibility that [it] was originally attached to the upper end of a wooden pole, as if it were a kind of puppet.'[15] Who or what this head depicts will never be known, but its face, which looks back at us from some 7,000 years ago, has a haunting and powerful – some may even say eerie – quality that is hard to deny.

Some 200 burials were discovered in the various occupation levels at Merimde Beni Salama, both outside and inside the floors of the houses, although whether the latter were interred in occupied or abandoned dwellings remains a contentious issue. The bodies were wrapped in woven mats or animal skins and placed in a contracted position in shallow, oval pit-graves and, unusually, very few grave goods were placed with the dead, most of which were women and children. This imbalance in the mortuary evidence led Junker to suggest that most of the men may have been buried away from the settlement after being killed during hunting expeditions or raids on enemy settlements. However, it is probably more likely that they were buried in cemeteries in or near the settlement that have not yet been discovered.

El-Omari

In the spring of 1924, a young Egyptian mineralogist named Amin El-Omari discovered a large Neolithic settlement just to the north of his native town of Helwan, some 12 miles south of Cairo. Tragically, he died shortly after his discovery and never had the chance to carry out the archaeological investigation of the site that he had planned, but Father Paul Bovier-Lapierre, who carried out the first archaeological investigation of this important site in 1925, named it El-Omari in his honour. Strictly speaking, El-Omari 'is not one site but an archaeological locality'[16] comprising three main areas (El-Omari A, El-Omari B and Gebel Hof) located at the foot of Gebel Tura, the desert mountain which provided the high-quality limestone for the huge blocks used in the construction of the awe-inspiring Giza Pyramids. El-Omari A and B are separate parts of a single village situated near the mouth of the Wadi Hof, while the Gebel Hof settlement is situated on a high terrace almost 100m above the floor of the wadi, perhaps as a defensive measure or because water was readily available nearby in natural rain-catchment basins. The many fascinating remnants of Neolithic life recovered from El-Omari and Gebel Hof have been dated to c.4600–4350 BCE, meaning that the settlement and funerary evidence found at these sites is contemporary with that of the final stage of settlement or *Jüngeren Merimdekultur* at Merimde Beni Salama.

Father Bovier-Lapierre only spent some two weeks working at El-Omari and only published two brief and unsatisfactory accounts of his excavations. It was not until the Second World War in 1943–44 that another French archaeologist, Fernand Debono, resumed the investigation of the site, which was seriously under threat from looters and 'sebakh' diggers[17] undertaking excavations in 1948 and 1951, although it was not until forty years later that the German Archaeological Institute in Cairo finally published a full account of Debono's work at El-Omari.

Debono discovered the remains of many oval and circular lightweight wooden huts that seem to have had walls comprising posts and mud-daubed wickerwork frames, and numerous objects, among which was a variety of simple pottery vessels made from a combination of two types of clay obtained from the nearby Wadi Hof. Interestingly, these pots compare more closely with those made by contemporary Palestinian potters, who also used two clays in the production of their ceramic vessels. The non-ceramic finds included objects such as small conical stone axes, ostrich eggshell containers, bone needles and fish hooks, winged arrowheads, limestone palettes, and a new and distinctive type of long flint knife with a curved back and a tang at the base, presumably to aid in their hafting; these knives were made from a grey imported flint. Also found were limestone spindle whorls and net sinkers for fishing, the base of a stone (basalt) vase with three feet that was probably imported from Palestine, and many items of jewellery, among which were pierced snail shells from the Red Sea, bone, stone and ostrich eggshell beads, and pierced fossils worn as earrings or pendants. Thanks to the exceedingly dry climate, as at Merimde Beni Salama, baskets used by the inhabitants of El-Omari had been preserved as well as pieces of linen (made from flax), lengths of string and a complete animal hide was even recovered from one of the houses. An interesting discovery was also made in one of the many small storage pits discovered at El-Omari and comprised fragments of lead ore that had been wrapped in an animal skin bag and placed underneath a pottery dish.

Like their counterparts at Merimde Beni Salama, the 'El-Omarians' were farmers and herders, as revealed by the discovery of many sheep, goat, cattle and pig bones and 'copious amounts of grains and ears of wheat and barley'.[18] It has been noted that the preserved remnants of cakes 'made of crushed wheat grains and bits of wheat and barley bread'[19] were not an uncommon find during Debono's archaeological investigations at El-Omari. Fishing also certainly played an important part in the daily diet of El-Omari's inhabitants, as revealed by the abundant amounts of Nile perch and catfish bones recovered from the settlement areas, with hunting attested by the bones of crocodiles, turtle, hippopotami and other wild animals. It is worth noting that El-Omari was the first Egyptian Stone Age site to yield what are probably the bones of domesticated donkeys, as some of the 'donkey specimens from…El Omari are small in size relative to their wild ancestors, a trait often used to identify early stages of domestication.'[20] These beasts of burden may well have been used in the transport of imported objects found at the site, such as Red Sea shells and the grey flint used to make the distinctive knife blades.

Debono's excavations at El-Omari A and B brought to light forty-three graves containing both adults and children, who were laid to rest in the foetal position in simple shallow pits with their faces towards the west and lying on or covered by mats. It also seems that a handful of the graves were covered by superstructures of some sort, as suggested by the post-holes surrounding them. Furthermore, Béatrix Midant-Reynes has remarked that the graves were obviously dug in abandoned parts of the settlement and that men, women and children were buried apart in separate areas.[21] Grave goods were scanty, but in nearly every grave there was a small pot, which was placed in front of the face or next to the body of the deceased. A few other finds were recovered from the burials: in one grave, a small clay box had been placed behind the head of its owner, while in another, the remains of a bouquet of flowers were found covering the deceased; ibex horns were also found placed in one of the children's graves.

The most interesting of the graves excavated by Debono was Grave A35, which contained the burial of an adult man who may well have held status of some sort at El-Omari:

> The skeleton of what is thought to be a local ruler was found holding in its hand a well-made wooden staff...some fourteen inches long, carved at both ends, one of the latter being pointed, the other flat. This so-called 'baton of command' has been compared with the *ames-*staff carried by Egyptian kings and gods and perhaps of prehistoric ancestry.[22]

Midant-Reynes' description of the man's 'baton of command' is a little different as she describes it as 'bulging at both ends, suggesting the shape of a phallus'.[23] Whatever the actual appearance of this intriguing object, as she has further noted: 'Its presence in the hands of a man suggests that it may have had a specific meaning.'[24]

Finally, it is worth noting that 'The existence of an unsuspected microlithic-style industry at El-Omari'[25] suggests that its Neolithic inhabitants may well have been directly descended from the earlier Epipaleolithic hunter-gatherers who once lived along the stretch of the Nile Valley in the neighbourhood of Helwan.

The Badarian Culture

Marking the earliest 'attestation of agriculture in Upper Egypt',[26] the Badarian culture is named after the site of el-Badari on the eastern bank of the central Nile Valley, where it was discovered in the 1920s by the English archaeologists Guy Brunton and Gertrude Caton Thompson who worked on the Badarian sites between 1922 and 1931 for the British School of Archaeology in Egypt. The archaeological evidence for the Badarian culture was retrieved from a series of cemeteries and settlement areas that were excavated along a c.20-mile stretch of the central Nile Valley in Middle Egypt in the 1920s. As Beatrix Midant-Reynes has remarked, 'With this culture we unexpectedly plunge straight into a symbolic universe of incredible richness, reflecting an increasingly structured and complex society'[27] which was revealed in the hundreds of graves excavated by Brunton.

Archaeologists have generally dated the Badarian culture to c.4500–4000 BCE, although thermoluminescence dates obtained from some sites have suggested that it may have already emerged by c.5000 BCE.

Badarian graves consist of simple pits that were dug into the low and narrow stretch of desert that fringes the cultivated land next to the River Nile, and the dead were mainly laid to rest on their left sides, heads to the south and facing westwards. Bodies were laid on woven mats and then completely wrapped in a mat or an animal skin, with the heads of the deceased (which often still had hair surviving on them) also sometimes resting on pillows of straw or rolled-up animal skins. Evidence has also been found to suggest that some type of loincloth or kilt, made from animal skin or linen, was sometimes worn by the dead. The remains of rudimentary coffins were even found in some of the graves, most notably in Grave No. 5716 in Cemetery 5700, which is documented in Brunton and Caton Thompson's *Badarian Civilisation*:[28]

> Undisturbed adult male in an almost rectangular grave, without pottery. With the burial was a quantity of wood and matting. As far as could be seen, the body lay on a tray of matting stiffened with sticks placed cross-wise. The ends of the sticks were lashed to stouter poles running north and south. There were sticks and matting above the bones as well, and probably we have here the remains of a kind of hamper coffin.[29]

From the same cemetery, there is also Grave No. 5710, which contained the body of a child aged about 10 who had been buried wearing shell, carnelian and steatite jewellery 'in a rush coffin'.[30]

Interestingly, modern scientific analysis carried out on skin and 'reed' wrappings, which were taken from bodies in the Badarian graves at the Mostagedda cemetery and subsequently sent back by Brunton to the Chadwick (now Bolton) museum, 'identified a pine resin, an aromatic plant extract, a plant gum/sugar, a natural petroleum source, and a plant oil/animal fat in [the] funerary wrappings.'[31] It has been remarked that 'Pre-dating the earliest scientific evidence by more than a millennium, these embalming agents constitute complex, processed recipes of the same natural products, in similar proportions, as those utilized at the zenith of Pharaonic mummification some 3,000 years later.'[32]

Various grave goods accompanied the dead, the most distinctive of which are black-topped pottery vessels with polished red or brown surfaces that are often viewed as the archaeological hallmark of the Badarian culture. These vases and bowls were very finely made with extremely thin walls, displaying the great technical skills possessed by Badarian potters which, in

Black-topped bowl of the Badarian culture. (*Metropolitan Museum of Art, Rogers Fund, 1932, Creative Commons, Public Domain*)

fact, were never surpassed by those of pharaonic Egypt. As noted: 'The most characteristic element of the Badarian pottery is the "rippled surface" that is present on the finest pottery, meaning that the surface had been combed with an instrument and afterwards polished, resulting in a very decorative effect;'[33] sometimes, simple floral motifs were also incised around the bottom of this black-topped ware. A small handful of unusual, bottle-shaped pottery vessels with loop-handles stand out from the rest of the Badarian pottery and are more akin to those found in the contemporary Ghassulian culture of the southern Levant.

In many Badarian graves, the skulls of cattle, sheep, antelopes, cats and jackals or dogs were interred alongside the dead. Sheep, dogs and antelopes were even sometimes buried alongside humans in separate graves in the cemeteries, 'thus indicating their social status and foreshadowing the role that the animal kingdom was to play in the symbolic and mythical worlds of the [ancient] Egyptians.'[34]

Many other items were placed in Badarian graves, among which were various objects made from bone and ivory such as needles, hairpins, beads, rings, long-toothed combs, spoons with their handles carved into animal forms and small spiral-carved rods of uncertain purpose. Also found in graves were decorated wooden throw-sticks, the remains of wickerwork baskets, ostrich eggshell containers, rectangular or oval stone palettes and pear-shaped mace-heads, small cosmetic jars, sometimes still stained by malachite or red ochre (with actual malachite found in one example), and beads made from pierced Red Sea shells, bone and various types of stone, which were found in their thousands and sometimes seem to have been worn on belts around the waist. Although scarce, small cylindrical or ring-like copper beads, cold-hammered from copper ore (perhaps from Sinai), were recovered from some Badarian graves, and it is interesting to note that the remains of small leather bags or baskets found with some burials still bore traces of green oxidization, suggesting 'the very early pillaging of these precious accoutrements'.[35] Several hippopotamus tusks were recovered from three graves, one of which had evidently been used as a malachite container, and in one grave ostrich feathers were even found, perhaps originally used to decorate a headdress. Although the lithic industry of the Badarian

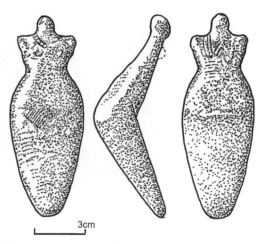

3cm

Schematic clay female figurine of the Badarian culture. (*Redrawn after Midant-Reynes, 2000*)

culture is mainly known from the settlements, finely-made flint sickles and winged and leaf-shaped arrowheads were reserved for burials.

The most striking objects recovered from the Badarian cemeteries are a small number of female figurines modelled in both hippopotamus ivory and baked clay (Plate 14). Aside from their obvious female attributes, the ivory figurines that have survived intact have over-large heads, with their facial features comprising huge staring eyes, wide prominent noses and thin mouths. The eyes and mouths were incised into the surface of the figurines and the former were perhaps originally filled with a coloured pigment of some sort. One of these clay figurines is very schematic in appearance and has a tiny head, no arms or feet and a huge, wide lower torso. It has been suggested that these figurines were perhaps intended 'to represent fertility, as a concept or as a deity, in order to assist the deceased in rebirth in the afterlife, or to provide maternal protection during that journey'.[36] Alternatively, perhaps these small and intriguing female figures 'represent the tomb owner herself returned to life and vitality'.[37]

A few hippopotamus figurines carved from the ivory tusks of the same animal and a possible antelope head also came to light during the excavation of the

Ivory vase of the Badarian culture in the form of a hippopotamus. (*Akhenatenator, Creative Commons*)

Badarian graves, as well as three clay boat models, which are probably the first reference to the River Nile found in a funerary context. It is worth noting that one of the hippopotamus figurines (found at the Mostagedda cemetery) was cleverly and skilfully carved out to form a vase, the neck of which emerges from the middle of the animal's back.

Bone, shell and serpentine beads from a Badarian grave. (*Metropolitan Museum of Art, Rogers Fund, 1932. Creative Commons, Public Domain*)

It is worth mentioning that detailed analysis of the 262 burials discovered at the cemeteries of the type-site of the Badarian culture, el-Badari, by Wendy Anderson, revealed that a small group of graves were more richly furnished than others and contained 'lavish burial offerings…not shared by other members of society'.[38] Anderson therefore plausibly concluded from her analysis that a minority of individuals in Badarian society held positions of high status and therefore its 'social system must be considered to have been inegalitarian'.[39]

The archaeological evidence relating to the settlements of the 'Badarian civilization' is 'somewhat less attractive'[40] than that recovered from its cemeteries, but the excavations carried out by Brunton and Caton Thompson revealed the existence of several small hamlets or villages, whose subsistence economies revolved around agriculture and animal husbandry; fishing was also obviously still an important part of the diet. No substantial dwellings were recovered from these sites, only lightweight temporary structures, perhaps suggesting that these were seasonal encampments and that the larger, permanent settlements may have once existed closer to the Nile floodplain but were subsequently washed away by later Nile floods or buried under the thick layers of alluvium deposited by these annual inundations.

Commonly found in the Badarian settlements were the remains of fairly substantial circular pits lined with basketry (c.1m deep and 1.3m wide), and many pottery vessels pushed into the ground, both of which served to store grain and other foodstuffs. An interesting find from the site of Matmar was a cache of six hippopotamus tusks, which presumably were intended to be used in the creation of various ivory objects. Other archaeological traces of daily life found at Badarian settlements include various stone tools and numerous pottery sherds. However, it is from their tombs that we have undoubtedly gleaned the most striking evidence of the people of the Badarian culture: the first farmers of Upper Egypt.

Chapter Eight

Prelude to Ancient Egypt:
The Naqada and Lower Egyptian Culture

I n the winter of 1894/95, Flinders Petrie and his colleague James Quibell excavated a massive burial ground located along a short stretch of the River Nile between Naqada and Ballas in Upper Egypt. More than 2,000 graves were discovered in three separate burial areas: Cemeteries B and T, and the 'Great New Race Cemetery/Cemetery N'. Petrie had never come across anything like this before, immediately recognizing that the Naqada graves and the artefacts that accompanied the dead were untypical of pharaonic Egypt:

> The first graves that I opened at Naqada shewed a position of the body which was obviously not that usual among Egyptians. The pottery and objects found were also different from any that we knew as belonging to dated periods in Egypt. So soon as I found that these were not casual and isolated peculiarities, but part of a large class, it seemed that we must regard them as belonging to an immigrant people. The longer we worked the more we marked the distinction between these immigrants and the regular Egyptians; and the longer we searched in vain for a single object of the many kinds so well known in Egyptian graves – the headrests, the canopic jars, the pottery, the amulets, the scarabs, the coffins – without finding a single example, the greater appeared the historical gulf between the two peoples.[1]

Petrie was a firm believer in the idea that ancient Egyptian civilization had been founded by an immigrant population, initially ascribing these graves to a 'New Race' that had invaded Egypt at the end of the Old Kingdom during the 'First Intermediate Period',[2] concluding that this 'sturdy hill people' who subjugated the native Egyptians hailed from Libya. Ironically, Petrie had to change his exciting theory after one of his great rivals, the French archaeologist Jacques de Morgan (director of the Egyptian Antiquities Service), discovered Naqada culture graves while excavating at Abydos in 1896 'and *immediately* recognized them as prehistoric'.[3] However, although this must have caused Petrie some consternation (and envy), it was the

Englishman who put in the hard work (which involved the discovery and excavation of more than 1,000 further Naqada culture graves at Hu and Abadiya) and carried out the painstaking analysis of a massive amount of archaeological material that eventually provided the first proof of the Egyptian Predynastic Period: 'In the five years since Naqada was published the evidence has accumulated, showing that the people there described are Predynastic, and constituted the oldest civilized people of the land, about 7000–5000 BC.'[4]

We now know that Petrie was way out with his dating of the Naqada culture, but his development of an ingenious dating system using hundreds of pottery vessels from the cemeteries of Hu and Abadiya allowed him to define three major cultural phases of his new Predynastic culture: the Amratian, Gerzean and Semainean. Although later archaeologists subsequently 'fine-tuned' the dates of the Amratian, Gerzean and Semainean, and redefined them as Naqada I, II and III respectively, these three stages of the Late Predynastic Period 'have never been fundamentally questioned, and today they still constitute the loom upon which Egyptian prehistory is woven.'[5]

Interestingly, it seems that many of the Naqada culture graves excavated by Petrie and Quibell had been rifled by robbers in the past, and the people responsible were probably the Naqadans themselves:

> There was evidence that much of the robbery had taken place soon after the making of the graves. For the plunderers had known of the position of the bodies, and had avoided working in the less profitable ends of the graves. The ends of the graves, where stood great masses of pottery but no small objects of metal, were often found intact, while the centre of the grave was disturbed.[6]

It is worth bearing in mind that numerous objects – how many we can never know – must have been lost as a result of this ancient pillaging and furthermore, that people also seem to have been plundering burials in the preceding Badarian culture. In her detailed reanalysis of hundreds of Badarian burials, Wendy Anderson identified that 'certain highly visible graves were subject to plundering [and that] the plunderers were apparently primarily engaged in removing luxury goods or "sociotechnic" artefacts (those that served to symbolize social rank or vertical social differentiation).'[7] Unfortunately, the Badarian and Naqadan grave-robbers stood at the start of a long tradition of tomb robbery that continued into the pharaonic period and well beyond, with the plundering of ancient burial (and other) sites still a serious problem in modern-day Egypt. Of course, accusations of tomb robbery can be levelled at many of the early archaeologists or antiquarians of the nineteenth century, who often came to Egypt looking for treasure rather than knowledge, and some people would even go as far as to say that modern archaeologists are little different to their forebears.

Archaeology of the Naqada Culture

Much of our knowledge of the Naqada culture comes from its cemeteries, although several Naqada settlements have been excavated, most notably the hugely important site of Hierakonpolis, which has provided a wealth of archaeological evidence with some remarkable discoveries made here over the years by archaeologists. The similarity seen between the burials of Naqada I communities and those of the Badarian culture has led many archaeologists to propose that it is in the latter that the origins of the Naqada culture lie. Like Badarian communities, those of the Naqada I period (c.4000–3600 BCE) buried their dead in simple grave-pits, covered with rudimentary roofs of branches and brushwood, and were laid to rest on reed mats on their left side in a contracted or foetal position, with their bodies (and often the grave goods as well) covered over with another mat or an animal skin, normally from a goat or gazelle. The funerary offerings placed in Naqada I or Amratian burials were also similar to those found in Badarian ones, although as pointed out, 'The Amratian culture particularly differs from the Badarian in terms of the diversity of types of grave goods and consequent signs of hierarchy.'[8]

A striking characteristic of Naqada I are the reddish-brown pottery vessels that have a lustrous black band around their rims ('Black-Topped pottery' or 'B-Ware'), which are somewhat similar to those of the Badarian culture (Plate 15). They became less common through time, and by the time of the Naqada III phase (c.3200–3000 BCE) were no longer being made by Naqadan potters. A new type of pottery known as 'Cross-Lined Ware' (C-Ware) also appears for the first time in Naqada I. This distinctive pottery comprises bowls, plates and narrow, rather elegant jars, which feature creamy-white decoration on their reddish surfaces. Cross-Lined Ware represents the earliest painted pottery in Egypt and is decorated with geometric, vegetal and animal motifs and, less frequently, depictions of boats. Human figures can also be seen on a limited number of C-Ware vessels and, as mentioned in Chapter 6, a few depict what are probably victorious warriors and their defeated enemies; such scenes became an essential part of pharaonic propaganda in ancient Egypt. More common are hunting scenes, such as the one shown on the well-known 'Moscow bowl' in the Pushkin Museum of Fine Arts, Moscow, which shows a hunter holding a bow in his right hand and four leashed greyhound-like dogs in his left. In Dynastic Egypt, hunting scenes were commonplace in the temples and tombs of royalty and their officials, with perhaps the most famous and beautiful example found in the Eighteenth Dynasty, New Kingdom tomb (c.1350 BCE) of Nebamun, who was a scribe and grain-counter at the famous Karnak temple at Luxor.

White Cross-Lined-ware beaker of Naqada I with crocodile motifs. (*Metropolitan Museum of Art, Rogers Fund, 1912, Creative Commons, Public Domain*)

Many other objects were made in Naqada I: for example, long-toothed combs with handles carved into animal forms, needles and hairpins made from bone, engraved hippopotamus tusks, small tags (made of ivory, bone, horn or alabaster) bearing human features but of unknown purpose, copper bracelets, beads, anklets, fish hooks and harpoons, and stone cosmetic palettes are often found in graves. The palettes were almost exclusively made from greywacke (siltstone/mudstone) sourced mainly from the Wadi Hammamat, an ancient dried-up river bed that runs from Koptos to Quseir on the Red Sea coast, an important trade route and quarrying area for the ancient Egyptians. Primarily rhomboidal in shape, some examples are embellished at one end with carvings of horns or birds and many examples have concavities on their surface, attesting to their long use before they were buried with their owners. In some cases, smooth brown or black pebbles of jasper accompanied palettes and these were used to grind up the pigments used for the cosmetics.

The skill of the Naqada I flint-knappers is revealed by two distinctive types of artefacts: long, delicate bifacially-flaked flint blades (some of which reach as much as 40cm in length), which often have a serrated edge, and 'fishtail lance-heads/knives' with bifurcated or forked blades. Petrie saw these artefacts as weapons that were used for close-range hunting, and it has also been noted that they 'look ahead to the Old Kingdom [2686–2160 BCE] forked instruments known as *pesesh-kef* used in the Opening of the Mouth funerary ceremony'.[9] This was basically a very elaborate funerary ritual performed by ancient Egyptian priests 'by which the deceased and his or her funerary statuette were brought to life [and] effectively transformed into vessels for the *KA* [life-force or soul] of the deceased.'[10] It has been argued, however, that there is no link between the fishtail knives and the later Opening of the Mouth Ceremony of Old Kingdom Egypt, and that they are status symbols 'most likely linked to the realm of the male world'.[11] Whatever the truth, fishtail knives continued to be made until late Naqada II times, with some examples also being fitted with bone, wood or ivory handles.

Pesesh-kef or 'Fish-tailed lance-head'. (*Brooklyn Museum, Charles Edwin Wilbour Fund, Creative Commons-BY*)

It may also be worth noting the small bird-shaped pendant that Petrie recovered from one of the graves of Naqada I, as this artefact perhaps represents the earliest faience object yet known from Egypt. Faience is basically a glazed ceramic made from crushed quartz and was very widely used by the ancient Egyptians, with countless artefacts made from this material used by both the 'lower' and 'upper' classes.

Symbols of power and prestige in the form of finely-made, disc-shaped or conical polished stone maceheads, pierced through the middle (for the attachment of handles), were also placed in Naqada I graves, and some examples may well have been used as lethal weapons in armed conflicts. They are often made from hard stone (e.g. black and white diorite porphyry), and a small number of maces have even survived with their handles attached, such as the one found in a grave at el-Mahasna that had a wooden handle or the two maces recovered from grave B86 at Abadiya; one had a handle made of ivory, while the other was furnished with a handle fashioned from an oryx horn.

Also appearing during Naqada I are cylindrical stone jars made from basalt that originated in Lower Egypt, which have high bases and two pierced handles or lugs near their rims (Plate 16). Representing the first stone vessels made in Egypt, these jars are 'certainly to be considered the production of specialized craftmanship'.[12] As Béatrix Midant-Reynes notes, 'This craftsmanship would eventually ensure that the Egyptian culture became the "civilization of stone" *par excellence*.'[13]

In the succeeding Naqada II or Gerzean phase (c.3600–3200 BCE), the Naqada culture expanded northwards into Upper Egypt, as revealed by the foundation of a cemetery at el-Gerzeh (giving its name to Petrie's Gerzean

Disc-shaped macehead of the Naqada 1/Amratian Period. (*Brooklyn Museum, Charles Edwin Wilbour Fund, Creative Commons-BY*)

culture) near the famous Meidum pyramid, a long way from the heartland of the Naqada culture which lay in the Upper Egyptian Nile Valley between Qena and Luxor. During this time, the Naqada culture also expanded southwards towards Nubia or northern Sudan, which was home to a late prehistoric Sudanese culture that archaeologists somewhat blandly refer to as the 'A-Group'. The presence of Naqadan artefacts in many A-Group burials attests to the substantial trade that took place between the two cultures.

For the most part, the burial traditions and material culture of Naqada II were similar to those of Naqada I. However, new items of material culture are found in Naqada II graves, such as the well-known 'wavy-handled' pottery jars and painted jars featuring simple but charming decoration comprising various figurative and geometric motifs. The fine stone vessels that first emerged appeared in Naqada I were becoming even more skilfully carved during this time, laying the foundations 'for the great achievements of pharaonic stone architecture'.[14] Depictions of long curved boats dominate the imagery on the painted jars, reflecting the importance of the River Nile to Naqada II communities,

Decorated Naqada II/Gerzean jar depicting a boat and human and animal figures. (*Metropolitan Museum of Art, Rogers Fund, 1920, Creative Commons, Public Domain*)

not only as a source of sustenance but also as an aquatic highway that facilitated trade and the expansion of the Naqada culture.

Other distinctive artefacts of the Naqada II phase are pear-shaped or 'piriform' maceheads which replaced the disc-shaped type, and stone cosmetic palettes carved into a variety of animal forms such as fish, turtles and birds. The disc-shaped macehead was also replaced by

Stone cosmetic palette of Naqada II/Gerzean, carved to represent a Nile tilapia fish. (*Brooklyn Museum of Art, Charles Edwin Wilbour Fund, Creative Commons-BY*)

the 'piriform' or pear-shaped type, the earliest examples of which date to the fifth millennium BCE and were recovered from Merimde Beni Salama. Why the pear-shaped macehead was adopted by Gerzean communities is something of a mystery, but it became 'one of the quintessential symbols of pharaonic domination'[15] in ancient Egypt, and pharaohs were often depicted on temple walls smiting their cowering enemies with these weapons. Also typical of the Naqada II period are the superb and delicate 'ripple-flaked' flint knives that were probably made with small copper tools and which, for Petrie, represented 'the finest examples of such work that are known from any country or age.'[16] Although this may be something of an over-exaggeration on his part, there is no doubt that these rather beautiful objects represent one of the finest examples of late prehistoric flint-knapping from anywhere in the world.

The Gebel el-Arak Knife

Some of the ripple-flaked knives of Naqada II, which continued to be made in Naqada III, were attached to decorated ivory handles, with around twenty examples discovered over the years.[17] Patricia Kim has remarked that these 'were elite objects, owned by individuals who were fully aware of the power, value and beauty of the blades alone' and their ivory handles contributed to the high-value status of these objects.[18]

The most famous ripple-flaked knife is the Gebel el-Arak Knife, which the curator of the Egyptology collection in the Louvre Museum, Georges Bénédite, purchased from an antiquities dealer in Cairo in 1914 (Plate 17). The authenticity of this stunning object has been questioned by a few scholars, but most agree that it was made in the later Naqada II period c.3300 BCE. Although the exact archaeological context of the knife is unknown, it probably came from Abydos rather than the site of Gebel el-Arak, as reported by the Cairo antiquities dealer who sold it to Bénédite.

Ripple-flaked Gerzean flint knife. (*Brooklyn Museum, Charles Edwin Wilbour Fund, Creative Commons-BY*)

There is some uncertainty as to whether the handle of the Gebel el-Arak Knife is made from elephant or hippopotamus ivory, but there can be little doubt that the low, carved relief that adorns it was executed by a masterful hand. Indeed, 'The knife-handle is exemplary of artistic and technical ingenuity, while its imagery exudes power, control and dominance.'[19] As has also been pointed out, 'The handle was either carved by a native artist familiar with Mesopotamian conventions or a foreign artisan.'[20]

On the front or obverse face of the handle (on which trace elements of gold foil have also been found), the top two registers of the finely-carved decoration depict nude male combatants engaged in hand-to-hand fighting, and below these figures, in the bottom three registers, dead warriors can be seen floating in the water between curved boats with cabins. On the reverse side of the handle, at the top, above a central knob or boss which is pierced for the attachment of a cord, a bearded and clothed individual flanked by

The carved decoration on the front and back faces of the Gebel el-Arak Knife handle. (*Rama, Creative Commons*)

or grappling two upright lions is depicted. This figure is similar to the 'Master of the Animals' motif, (identified with the Mesopotamian god El) commonly seen in the art of the Uruk period in ancient Mesopotamia. It has been pointed out that 'While it is correct to use the term Mesopotamian, a more precise description of the style is Sumerian. It is likely the figure is not actually El, but the Sumerian King of Uruk wearing the traditional symbol of his kingship, a shepherd cap.'[21] Immediately below this individual, two dogs with raised paws can be seen, and below these, in the two middle registers either side of and below the pierced boss, horned animals (probably Barbary sheep and antelopes) are shown, one of which is being mauled by a lioness. In the final register at the bottom of the handle, two dog-like creatures are depicted, one of which is on a leash held by a naked man who can be partially seen on the handle's edge.

Naqada Culture Figurines

Although they have only been found in very small numbers (c.120), mainly in graves, the so-called 'bird-headed' clay female figurines made during Naqada I and II represent one of the most enigmatic features of the Naqada culture, one of the most famous examples being the graceful 'bird lady' of Brooklyn Museum, New York (recovered from a grave at Ma'marya, Upper Egypt) (Plate 18). These curious objects take 'their name from their abstracted facial features, which are attenuated to a simple downward curve',[22] which somewhat resemble the large curving beak of a bird of prey and, as pointed out:

> The bodies of a few of these evocative bird-faced figurines capture a very particular posture: their slender torsos stretch upwards from their neat waists, their buttocks are thrust outwards, their arms (where present) curve upwards behind their heads terminating in long fingers, and their elongated legs are pressed tightly together and are frequently abbreviated to a conical form that tapers towards a rounded base without any representation of the feet. The naked upper torso is often painted red while the lower body in a few cases was coloured white [perhaps representing a dress of some sort].[23]

Carved ivory figurine of the Naqada culture. (*Metropolitan Museum of Art, Rogers Fund, 1954, Creative Commons*)

The true meaning of these figurines eludes us, but they have been variously interpreted as a representation of a Mother Goddess connected with fertility, dancers, worshippers, 'magical' servants placed in the graves to serve the dead in the next life (much like the famous *shabti* figurines that were deposited in ancient Egyptian tombs) and votive offerings made to deities.

It was not only bird-headed figurines that were a feature of the Naqada culture, as 'The more or less schematically rendered heads of bearded men seem to constitute another new category of human representation in Naqada I, which was to be further developed in Naqada II.'[24] These figurines were carved from hippopotamus or elephant ivory and the pointed beards and incised eyes, which were carved into their surfaces, do indeed give these small but intriguing objects 'a strange bird-like appearance'.[25] It has been suggested that the beard was a symbol of male power in the Naqada culture, and also noted that in later pharaonic Egypt, the ceremonial 'false beard' was the sole preserve of kings and gods.[26]

Tomb T5: Cannibalism or Ritual Sacrifice in the Naqada Culture?

Already in Naqada I there are signs of a late prehistoric society undergoing significant social change, with some graves 'wealthier' than others and reserved for the burial of elite individuals. This trend accelerated significantly in Naqada II, with the appearance of 'larger, more elaborate tombs containing richer and more abundant offerings. Cemetery T at Naqada and Tomb 100 (the so-called 'Painted or Decorated Tomb') at Hierakonpolis are good examples of this overall trend',[27] and we will return to look in more detail at Tomb 100 and other Naqada culture burials that have been discovered at this famous site below.

Tomb T5, in Cemetery T, represents one of the largest (c.11m²) and richest of the Naqada culture graves that Petrie discovered and is particularly interesting. Not only was Tomb T5 intact and lined with mud-brick, it yielded various artefacts: six stone vases, a 'forehead pendant', a stone cosmetic palette decorated at either end with a bird's head, and beads made from gold and lapis lazuli. T5 also contained the skeletal remains of several individuals displaying evidence of unusual funerary rituals and these had been piled along the walls of the tomb, indicating that they were secondary burials. Petrie tells us:

> But one of the most conclusive and important graves is that marked as T5.... This grave is one of the largest, but had every appearance of never having been opened. The valuable polished stone vases stood in perfect order, upright on the floor...the pottery vases were ranged intact along

the sides; and the filling shewed no signs of disturbance. Six skulls lay in the grave, and a large quantity of bones; but not a single bone lay in connection with its fellow. The skulls lay on the floor, some close to the upright stone jars on either side of them. A mass of bones, mainly broken at the ends, and some split, lay together on the floor in a heap about two feet across and seven inches high; while round the sides of the grave were many bones, nearly all with ends broken, lying scattered apart. Three arm bones and one thigh, broken, lay in the N.W. corner; and in another place were ten shin bones lying parallel, with one thigh.

Not only were the ends broken off, but in some bones the cellular structure had been scooped out forcibly, what remained of it being very firm and strong; and beside this there were grooves left by gnawing on the bones. That this disturbance could not be due to any animals that might have got at the bodies, either before or after burial, is proved by the scooping out of the cellular structure of the long bones; and by the heaping together of the bones in a pile, all dissevered and broken.[28]

Petrie concluded from the skeletal evidence found in Tomb T5 'that bodies were sometimes – with all respect – cut up and partly eaten'.[29] However, later scholars have criticized Petrie's cannibalism theory, with Michael Hoffman, for example, pointing out that it is not clear whether the teeth marks visible on the bones were human or animal and furthermore, there are no signs of burning on them, arguing against cannibalism.[30] Also, Hoffman came up with an alternative suggestion that is perhaps worth considering: 'It is quite possible that the inhabitants of the tomb were victims of human sacrifice – a practice that reached its peak early in Dynastic times and then quickly disappeared.'[31] In this respect, Toby Wilkinson has noted that

The tombs of the early First Dynasty kings, especially Aha, Djer and Djet, were accompanied by numerous graves of retainers; analysis of the skeletons points to these most loyal of servants having been sacrificed (willingly or unwillingly) at the time of their master's death, so that they might accompany him into the afterlife.... Hence the king's power of life and death was given very visible expression in the royal mortuary complex. Later in the First Dynasty, by contrast, the number of subsidiary burials was sharply reduced – although the practice of retainer sacrifice did not die out entirely until the beginning of the Second Dynasty.[32]

The sacrifice of slaves or servants was certainly not unknown in other ancient societies around the world. In the early 1900s, a renowned example of this shocking practice was discovered by the famous American Egyptologist George Reisner at the site of Kerma, the capital of the Kushite kingdom of ancient Nubia and the type-site of the Kerma culture (c.3000–1500 BCE), whose rulers were frequently at war with Egypt's pharaohs. During the 'classic' Kerma period (c.1750–1500 BCE), the kings of Kerma built huge burial mounds for themselves, under which Reisner found corridors containing the skeletal remains of hundreds of individuals. Some scholars have suggested that these 'corridor people' represent prisoners of war who had been captured on raids carried out in Egypt and who were subsequently ritually executed, rather than servants who had been killed to serve their king in the next life. However, a recent reanalysis of these remains by Margaret Judd and Joel Irish suggests that the latter is more likely: [The] findings suggest that large numbers of Kermans did accompany their king in death, but whether this was done willingly or not is unknown. There was no skeletal evidence of physical force to subdue reluctant participants, although soft tissue trauma resulting in death remains a possibility. A sedative may also have been involved.[33]

Whether or not the human remains found in Tomb T5 provide evidence of human sacrifice, another notable grave found in Cemetery T was Tomb T4. Also lined with mud-brick and measuring c.7m^2, T4 contained a wooden box with a skeleton still in place, with a row of black-topped and red burnished jars arranged along the head of this rudimentary coffin. Three skulls also lay on the floor and in one corner of the grave, three stone palettes were found still tied together with a cord after thousands of years. Next to them were a crushed ostrich eggshell and two engraved ivory tusks.

There were fewer than 100 graves located in Cemetery T, and these were both larger than the others found at Naqada and contained a greater wealth of grave goods. It has also been noted that Cemetery T was spatially separate from the other cemeteries[34] and it therefore seems likely, as many scholars have suggested, that the cemetery was reserved as the burial place of an elite group who were able to build bigger and more richly-furnished tombs.

It is worth mentioning that Petrie and Quibell discovered two distinct settlement areas ('Zawayda-South Town' and 'Nubt-North Town'). At the former, Petrie excavated the remains of a huge rectangular structure (c.50m by 30m), which perhaps represented the remains of a temple or the residence of a local ruler. A smaller, rectangular structure subdivided into several rooms (perhaps workshops or a storage area) and the remains of an enclosure wall c.2m wide can also be seen to the south of this substantial structure on a plan included in the 1896 report on Petrie and Quibell's excavations. Unfortunately, little remains of the South Town today: archaeologists of the Washington State University 'Predynastic of Naqada' project (1978–81) discovered that the site had been 'systematically looted and used by local farmers for *sebakh* [decomposed mud-brick used as fertilizer], leaving the desert edge site looking like a ploughed field and moving the remaining objects from their original context. Undoubtedly many of the objects from this site were sold on the black market.'[35] Radiocarbon dates obtained from undisturbed deposits in the South Town suggest that it was established around c.3500 BCE in Naqada II.

By the time of Quibell's excavation investigation of the site, little remained of the North Town settlement area: 'The layer of ruins was extremely thin, varying from half an inch to two feet, in most places not more than one foot. This layer consisted of clay dust, ashes and potsherds.'[36] A few objects (e.g. bone bodkins perhaps used for leather-working, limestone spindle whorls and two fine alabaster vases) were nevertheless found, as well as several small pit-graves containing the burials of young children and black-topped bowls and beakers.

The Coptos Colossi

In the Egyptian winter of 1893/94, just before they uncovered the vast burial ground of the Naqada culture that famously came to prove the existence of an Egypt before the pharaohs, Flinders Petrie and James Quibell carried out excavations below the Ptolemaic/Roman temple of the god and goddess, Min and Isis, at Coptos (Qift), which lay across the Nile from Naqada. Petrie unearthed numerous objects dating to the Late Predynastic/Early Dynastic, including fragments from two life-size lion statues and a huge falcon statue. However, the most notable of the many discoveries were pieces from three quite remarkable colossal limestone statues (the legs and torsos of two and the head of another) that Petrie attributed to his 'Eastern Invaders', the people he believed at the time to be the founders of pharaonic Egypt:

> Then in a hole against the south wall of the temple area I saw a long block of limestone, lying deep down in some sand bed of foundations. I thought it was pieces of [a] clustered pillar. At last when it was cleared I found some carving, and on turning it I saw it to be the legs of a statue of Khem (or Min as we should now write); and to my delight it was a primitive statue of the temple, perhaps the oldest sculpture in Egypt.... The whole thing seems to have been a rude block only roughly shaped... and then occasionally decorated with strange carvings. From all these considerations I believed that I saw before me one of the primitive idols

of Egypt, which may date from the days of the first settlements of dynastic peoples. May we soon find the remainder of it![37]

The statues may not have been the work of 'Eastern Invaders', but Petrie was not that far off in his dating of them as 'they are now generally accepted to date to the beginning of the Naqada III period [c.3200 BCE].'[38]

Although crude in comparison to the statues carved by the master masons of later Dynastic Egypt, the 'Coptos Colossi', when complete and standing in their original locations, must have been a rather awe-inspiring sight as they would have measured c.4m tall (and thus probably weighed around 2 tons). The statues embody early representations of the important Egyptian fertility god Min, and are depicted as bald and heavily-bearded men wearing broad girdles or belts around their waists, right arms pressed close to their sides and pierced so as to hold an object of some sort, with the hands of their left gripping huge erect stone penises that had been made separately and inserted into specially-made holes. Although these had long since snapped off by the time Petrie discovered the statues, a stump remained on one of the statues and Petrie also found a complete example (20cm) during his excavations at Coptos, although it may not have originally belonged to one of the statues. Given the prudish nature of late Victorian society, Petrie was perhaps understandably coy regarding the striking sexuality of the Coptos Colossi and failed to mention this obvious feature of the statues in the manuscript journal that he wrote while digging at Coptos in 1893–94, instalments of which were sent back to readers in England:

> The attitude is not that sanctioned by regular use, no back pillar, and one hand being at the side: differing therefore from all known figures of Khem, although there is enough of it to prove it to be of him. The hand at the side is very rude and elementary, and pierced through to tie

Reconstruction drawing of the Coptos Colossi shrine. (*Redrawn after Kemp, 2010*)

things onto the statue. And on the surface on one side are several low-relief carvings, most like the prehistoric rock figures of the Nile cliffs.[39]

The low-relief carvings mentioned by Petrie in his journal were carved down the right side of each statue and 'cover a curious range of subjects'[40] such as a pair of Min-standards on poles, Red Sea shells (*Lambis truncata*, giant spider conch), a lion or a dog, trees or plants, and an elephant and bull standing on mountains. In his study of the statue that the Egyptian Museum in Cairo took for its collection, at the end of Petrie and Quibell's dig at Coptos, Bruce Williams identified the *serekh* of the famous King Narmer, although Barry Kemp has questioned this identification.[41] Whatever the case, Kemp has suggested that rather than originally standing under a roofed temple building, it is more likely that the Coptos Colossi stood 'in a courtyard surrounded by a low wall, perhaps on an artificial mound, although substantial foundations would then have been required to hold the ground firm beneath their weight.'[42]

Early Discoveries at Hierakonpolis

As has been noted, 'The famous site of Hierakonpolis is located between the modern towns of Esna and Edfu in Upper Egypt.... Occupied from at least 4000 BC onward, it is the largest Predynastic site still extant and accessible anywhere in Egypt.'[43] Deep archaeological coring of sediments 6m below the surface has revealed that the origins of Hierakonpolis, or 'Nekhen' as it was known by the ancient Egyptians, lie in the Badarian period c.4500 BCE. At its peak in Naqada I, c.3800–3500 BCE, this prehistoric town must have been an impressive sight as it was spread out over an area that 'stretched for over 2.5 kilometres along the edge of the desert and back almost 3 kilometres into the great wadi that bisects the site, extending for an unknown distance into the cultivated land, where it is now deeply buried below the accumulated Nile silts.'[44] Although by the time of Naqada III Hierakonpolis had shrunk in size and declined in importance, being eclipsed by Abydos in the north, it continued to be occupied into the Early Dynastic period. Pharaohs of the later Dynastic period, such as Hatshepsut and Thutmose III, also built temples to the Egyptian hawk-god Horus at Hierakonpolis, which was probably an important centre of Horus even in the Late Predynastic and Early Dynastic periods. Known as Nekhen by the ancient Egyptians and today as Kom el-Ahmar ('the Red Mound') by modern ones, this huge urban centre was named Hierakonpolis by the ancient Greeks and means 'City of the Hawk'.

Archaeologists have now been conducting excavations at Hierakonpolis for more than a century, and as a result have made numerous discoveries at this hugely important site, which 'in its day must have been one of, if not the largest urban units along the Nile',[45] and also the power-base of a ruling Naqadan elite. Perhaps the most famous discovery from Hierakonpolis dates to the early days of archaeological exploration at the site and was unearthed during the excavations undertaken there between 1897 and 1899 by James Quibell and Frederick Green.

The Narmer Palette

Quibell and Green made many spectacular finds at Hierakonpolis, such as an exquisite falcon's head made from sheet gold (probably dating from the Sixth Dynasty of the Old Kingdom, 2686–2160 BCE), two somewhat haunting, near life-sized copper-plate statues depicting King Pepy I and his son Merenre of the Sixth Dynasty and a superb greenstone statue of King Khasekhemwy of the Second Dynasty (2890–2686 BCE). Quibell and Green unearthed many other fine artefacts at Hierakonpolis and these are important in their own right, but from a historical viewpoint, the most significant find they made was the famous 'Narmer Palette', which has been labelled 'the earliest historical record from Egypt'.[46]

This superb ceremonial object, which was probably found among or near a superb cache of objects known as the 'Main Deposit', has been dated to Naqada III (c.3200–3000 BCE), the end of the Egyptian Predynastic period (Plate 19). Kathryn Bard has remarked that 'It was during this period that Egypt was first unified into a large territorial state, and the political consolidation that laid the foundations for the Early Dynastic state of the First and Second Dynasties must have occurred then.'[47] Made from dark grey-green silt or mudstone and measuring almost 64cm long, the Narmer Palette is basically a larger and 'fancier' version of the cosmetic palettes placed in many Naqada culture graves, which were used to grind the green malachite ore that was used as eye make-up.

The palette is shield-shaped and decorated on both faces with scenes that have been superbly carved in low-relief, which as David O'Connor has noted 'have a monumental quality; boldly modelled figures of men and other creatures, some on a comparatively large scale, are arranged in formally well-organized compositions.'[48] On the obverse or front face of the palette, in the upper register, a king wearing the red crown (in Dynastic times known as the *deshret*) of northern or Lower Egypt is depicted with his standard-bearers approaching two rows of ten headless corpses, their arms bound at their sides and their severed heads neatly placed between their feet (this scene is made all the more grisly by the fact that all but one of the dead have their severed penises topping their heads). Below this scene and forming the central circular 'well' used for grinding cosmetics, two fantastical creatures with huge, serpent-like necks are depicted, each of which is being restrained by leashes grasped by human figures. Known as 'Serpopards', these strange beasts were derived from contemporary Mesopotamian royal iconography. Below the Serpopards, in the bottom panel, a rampaging bull can be seen attacking a walled town and trampling the corpse of a bearded and naked man.

The reverse and more commonly seen face of the palette is dominated by the towering figure of the king, who is now shown wearing the white crown (*hedjet*) of southern or Upper Egypt and grasping the hair of a bearded and kneeling 'man of un-Egyptian type'[49] who, it seems, is about to be violently dispatched by the king, who holds a pear-shaped mace aloft in his right hand. Immediately above this unfortunate individual, the hawk-god Horus is depicted perched on top of a papyrus thicket holding a rope in one of his talons, which is attached to the nose of a bearded individual shown emerging from the papyrus stalks below. In the bottom panel, below the king and his doomed captive, two naked men, again 'un-Egyptian' in appearance, are depicted lying sprawled on the ground, one of whom lacks a penis and scrotum. Next to the head of the individual on the left can be seen a symbol depicting a town with fortified walls, while next to the head of the individual on the right is a knot symbol, perhaps naming this settlement which had been conquered by the king.

On both sides of the palette at the top, on either side there are human heads adorned with impressive curving horns and bovine ears, representing the goddess Bat and perhaps in this context signifying 'heaven'.[50] Between these opposing pairs of horned heads, small *serekh* frames (symbolizing the façades of early mud-brick palaces) containing catfish and chisel hieroglyphs represent the phonetic spelling of the name Narmer, which has sometimes been translated as 'fighting catfish'.

Traditionally, the scenes on the Narmer Palette have been seen as recording actual events: the military conquest of the Libyans and/or northern Egyptians of the Delta by King Narmer, and the subsequent unification of Upper and Lower Egypt. This interpretation has now fallen somewhat out of favour and more scholars now probably see the scenes on the palette as being a 'cosmological' rather than historical narrative, basically displaying

Decoration on the Narmer Palette. (*Drawing by J.E. Quibell, 1900. Creative Commons, Public Domain*)

the central role that the king played in defeating the dangerous forces of chaos that threatened Egypt.

Quibell and Green found another large, ceremonial cosmetic palette during their excavation of the Main Deposit. Known as the 'Two-Dogs Palette', like the Narmer Palette, it is carved with stunning low-relief decoration, although unlike the latter, it has a more 'chaotic' feel, as noted on the web page of the Ashmolean Museum, Oxford, which is now the privileged guardian of this superb artefact:

> On the reverse of the palette, a mixture of fabulous and real wild animals occupy the left-hand side of the scene from where they attack a range of herbivores native to North Africa. From the top, there are a pair of lions, a serpopard, a leopard, a hyena and a griffin with comb-like wings. At the bottom is a long-tailed dog-like creature wearing a belt and playing an end-blown flute. Presumably some of the imagery was carried to Egypt along trade routes, perhaps as seal impressions on containers, and the exotic creatures were adopted by Egypt's early kings to express their otherworldly status and power.[51]

The Two Dogs Palette.
(*Akhenatenator, Creative Commons*)

The Narmer and Scorpion Maceheads

Also found in the Main Deposit are two superbly-decorated, pear-shaped limestone maceheads, one associated with the King Narmer, the other with the somewhat mysterious King 'Scorpion', who some scholars view as the predecessor of the former. The Narmer Macehead is the better-preserved of the two, and as N.B. Millet has said, 'The wide range of interpretations that have been put upon it has...simply served to underline our real ignorance of the dim period in human history during which it was made.'[52] Nevertheless, Flinders Petrie suggested that the scenes that have been beautifully carved into its surface in low-relief 'commemorate the symbolic wedding of the king to the heiress of the crown of Lower Egypt and the legitimization by marriage of his military conquest'[53] and this interpretation still finds favour with some scholars. Alternatively, it has been argued that this explanation is perhaps too extravagant and that it is more likely that the main purpose of the decoration on the palette 'is to signalize the date of the objects' manufacture and presentation to the temple rather than to extol the intrinsic importance of the events mentioned.'[54]

Whatever the case, the main focus of the decoration on the Narmer Macehead is a scene showing the cloaked figure of the king wearing the Red Crown, and sitting on his throne on a high, canopied dais with steps, with his fan-bearers below and royal bodyguard armed with long staves behind (above which is the *serekh* of Narmer). In front of Narmer, a figure of uncertain sex (perhaps a princess or a female/male child of the king) sits in a

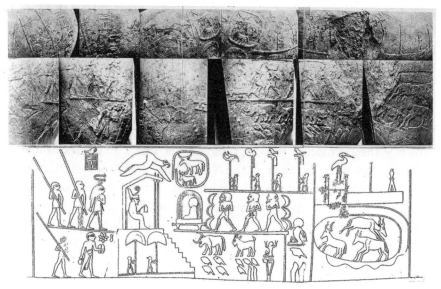

Decoration on the Narmer Macehead. (*Creative Commons, Public Domain*)

covered litter, which is followed by three bearded men running or walking. Behind and below these figures can be seen a bearded captive squatting on the floor and in front of him a goat and cow, with these motifs perhaps representing the details of booty taken in a military conquest. However, the figures recorded for this possible booty seem rather 'extravagant', as the number 120,000 is associated with the squatting captive and the numbers 400,000 and 1,422,000 with the goat and cattle respectively.

Only fragments of the Scorpion Macehead were found by Quibell and Green, but the surviving decoration depicts a king wearing the White Crown standing at the edge of a strip of water and carrying a hoe, 'perhaps inaugurating some form of early irrigation project'.[55] Two servants can be seen in front of the king, one carrying a basket, the other a sheaf of cereal, and above them two standard-bearers are depicted. Immediately in front of the king's face is a scorpion hieroglyph, with a rosette above. Behind the king is a possible group of dancing (?) women,

The Scorpion Macehead. (*John Bodsworth, Creative Commons*)

and above these, an individual with a cricket bat-like implement standing in front of seated individuals. Perhaps the most striking scene is that in the top-most register of the surviving decoration, which shows a group of *rekhyt-*birds hanging by their necks from a row of standards, with these strung-up birds 'representing conquered peoples'.[56]

In respect of the finely-sculpted decoration that adorns the Narmer Palette and the Narmer and Scorpion Maceheads, Kathryn Bard has argued:

> While the unification of Upper and Lower Egypt is too specific an interpretation of the scenes on the Narmer Palette, the scenes illustrate dead enemies and vanquished settlements. Scenes and signs on the Narmer Macehead represent war captives and booty, and conquered peoples are also represented on the Scorpion Macehead. Such scenes suggest that warfare played a role at some point in the forging of the early state in Egypt.[57]

Tomb 100

Discovered in the winter of 1898/99 by Frederick Green and commonly referred to as the 'Decorated' or 'Painted' tomb on account of the remarkable mural that covered one of its walls, Tomb 100 represents one of the most important and most famous archaeological discoveries from prehistoric Egypt. Indeed, it is also the oldest painted tomb yet known in the world. Tomb 100 comprised a rectangular pit measuring c.6m × 3m in area and some 1.5m deep, its walls were lined with mud-brick and coated with plaster, and a free-standing mud-brick wall also projected about halfway across the burial chamber from its eastern wall. Although Tomb 100 has now been lost beneath modern housing, the wall paintings were removed and survive in the Egyptian Museum, Cairo. Fortunately, Frederick Green also made a full-size copy of this prehistoric mural, which survives in the Griffith Institute, Oxford (Plate 20). Tomb 100 has been dated to Naqada II or the Gerzean culture by the style of its paintings, and by the remaining artefacts Green found in its burial chamber. Unfortunately, the tomb had been plundered some time before its discovery and all that Green found were a few miniature stone vases, about twenty various pottery vessels, several pottery sherds and a fishtail lance-head or knife. Somewhat strangely, perhaps, no human remains were found in the burial chamber, leading some earlier scholars to suggest that it was a shrine or, even less plausibly, a subterranean dwelling. However, the now widely accepted view is that the 'Painted Tomb' was the burial place of 'a powerful member of the Hierakonpolitan elite'.[58]

Turning to the prehistoric paintings that adorned the tomb, which have been described as 'an astonishing visual demonstration [of the] new social and economic structures'[59] that were established in Naqada II, these were executed in black, red and white pigments on an ochre background. Whatever the 'story' behind the mural in Tomb 100, it is dominated by the depiction of six huge boats (five coloured white and one black), around which are organized various scenes featuring smaller human and animal figures, which essentially deal 'with the themes of hunting and warfare'.[60] Also depicted are two men 'carrying symbols of authority similar to crooks, but uncrowned and with no other royal regalia suggesting kingly status [and who are thus] more likely to be chieftains than kings'.[61]

One of the most striking scenes relating to warfare in Tomb 100 shows three prisoners kneeling on the ground and probably bound together with a rope, while to their left a much larger standing figure can be seen. This individual holds a war club above his head and seems to be grabbing the prisoner nearest to him by the hair, who rather than being roughly treated and threatened by his captor may about to be executed. This simple but powerful scene is echoed in the 'smiting' scenes often found on the walls of later Egyptian temples, which depict pharaohs dispatching the traditional enemies of Egypt with their maces. Another interesting painting is the one showing a figure painted in red, who is holding or grappling two upright lions by their necks. Although crude in comparison, it is hard not to look at this male figure and the pair of warriors to his left, who appear to be engaged in single combat, 'without recalling the decoration of the Gebel el-Arak Knife handle'.[62]

Whether or not the paintings in Tomb 100 represent a visual narrative of real events or are connected to religious and social themes and beliefs remains a matter of debate, but more scholars probably favour the former idea. Nevertheless, it may still be worth considering the interesting suggestion that 'the Hierakonpolis mural, like the Gebel-el-Arak Knife, depicts a seaborne invasion of Egypt by the Sumerians.'[63] Humphrey Case and Joan Crowfoot pursued a similar line of reasoning in their 1962 article on Tomb 100, also comparing the scenes in its mural to those carved into the Gebel el-Arak Knife handle: 'The painted tomb shows similar aggressors of Asiatic affiliation intruding far into the south of Upper Egypt.'[64]

Further Finds from Hierakonpolis

Ever since Quibell and Green's fabulous discoveries at Hierakonpolis at the end of the nineteenth century, archaeologists have uncovered an abundance of fascinating archaeological material associated with the Naqada culture. For example, the late Michael Hoffman,[65] whose *Egypt Before the Pharaohs* should be on the bookshelf of anyone interested in the prehistory of Egypt and whose 'work at the site put Hierakonpolis on the map as the premier site for understanding Egypt's formative period'[66] made many important discoveries here. One of Hoffman's most significant discoveries was made in 1978,[67] when he unearthed the remains of a house dating to the Naqada I period at 'Locality 29'. As Hoffman wrote in the 1980 report on his excavation of this ancient dwelling: 'I will confine myself to the description of one of the more important individual finds of the 1978 season – the first clearly rectangular Predynastic house to be excavated scientifically.'[68] The house basically consisted of a single mud-brick-lined room (measuring c.4m × 3.5m) with a partially sunken floor, above which there had been a light wattle-and-daub superstructure. Inside the house, which had burned down some time after its construction, the base of an oval oven made of mud-brick and a partially destroyed very large pottery storage vessel (at least 35cm high and c.50cm wide) were discovered, and a fragment of a stone disc-shaped macehead was also found nearby.

The Elite Cemetery (HK6)

However, it is the Hierakonpolis Expedition led by Renée Friedman and Barbara Adams[69] which has thrown the most light on Late Predynastic life at this famous site, with the expedition beginning its archaeological exploration of Hierakonpolis in the mid-1980s and continuing to this day.[70] As Renée Friedman has said:

> Bit by bit, we are lifting the lid on the treasure chest we call Hierakonpolis. We don't mean to go slowly, but it just takes time to tease out all of the secrets hidden in our remarkable range of finds – some as small as a starch grain, others as large as an elephant.[71]

Some of the most fascinating discoveries of the Hierakonpolis Expedition have been made in the HK6 or 'elite' cemetery, where high-status individuals of the Naqada culture were buried. The cemetery is located away from the settlement area, about 1.3 miles into the desert. Excavations undertaken here in recent years 'have revealed how much further the Hierakonpolis elite took the display of their status by placing their sizeable tombs within impressive architectural settings and surrounding them with subsidiary graves containing an intriguing array of human and animal associates.'[72]

One of the most impressive tombs in the elite cemetery is Tomb 16 (dated to around 3600 BCE), which measures c.4.3m × 2.6m and about 1.5m deep and originally surrounded with an 'interconnected network of wooden enclosures [c.60m × 40m in extent] containing the graves of associates which surround the tomb on all four sides in an arrangement that anticipates the rows of subsidiary graves around the tombs of the First Dynasty kings at Abydos.'[73] Post-holes found around the edge of the tomb indicate that it was contained within a hall-like wooden superstructure which was presumably roofed.

The subsidiary graves contained both animal and human burials, with the former comprising a quite remarkable range of species and totalling forty-five animals: an African elephant, a wild bull (aurochs), hippopotamus, hartebeest, three baboons, three domestic cattle (bull, cow and calf), two goats, twenty-seven dogs and six cats. Sadly, there can be little doubt that these animals were sacrificed to accompany their owners in the next life, and there is also a strong suspicion that the same can be said of their human counterparts as two-thirds of the thirty-six individuals found in the thirteen subsidiary graves adjacent to Tomb 16 were juveniles under 15 years of age, and young women buried with fine grave goods such as beads made from semi-precious stones, ivory hair combs and delicate black-topped pottery. Although as has been noted, this skeletal sample is limited, it provides evidence of 'far from normal mortality'.[74] In the other subsidiary graves, young men equipped with weapons for the hunt (or for war?) were buried.

Like many ancient burial sites in Egypt, Tomb 16 had been plundered at some point, and although many fine artefacts were probably taken by its robbers, more than 115 pottery vessels remained in its burial chamber, one of which was incised with the earliest-known motif of the goddess Bat. Also surviving the attentions of the tomb-robbers were two well-preserved and rather eerie curved clay masks that were meant to be worn over the face (attached to the head by string passed through holes drilled behind the ears). Several fragments from other similar masks (representing at least six examples) were found elsewhere in the elite cemetery and probably represent the earliest funerary masks from Egypt, the forerunners of the mummy masks of pharaonic Egypt, the finest example of which was found covering the face of the famous boy-king Tutankhamen.

Perhaps the most remarkable range of grave goods recovered from the elite cemetery came from the almost intact Tomb 72, the earliest ones found being hollow hippopotamus tusks that had small holes drilled around their rims, and twenty-nine flint bladelets that were probably made at the time

Mask 'A' from Tomb
16, Elite Cemetery,
Hierakonpolis. (*Redrawn
after Rossiter, 2014*)

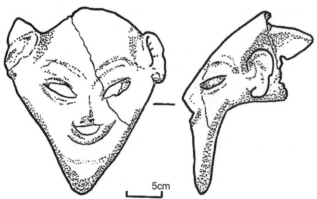

5cm

of the funeral. Traces of yellow ochre were identified in the tusks, revealing that they had been used as pigment containers. Further finds followed as excavation of the tomb progressed and, for example, there was a crude human figurine made of clay, a large trapezoidal palette made of diorite (more commonly found in contemporary Nubian graves), a superb flint spearhead and several long-toothed ivory combs, one of which was surmounted by the carving of a donkey, and another, a hippopotamus. The most notable finds from Tomb 72, however, comprised an ivory figurine of a standing, bearded male figure (32cm tall), carved from a hippopotamus tusk, and a fine pottery jar that had the large silhouette of a lion incised into its surface. Again, as with the trapezoidal palette, a Nubian connection was suggested by this unusual pottery vessel. In respect of the rare ivory figurine, its excavator Liam McNamara has said:

> Who does the new Hierakonpolis statuette represent? A god or a spirit; an early ruler; the tomb owner; a member of his family or court; a friend or foe? Why was it deposited in the tomb? As a representation of the deceased; to act on his behalf in the afterlife; as part of the funerary rituals performed at the time of the burial; to protect the deceased against attacks from enemies? Interpreting the function of such early statuettes is extremely speculative.[75]

Mention should also be made of Tomb 23, the largest in the elite cemetery (c.5m × 3m) which, like the nearby Tomb 16 (and others in the elite cemetery), was probably originally covered by a roofed wooden superstructure and contained within a larger wooden enclosure. The tomb yielded an impressive range of artefacts such as a large siltstone cosmetic palette featuring a carved bird's head on one of its corners, beautifully made bifacial flint arrowheads, and limestone and calcite amulets modelled in the shape of a scorpion. Also found in Tomb 23 and the surrounding area were the remains of a shattered life-sized statue comprising some 500 fragments of limestone. Unfortunately, only the ears and nose could be identified, as well as what may be part of a stand or throne. It is therefore impossible to tell who the statue was meant to represent in its original form, although it seems likely that they were either a 'royal' or divine personage.

In the central area of Cemetery HK6, in what seems to have been the focal point around which the elite burials clustered, the archaeologists of the Hierakonpolis Expedition discovered the remains of a remarkable group of pillared wooden halls, which are thought to have been early mortuary temples. Eight separate structures have been identified (not all contemporary), with the largest example being Structure 07 measuring 15m long and 10.5m wide. An assortment of objects was recovered from its corners, with one of the most notable part of a unique ivory 'wand' that has a procession of hippopotami carved along its top edge. There was also a complete ostrich egg engraved with a hunting scene, a collection of rather beautiful and superbly-made winged flint arrowheads, and a group of flint animal figures, with an elegant ibex the stand-out piece. Also found were a falcon figurine, 'masterfully carved from brittle malachite', which is the earliest yet known image of a falcon from Egypt and also probably symbolic of the local god Horus.[76]

Urban Evidence

The Hierakonpolis Expedition has also made many archaeological discoveries relating to daily life within the urban limits of the Predynastic town, such as the remains of several installations dedicated to the production of two major staples: beer and porridge. Each of these installations was fitted out with six to ten conical vats and their workforces would have been able to produce 100–200 gallons of beer or porridge per day, with the remains of pottery kilns found nearby used to make the large jars that were needed to hold these staples. More than ten beer-producing installations have been identified, some of which date back to c.3600 BCE, making them the oldest breweries yet discovered in the world. It is suspected that control of the food supply and its surplus was in the hands of a small but powerful few at Hierakonpolis, and that they oversaw a redistributive economy much like that of pharaonic Egypt, with agricultural produce centrally collected and redistributed to the general populace as 'wages'.

Whether or not this was the case, in the centre of Hierakonpolis, archaeologists of the Hierakonpolis Expedition discovered the post-holes from a huge palisade wall built from logs, which they traced for over 50m and which is likely to have enclosed an area measuring a substantial c.2.5 acres. Inside the enclosure, the remains of a palace or administrative centre were uncovered, which contained the remains of workshops where high-quality products in the form of flint tools, semi-precious beads and carved stone vessels were produced. They also unearthed the western end of a huge 'ceremonial centre' (c.45m long and 13m wide) that was first identified in the 1980s by Michael Hoffman and which featured a monumental gateway (c.13m wide) on its southern side, framed by four massive wooden posts. The ceremonial centre was constructed in Naqada II and was in use for some 500 years until the end of the Predynastic period and, as has been nicely noted, its 'caretakers were fastidious housekeepers'. This was revealed by the discovery of numerous rubbish pits around its peripheries, the contents of which have provided fascinating evidence of the cultic practices of the Predynastic.[77]

Around 38,000 animal bones from both domestic animals (young cattle, sheep and goats), fish and a wide variety of wild species (e.g. crocodile, turtle, hippopotamus, gazelle, Barbary sheep) were discovered in the pits, and the debris from the sharpening of fine flint knives which were probably used to butcher the many unfortunate animals who were killed within the precincts of the ceremonial centre. The numerous bones of domesticated animals and fish found in the pits point to the feasting that took place here over hundreds of years. However, as Renée Friedman has remarked, the many wild animal bones also recovered from the pits indicate 'something more than just fine dining [and] this collection of wild and often dangerous game had a much more important purpose – the control of chaos, the most important role of later pharaohs.'[78]

Naqada Culture Burials at Cemetery U, Abydos

The famous site of Abydos in northern or Lower Egypt is one of Egypt's most important archaeological sites, and the numerous temples and tombs found here reflect its role as the cult centre of the god Osiris for much of the pharaonic period, with a significant group of early dynastic tombs also found here. Abydos is also home to one of the most important burial places of the Naqada culture: Cemetery U at Umm el-Qa'ab ('mother of pots'; many thousands of ancient pottery sherds litter the surface of the site), which was completely excavated between 1985 and 2001 by the German Archaeological Institute, Cairo. Approximately 600 graves dating from Naqada I to III were excavated during this period by the German expedition and 'Despite the

Umm el-Qaab Abydos. Thousands of pottery sherds can be seen in the foreground. (*Image courtesy of Markh, Creative Commons*)

looting of the cemetery and two previous excavations, Cemetery U yielded a surprising number of finds, which clearly indicate the presence of elite tombs from earliest times onwards.'[79]

Two of the most notable tombs from Cemetery U are U 279 and U 127, with both of these grave-pits (measuring c.2.4m × 1.6m and 4.5m × 1.7m respectively) yielding a wide range of impressive grave goods. In U 279 (which originally was probably lined with wood and contained a wooden coffin), there were more than a dozen pottery vessels, one of which was unusually decorated with snakes that had been modelled in low-relief on its surface. Also found in the tomb were gypsum gaming pieces, a bone comb, a model of poppy seeds, several copper and ivory fragments and a superb fishtail lance-head/knife measuring c.13cm long, which still bore traces of the material in which it had been wrapped when it was placed in the grave. The bones of two goats were also found in the grave and are thought to represent a food offering for the deceased.

In Tomb U 127, the deceased had been placed in a wooden coffin and there was an impressive array of grave goods, which included items such as 100 threads of gold, gaming pieces and several fragments of a decorated ivory knife handle. On one of the fragments, a row of gift-bearers with long hair is depicted, and on the other, a row of at least four kneeling prisoners are depicted with their arms probably tied behind their backs, who are being led by a standing naked figure. Underneath these figures, a further row of captives are shown with their captors and 'Both scenes tell a story of victory and defeat.'[80] Animals such as cattle, lion and sheep/goats can be seen on other fragments of the handle. Various lithic artefacts also accompanied the deceased, with twenty 'micro end-scrapers', a fishtail lance-head/knife and four bladelets found close together that were probably originally contained within an organic container of some sort'. The most impressive lithic artefact recovered from U 127 was a ripple-flaked flint knife measuring c.15cm long by 6cm wide, with a narrower tang on the end which would originally have facilitated the attachment of a wooden or ivory handle. It is also worth noting the fifty-five 'transverse' arrowheads (trapezoidal in shape), which would originally have been attached to reed arrow shafts that were found in Tomb U 141. Discoveries such as these, when considered alongside the decorated knife handle from U 279 with its scenes of subjugated prisoners, hint 'that we are dealing with concepts related to the male world and especially those related to hunting and warfare.'[81]

Perhaps also worth briefly mentioning here is the impressive bone comb that was found in Tomb U 650, a simple pit-grave probably dating to Naqada I, which contained the burial of a child aged 6 to 8 years. The comb, which was probably made of a cow's rib-bone, has nine long teeth and measures c.18cm long, which is in itself notable, but the most striking thing about this ancient object is that there is a carving of a rhinoceros with very long legs adorning its top. To date, this comb finds no parallels among the numerous others recovered from Naqada culture graves.

Tomb U-J

The stand-out tomb in Cemetery U is undoubtedly Tomb U-j, which not only 'represents one of our best sources for early Egypt',[82] but is also the largest and most richly-furnished tomb of a Late Predynastic ruler yet found in Egypt. Tomb U-j was discovered by the German Archaeological Institute in 1988 on the southern edge of Cemetery U, with radiocarbon dates obtained from material in the tomb placing its construction in Naqada III, c.3200–3150 BCE. Made from mud-brick, the tomb is square in plan, with its northern and southern walls measuring c.11m long and its eastern and western ones c.8m; the corners of the walls are roughly orientated on the cardinal points of the compass (the tomb was actually built in two phases of construction, with the first phase slightly smaller than the second).

The tomb's interior comprises four separate burial chambers, one of which is further subdivided into nine smaller compartments, with fragments of its roof (which comprised beams of acacia wood covered with reed mats and a final mud coating) preserved in some places. It is also thought likely that the large amount of earth from the pit in which the tomb was constructed was originally placed over the roof of the tomb to form a substantial tumulus that marked its location and perhaps symbolized the primordial or primeval mound which, in ancient Egyptian religion, was the place where the creation of the world began.

An interesting architectural feature of Tomb U-j is the slit-like openings in the walls of the chambers that connect them together, with these narrow entrances acting as symbolic doorways through which the deceased could pass to access the many grave goods that were placed in the chambers by the living. In effect, Tomb U-j functioned as a dwelling for the deceased, with all of its trappings and furnishings intended to keep him content in the afterlife.

Unfortunately but not unsurprisingly, Tomb U-j was plundered by grave-robbers, probably in the early Dynastic period, and was perhaps also partially emptied by Émile Amélineau in the late nineteenth century. However, when Tomb U-j was rediscovered by its German excavators in the late 1980s, it still contained hundreds of pottery vessels of various types (around 2,000 in total), among which were some 300 wine jars imported from Palestine that were stacked on top of each other in four layers in chambers 7 and 10.

In the largest chamber, the remains of a large wooden shrine (and coffin?) were found along with various items such as an ivory sceptre with a curved top shaped like a bird's head, decorative ivory pins, an obsidian blade, carnelian and turquoise beads, two gold pins and a piece of gold leaf. These finds hint at the great wealth of high-quality objects originally placed in this 'royal chamber', but which were subsequently stolen by the later grave-robbers who emptied Tomb U-j of most of its original contents. Chamber 11 'served as a sort of treasury with special grave goods',[83] and contained fragments from finely-carved stone bowls, ivory gaming pieces and decorated ivory game sticks that were used like dice, the remains of cedar chests and, most notable of all, a large obsidian dish featuring a pair of human hands carved in low-relief on its surface. The raw material for this rare object was probably imported from Ethiopia.

As Günter Dreyer has pointed out, 'The most important group of finds from Tomb U-j are the approximately 125 clay vessels and fragments of vessels with ink inscriptions and the approximately 160 tags of bone or ivory with incised characters.'[84] Elise MacArthur has noted that scholars have divided the signs on the vessels 'into two groups: "main signs" (e.g. scorpions, Red

Sea shells, fish, falcons and ships) and "secondary signs" (e.g. trees, reeds, horizontal and vertical strokes).'[85] The tags feature small drilled holes in their corners, indicating that they functioned as labels, and animal and human figures, as well as rows of dice-like notations which are thought to represent quantities of cloth and grain. Therefore, scholars plausibly suggest that the inscriptions on the jars represent the names of economic establishments or agricultural estates founded by various kings, the most common one being the scorpion motif. Tomb U-j was thus perhaps the final resting-place of an early Egyptian ruler known as 'King Scorpion', but whatever the truth, the inscriptions on the vessels can be viewed as 'proto-hieroglyphs' and represent the earliest-known examples of writing in Egypt.

Tell el-Farkha and Maadi

The Lower Egyptian culture (c.4000–3600 BCE) of northern Egypt is often seen as something of a poorer Predynastic cousin to the Naqada culture, and lacking the sophistication and complexity of its southern counterpart. However, while there is some truth to this view it is also a little unfair, as the communities of the Lower Egyptian culture have left us with various strands of archaeological evidence that somewhat contradicts it. For example, at the recently-excavated site of Tell el-Farkha in the Eastern part of the Nile Delta, the remains of large timber-framed houses with wickerwork walls were discovered, some of which had been grouped together in rows along lanes or streets, as well as the remains of a series of large brewing vats made from mud-brick and dating to c.3500–3350 BCE. From the inception of the Tell el-Farkha settlement around 3700 BCE, its inhabitants were also involved in a trade and exchange network with the Levant, as evidenced by the presence of pottery and other artefacts of Levantine origin.

It should also be mentioned that around 3300 BCE, Naqada culture settlers from the south arrived at Tell el-Farkha and 'After a short time of coexistence, the Naqadians gained the clear advantage over the local inhabitants of the area, whose fate after this point is a mystery.'[86] Some quite spectacular evidence was left by the 'Naqadians' who inhabited Tell el-Farkha in c.3000–3000 BCE, such as the remains of the largest monumental mud-brick building known from the Late Predynastic Period. The part of the structure that was excavated covers several hundred square metres and although its function is unclear, it may have been the residence of a powerful individual who oversaw the trading activities of the settlement. Interestingly, the building was destroyed by a fire around 3200 BCE which may have been a deliberate act 'related to the growing rivalry between the major political centres [of the Naqada culture].'[87]

Also found during the Tell el-Farkha excavations were votive deposits, each of which was discovered in the remains of two separate 'chapels' and contained an amazing array of figurines made of faience clay, stone and ivory, some of which 'are unique works of art of a style previously unknown in such an early period of Egyptian history'.[88] These figurines depict both people and animals (e.g. baboons, lions, dogs, falcons) and fantastical creatures such as a griffin-like creature holding a jug that has the body of a cat, female breasts and a hawk's head, and a cobra with the face of a woman. Among the human figurines (most of which are made from hippopotamus ivory) are women with children sitting on their laps or shoulders, and beautifully modelled figures of young boys seated on the ground with their knees drawn up and right fingers in their mouths, a motif that became common in pharaonic art. Thirteen dwarf figurines were also recovered (the largest group of such figurines yet found in Egypt), as well as male figurines, one of which wears a cloak and possibly represents an early king, and a group depicting probable war captives whose hands are tied behind their backs.

The most remarkable of the Late Predynastic finds from Tell el-Farkha, however, has to be the remains of two sheet-gold statuettes, which were reconstructed to show two naked men, perhaps representing an early king and his son. One figure stands c.60cm high and the other around 30cm, with the lapis lazuli used for their eyes probably imported from Afghanistan.

Maadi

The Lower Egyptian culture was first brought to light at the settlement of Maadi (giving rise to its original designation as the Maadian culture), and remains the major site of this Late Predynastic cultural complex. Discovered in 1913 by the French Jesuit archaeologist Father Paul Bovier-Lapierre in a southern suburb of Cairo, Maadi has been referred to as 'the major economic power centre of the northern Nile Valley in the period 3800–3500 BC,'[89] and was mainly excavated between 1930 and 1953 by archaeologists Mustafa Amer, Oswald Menghin and Ibrahim Rizkana of the University of Cairo. Covering some 4000m², the archaeological deposits measured up to 2m in depth, and many remnants relating to life in this Late Predynastic northern Egyptian town were uncovered. The archaeological evidence from Maadi reveals strong cultural links with the southern Levant, and this is most strikingly seen with the four subterranean houses that were found by the Egyptian archaeologists. These dwellings consisted of oval-shaped structures that were sunk 2m to 3m below the ground surface, accessed by stepped passageways and roofed by wooden superstructures as indicated by the post-holes found around the interiors of the deep pits that formed their living spaces. Some researchers have suggested that these were not houses but were ceremonial structures similar to the *kivas* built by the Pueblo Indians of south-western America, but the presence of hearths, sunken storage jars and domestic debris found inside them argues against this.

The subterranean houses at Maadi are unique in Egypt, but 'parallels are found in the Be'er Sheva region [the Negev Desert] during the Late Chalcolithic and the initial Early Bronze I periods; indeed, Maadi seems to have displayed the characteristics of a south Levantine community from its inception.'[90] In other words, it is quite possible – as some researchers believe – that Maadi was founded by settlers from here. Whatever the case, further evidence of this Levantine connection at Maadi is provided by the distinctive ceramic vessels found at the site, which were imported from the southern Levant and originally contained products such as oil, wine and resin. As Michael Hoffman remarks: 'The fact that Maadi has produced some of the earliest domesticated donkey remains in prehistoric Egypt goes a long way to explaining how these containers might have been brought to Egypt from southern Palestine.'[91] The stone-tool industry of Maadi also displays clear Palestinian influence in the large circular flint scrapers and Canaanite blades found at the site, although objects such as bone combs, stone cosmetic palettes and disc-shaped maceheads were also imported from Naqada communities in Upper Egypt.

A wide variety of other artefacts were unearthed at Maadi, such as thick walled limestone vessels that are thought to have been used as incense-burners, many copper objects (e.g. needles, harpoons, axes), large quantities of copper ore from the Sinai Peninsula, finely-carved wooden plates, personal ornaments such as pierced fossil sharks' teeth and river and sea shells, crude T-shaped clay objects that perhaps represented bulls' heads, ivory 'clap-sticks' and storage jars still containing hundreds of spines taken from the pectoral and dorsal fins of catfish. These fishbones, which were used as projectiles, seem to have been exported to Palestine from Maadi, as suggested by their discovery at the site of Wadi Gaza in the north-western Negev. Also found were huge storage jars or *pithoi* still found at Maadi, which were sunk up to their necks in the ground and used to store grain, wheat and other foodstuffs such as cooked mutton.

Although the hundreds of simple graves found at the Maadi South cemetery (located about 0.5 miles from the main settlement) and those of

Ivory 'clap-stick' from Maadi. (*Image courtesy of Guillaume Bouchard, Creative Commons*)

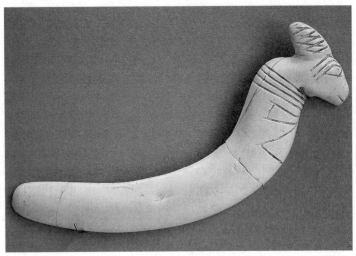

the Lower Egyptian culture in general never display the 'conspicuous luxury' seen in those of the Naqada culture, some were more richly-furnished than others, pointing towards social stratification.[92] Items such as ceramic pots and stone vases, cosmetic palettes, shells used as pigment containers and beads made from carnelian and other semi-precious stones were found with the dead in the Maadi South cemetery, as well as the skeletons of sacrificed dogs and gazelles. Premature or newborn infants were also found buried under houses in the settlement, 'perhaps as a magical means of warding off future miscarriages and stillbirths'.[93] The bodies of the premature infants were placed in pottery jars and it is interesting to note that one of these burial jars featured small circular holes near its inverted base, which may well have been intended as eye holes 'through which the deceased's gaze could be directed outwards'.[94]

Towards the end of the Naqada II period, the Lower Egyptian culture began to be assimilated into the Naqada culture. Whether this was achieved peaceably or through violent force remains a matter of debate, although most archaeologists perhaps favour the idea that this was a peaceful process. However, there is perhaps evidence to suggest that at Maadi at least, this may have not been the case, for as Michael Hoffman has said: 'Some archaeologists believe that Maadi met a violent end as witnessed by widespread ash and human bones scattered over the settlement.'[95] Whatever the truth, by the end of Naqada III, Egypt was well on its way to becoming what was undoubtedly one of the world's greatest ancient civilizations, the roots of which, it should not be forgotten, lay deep in the prehistoric past.

Notes

Introduction

1. Sir John Lubbock was a leading light in Victorian society and science, and was not only a keen archaeologist (or 'antiquarian' as the early archaeologists of the nineteenth century are known), natural historian and biologist, but also a social reformer, being responsible for the introduction of the Bank Holidays Act in 1871 which, if only a little bit, lightened the load of the Victorian workforce. Lubbock's most significant work as a politician – at least from an archaeological viewpoint – is that he introduced the Ancient Monuments Act (1882), a forerunner of English Heritage and the other heritage organizations that are dedicated to preserving and protecting Britain's past.
2. Pettit & White 2013, 35.
3. Brewer 2012, 21.
4. Hoffman 1980, 51.
5. Brewer 2012, 21.
6. Corbey et al. 2016, 6.
7. Schick & Toth 1995, 231.
8. The human fossils found at the site of Omo Kibish in Ethiopia are commonly seen as providing the earliest evidence of *Homo sapiens* and are approximately 195,000 years old.
9. Richter et al. 2012, 10.
10. Richter et al. 2017, 296.
11. 'The first of our kind: Scientists discover the oldest *Homo sapiens* fossils at Jebel Irhoud, Morocco.' Max-Planck-Gesellschaft.https://www.mpg.de/11322481/oldest-homo-sapiens-fossils-at-jebel-irhoud-morocco?fbclid=IwAR0JziQbi6hVZ4sFi3FM0opiyeSbimiLMAwkmdDYeuyBFbuUDvutdxqrYxY
12. Sample 2017.
13. The origins of the Levallois technique lie in the Late Lower Palaeolithic, as notably revealed at Jebel Irhoud, with this new technology used to make many of the stone tools found here. Many archaeologists have thus seen the introduction of the Levallois technique as going hand-in-hand with the emergence of *Homo sapiens* in Africa.
14. Hoffman 1980, 59–60.
15. Midant-Reynes 2000, 33.
16. Hoffman 1980, 59–60.
17. Hikade 2010, 2–3.
18. The Mousterian is named after the type-site of the industry, Le Moustier, in the Dordogne, south-western France. The site comprises two caves, one above the other, located in a cliff face above the village of Peyzac-le-Moustier. In 1863 the antiquarians Henry Christy and Édouard Lartet (one of the 'founding fathers'

of Palaeolithic archaeology) found a superb collection of Mousterian tools in the upper cave and further excavations carried out in the lower cave in the early twentieth century unearthed two Neanderthal skeletons: one an adolescent, the other a newborn (found in 1908 and 1914 respectively).

19. Garcea 2004, 31.
20. Rowland & Tassie 2014, 57.
21. Bard 1999, 9.
22. Bard 1999, 11.
23. Goder-Goldberger 2013, 184.
24. Scerri & Spinapolice 2019, 18.
25. Midant-Reynes 2000, 34.
26. Holl in Hardesty 2010, 38.
27. Scerri 2013, 115.
28. Gertrude Caton Thompson (1888–1985) was an archaeological pioneer ahead of her time and she worked on many archaeological projects over the course of her long and productive life, most notably at the stunning ruins of Great Zimbabwe, Africa. She began working in Egypt in the 1920s with the famous Flinders Petrie and the British School of Archaeology and was something of a rarity in the male-dominated world of early twentieth-century archaeology. She excavated the huge and important Predynastic site of Hemamieh and carried out extensive archaeological surveys at the Kharga and Fayum oases.
29. Bard 1999, 9.
30. Bard 1999, 11.
31. Hikade 2010, 4.
32. Bard 1999, 12–13.
33. Smith 1976, 35.
34. Smith 1975, 37.
35. Pierre Vermeersch is a leading authority on Egyptian prehistory and has investigated many important Palaeolithic sites in Egypt.
36. Hendrickx & Vermeersch 2000, 35.
37. Kuper & Kröpelin 2006, 805.
38. Hendrickx & Vermeersch 2000, 33.
39. Hendrickx, Huyge & Wendrich 2015, 18.
40. Hendrickx & Huyge 2014, 242.
41. Ibid.
42. With the outbreak of the Second World War, Junker was no longer able to continue his archaeological investigation of this significant site and he never returned to Egypt to do so, although the German Institute of Archaeology at Cairo returned to continue excavations at Merimde Beni Salama in 1977–1983.
43. Midant-Reynes 2014, 6.
44. Sir William Flinders Petrie (1853–1942) looms large in the story of Egyptology, and also in the development of archaeology as a scientific discipline. Petrie was a careful and meticulous excavator way ahead of other early archaeologists working in Egypt in the late nineteenth/early twentieth century and made many important archaeological discoveries throughout Egypt during the forty or so years he worked here.
45. Midant-Reynes 2000, 48.
46. Anđelković 2011, 29.

Chapter One

1. Some experts have reclassified African *Homo erectus* as a separate early hominid species known as *Homo ergaster* ('working man'), confining *Homo erectus* to Europe and Asia, although this remains a much-debated issue.
2. De la Torre 2016, 10.
3. An alternative theory is that *Homo erectus* evolved in Asia and subsequently migrated to Africa, although most palaeoanthroplogists probably favour the 'Out of Africa' theory for the early migration of *Homo erectus*.
4. Spikins et al. 2010, 309.
5. Klein 2009, 87.
6. Graves et al. 2010, 542.
7. Klein 2009, 87–88.
8. Schick & Toth 1993, 71.
9. Bradshaw Foundation, *Exploring the Fossil Record: Stone Tools*.
10. Debono 1981, 634–625.
11. Hendrickx & Vermeersch 2000, 18.
12. Midant-Reynes 2000, 26.
13. Brewer 2000, 20.
14. Brewer 2000, 20–21.
15. Hoffman 1980, 37.
16. Lubbock 1873, 217.
17. Sackett 2014, 3.
18. Hoffman 1980, 18–19.
19. Gamble and Krusynski 2009, 467.
20. Acheulean handaxes were found alongside extinct animal bones at Hoxne (a brick clay pit in Suffolk) in the late 1870s, and were described by the early antiquarian John Frere (the great-great-great grandfather of Mary Leakey) in a short article published by the Society of Antiquaries of London in 1800. Frere remarked that the handaxes 'were weapons of war, fabricated by and used by a people who had not the use of metals…the situation in which these weapons were found may tempt us to refer them to a very remote period indeed; even before that of the present world.' It is not exactly clear what Frere meant by these words, but he may well have had more than an inkling, some time before Boucher de Perthes, that humanity was far older than the Book of Genesis claimed.
21. Hoffman 1980, 20.
22. Daniel 1967, 123.
23. De la Torre 2016, 2.
24. Ramesses II also built a smaller but still spectacular temple at Abu Simbel that he dedicated to his chief wife, Nefertari. Some readers may not be aware that the two temples were, in an amazing feat of engineering, relocated in their entirety some 65m from their original location in 1968. This was because they would have been submerged under the waters of Lake Nasser, the huge water reservoir that was created during the construction of the Aswan High Dam in 1960–1970.
25. Brewer 2000, 21.
26. Vermeersch et al. 2000, 57.
27. Roe et al. 1982, 89.
28. Ibid.
29. Roe et al. 1982, 88.

30. A 500-kiloton airburst occurred when a meteor exploded over the central Russian city of Chelyabinsk on 15 February 2013. Somewhat remarkably, nobody was killed; nevertheless, 1,500 people were injured and thousands of buildings were damaged. The meteor was only 20m wide, indicating what will happen if a *really big* meteor hits Earth!
31. Temming 2015.
32. Vermeersch et al. 2000, 73.
33. Hill 2000, 66.
34. Caton Thompson 1932, 132.
35. Ibid.
36. McHugh 1975, 32.
37. Bagnold 1939, 290.
38. Wendorf et al. 1981, 178.
39. McHugh et al. 1988, 368.
40. These channels were found by a newer version of the Space Shuttle's Imaging Radar (SIR-C).
41. Haynes et al. 1997, 821. How far back in time this ancient trade route (known as the '40-day road') dates is unknown but it is probably of prehistoric origin and only stopped being used in 1899 when the British government abolished the slave trade.
42. Olszewski et al. 2005, 288.
43. Olszewski et al. 2001, 35.
44. Hoffman 1980, 56–57.
45. Machin et al. 2005, 23.
46. Binneman & Beaumont 1992, 94.
47. O'Brien 1981, 76.
48. O'Brien 1981, 79.
49. Whittaker & McCall 2001, 572.
50. Ibid.
51. Pope et al. 2006, 45.
52. Kohn & Mithen 1999, 521.
53. Kohn & Mithen, 1999, 519.
54. Hayden & Villeneuve 2009, 1167.
55. Wynn & Gowlett 2018, 23.
56. McNabb & Cole 2015, 105.
57. Wenban-Smith 2004, 14.
58. Machin 2008, 761.

Chapter Two

1. The Belgian Middle Egypt Prehistoric Project was created in 1976 by Professors Pierre Vermeersch and Etienne Paulissen, who through their work have shed much light on the Egyptian Palaeolithic. Another important figure in the study of Palaeolithic Egypt, Professor Philip Van Peer, has since taken over the reins of the project.
2. Vermeersch et al. 1990, 78–79. We might also wonder whether Palaeolithic women and children were also involved in seeking out these chert cobbles.
3. Most of these cobbles originate from the Red Sea Mountains of the Eastern Desert.

4. Vermeersch 2010, 69.
5. Van Peer 1998, 121.
6. Leplogeon & Pleurdeau 2011, 218.
7. Wurz & Van Peer 2012, 172.
8. Trinkaus 2005, 210. Fossil evidence of an even earlier arrival of early or 'archaic' modern humans in the Levant appears to be provided by the discovery in 2002 of part of an upper jaw bone and teeth at Misliya Cave, which lies close to Qafzeh Cave on Mount Carmel, Israel. There is general agreement among experts that the jaw fragment belonged to an early modern human, and scientific dating of the fossil has given a date range of 177,000 to 194,000 years ago. It has been claimed by some researchers that a human skull fragment found in Apidima Cave, Greece came from an early modern human who died some 200,000 years ago, but it may be more likely that the fragment came from a Neanderthal skull.
9. Van Peer 2010, 224.
10. Grine 2016, 254.
11. Van Peer et al. 2010, 224.
12. Garcea 2012, 119.
13. Vermeersch et al. 1990, 85.
14. Van Peer 1998, 121.
15. Vermeersch 2010, 67.
16. Van Peer et al. 2008, 247.
17. Dart & Beaumont 1969, 127. Original radiocarbon dates obtained on charcoal taken from the mine suggested that the Upper Palaeolithic mining activity at Lion Cavern took place between c.20,000–30,000 BCE. However, more recent dating has indicated that the Upper Palaeolithic mining dates to at least c.40,000 BCE. It is likely that the red ochre was used for rituals and ceremonies, many probably of a religious nature.
18. The site was given this name by the Belgian archaeologists because of the unusual scattering of large limestone boulders covering the surface of the hill. They previously found three ancient human skull fragments during a survey of the hill in 1978.
19. Vermeersch 2002, 277.
20. Vermeersch 2002, 276.
21. Vermeersch 2002, 278.
22. Crèvecoeur 2012, 205.
23. Vermeersch 2002, 278.
24. Crèvecoeur 2002, 206.
25. Vermeersch 2002, 281.
26. Crèvecoeur 2002, 205.
27. Crèvecoeur 2002, 216.
28. Crèvecoeur 2002, 217. Crèvecoeur also determined that Nazlet Khater Man was aged between 20 and 29 when he died and was a rather small individual, only measuring 1.6m (c.5ft 3in) in height.
29. Thoma 1984, 290.
30. Thoma 1984, 296.
31. Deflational basins or 'blow-outs' are hollows formed by the removal of particles of sand by wind action.
32. Directed by the renowned American archaeologist Fred Wendorf, a distinguished scholar who also fought against the Germans in the Second World War; he was

a second lieutenant in the 86th Regiment, 10th Mountain Division, and was seriously wounded in the right arm (ending his participation in the war), while leading his men against the Germans in the Apennine Mountains of northern Italy. He was awarded the Bronze Heart and Purple Star for his bravery.

33. Wendorf et al. 1987, 50.
34. Gautier 1993, 126.
35. Wendorf et al. 1987, 49.
36. Hoffman 1980, 68.
37. Ibid.
38. Gautier 1993, 125–126.
39. The survey involved archaeologists from the Czech Institute of Egyptology, Charles University, Prague and the Palaeolithic and Palaeoethnology Research Centre at the Institute of Archaeology, Brno.
40. Svoboda 2004, 266.
41. Vermeersch et al. 1994, 38.
42. The Emiran Industry was first defined by the English archaeologist Dorothy Garrod in the mid-twentieth century.
43. Rose & Marks 2014, 64.
44. This huge region, which is noted for its important cultural and natural heritage, was declared a National Park by the Egyptian government in 2007 and attracts the more 'adventurous' type of tourist to Egypt.
45. Le Quellec 2013, 241.
46. Le Quellec 2013, 241–242.

Chapter Three

1. Not all archaeologists are comfortable with describing prehistoric carvings such as that found at Qurta as 'art' because of the Western connotations of this word. However, 'art' remains the most convenient label for the ancient images that Stone Age people throughout the world carved and painted on open-air sites, caves and rock-shelters.
2. Huyge 2009, 110.
3. Huyge et al. 2011, 1186.
4. Huyge et al. 2011, 1190.
5. Huyge 2013, 41.
6. Huyge 2013, 40.
7. Ibid.
8. Huyge & Ikram 2009, 8.
9. Huyge 2008, 421.
10. Huyge 2013, 39.
11. Storemyr et al. 2008, 157.
12. Kelany 2012, 5.
13. Storemyr 2012. He has also noted that the Wadi Subeira rock art 'is extremely threatened by modern mining, which lately has proven to be even more widespread than was previously thought: A truly unique testimony of mankind's early art is now on the verge of destruction.'
14. Storemyr et al. 2008, 156.
15. Kelany 2014, 108.
16. Kelany 2014, 109.

17. Kelany 2014, 110.
18. Kelany 2014, 112.
19. Like many late-nineteenth-century clergymen, Greville was also a keen scholar with interests ranging from natural history to archaeology and he was particularly interested in the burgeoning field of Egyptology, visiting Egypt many times and making friends with Flinders Petrie on his thirty-eighth visit to the country. Although Greville wrote many archaeological articles (e.g. one on the rock art at el-Hosh that was published in the *Archaeological Journal* 1892), he is best-known as being a collector of Egyptian antiquities, with many of the objects that he purchased in Egypt obtained for the British Museum and other museums such as the Fitzwilliam, Cambridge.
20. Polkowski et al. 2013, 102.
21. Huyge 2005, 3.
22. Huyge & Storemyr 2013, 26.
23. Huyge 2005, 6.
24. Huyge & Storemyr 2013, 30.
25. Huyge 2005, 11.
26. Ibid.
27. Huyge & Storemyr 2013, 26.
28. Huyge & Storemyr 2013, 24.
29. Huyge & Storemyr 2013, 28.
30. Zboray 2012, 163.
31. Ibid.
32. Zboray 2012, 165.
33. Storemyr 2008, 63.
34. Storemyr 2008, 65.
35. Storemyr 2008, 66–67.
36. Storemyr 2008, 74.
37. Ibid.
38. Strictly speaking, the Cave of Swimmers and Cave of Beasts are large, open rock shelters rather than true caves, which archaeologists have more prosaically labelled Wadi Sura I and Wadi Sura II.
39. See Förster et al. 2010 for more.
40. Bárta 2010, 21.
41. As mentioned in the introduction some scholars prefer not to use this term, as although they made pottery and kept some domesticated animals, prehistoric communities did not grow crops and still largely followed a hunter-gatherer lifestyle during the Western Desert Neolithic.
42. Förster et al. 2010, 205.
43. Quoted in Le Quellec 2008, 26.
44. Ibid.
45. Ibid.
46. Bárta 2015, 488.
47. See Bárta 2015.
48. Negative hand-prints such as these and also 'positive' prints made by hands covered in paint (much like primary school children love to produce) have been recorded at numerous ancient rock art sites around the world, and perhaps the most famous examples are found in the celebrated decorated caves of Upper Palaeolithic Europe.

49. Lewis-Williams quoted in Le Quellec 2008, 27.
50. Förster & Scheid 2015, 301.
51. Between 2009 and 2015, the Wadi Sura Project painstakingly analyzed and recorded the rock art found in the Cave of Beasts. Detailed and fascinating reports of this work and more besides can be found at http://www.wadisura.uni-koeln.de. In 2011, the archaeologists of the Wadi Sura Project made a new and important discovery in the Cave of Beasts, uncovering a previously unrecorded rock art panel that depicted wild animals such as giraffes alongside what seem to be representations of domesticated animals (goats and a possible cow).
52. Förster & Scheid 2015, 309.
53. Ibid.
54. Förster & Scheid 2015, 307.
55. Bárta 2010, 65.
56. See Honoré et al. 2016.
57. Honoré et al. 2016, 246.
58. Förster & Scheid 2015, 303.
59. Förster & Kuper 2013, 24.
60. Ibid.
61. Förster & Kuper 2013, 25.
62. Ibid.
63. Bárta 2010, 15.
64. Bárta 2010, 35.
65. Bárta 2010, 37.
66. D'Huy 2009, 126.
67. 'Arid Climate, Adaptation and Cultural Innovation in Africa'.
68. Claassen 2009, 62.
69. D'Huy & Le Quellec 2009.
70. Barich 2014, 391.
71. Le Quellec & Huyge 2008, 92.
72. Barich 2014, 395.
73. A date of c.3500 BCE was also obtained from charcoal found in the upper layer of the deposit, indicating ritual or secular activity in the cave in the Naqada/Late Predynastic period.
74. Ibid.
75. Barich 2014, 385.
76. Ikram 2009, 69.
77. Ikram 2009, 267.
78. Ibid.
79. Ikram 2009, 270.
80. Quoted in Ikram 2009, 269.
81. Ikram 2009, 270.
82. Ikram 2009, 70.
83. This figure appears to have a penis or penis sheath dangling between its legs, and although it possible that rather than depicting a man with his arms spread wide, this motif depicts a lizard seen from above, this unlikely as its tail is rather short if so.
84. Ikram 2009, 79.
85. Ikram 2009, 80.

86. Ikram 2013, 95.
87. Ikram 2009, 78.
88. Ikram 2013, 99.
89. Ibid.
90. Ibid.
91. Polkowski 2013, 105.
92. Polkowski 2013, 106.
93. Polkowski 2013, 108.
94. Polkowski 2013, 109–110.
95. Huyge 2003, 65.
96. Cape hunting dogs are a species of wild dog native to sub-Saharan Africa.
97. Darnell 2009, 88.
98. Darnell 2009, 87.
99. Radford 2000.
100. Huyge 2003, 60.

Chapter Four

1. As mentioned in the Introduction, some archaeologists have questioned the use of the term 'Neolithic' to describe the late prehistoric communities who lived in the Western Desert between c.9000 and 4000 BCE, as even though they used pottery and to some extent kept some domesticated cattle and sheep/goats, they still largely followed a semi-nomadic lifestyle based on the hunting and gathering of wild food resources.
2. Jórdeczka 2015, 3.
3. The Combined Prehistoric Expedition was led for many years by Professor Fred Wendorf of the Southern Methodist University, Texas, and the numerous archaeological projects that this renowned American archaeologist directed in Lower Nubia and Egypt have made a huge contribution to our understanding of the Stone Age in north-east Africa.
4. Wendorf & Schild 1998, 100.
5. Brass 2003, 103.
6. Wendorf & Schild 1998, 101.
7. Bard 2015, 85.
8. Wendorf & Schild 1998, 101.
9. Gatto 2011, 23.
10. Brass 2003, 103–104.
11. Wendorf & Schild 1998, 104.
12. Jórdeczka et al. 2013, 257.
13. Jórdeczka et al. 2013, 280.
14. Jórdeczka et al. 2013, 276.
15. Ibid.
16. Jórdeczka et al. 2015, 21.
17. Jórdeczka et al. 2015, 20.
18. Jórdeczka et al. 2015, 20.
19. Jórdeczka et al. 2015, 15.
20. Wendorf & Schild 1998, 105.
21. Wendorf & Schild 1998, 106.
22. Ibid.

23. Nelson & Khalifa 2010, 136.
24. Nelson & Khalifa 2010, 140.
25. Barich 2008, 147.
26. Shirai 2016, 24.
27. Lucarini 2006, 466.
28. Lucarini 2014, 279.
29. Cristiani 2014, 304.
30. Cristiani 2014, 306.
31. Barich 2014, 201.
32. Barich 2014, 186.
33. Barich 2014, 178.
34. Barich et al. 2014, 257.
35. Barich et al. 2014, 262.
36. Barich et al. 2014, 263.
37. Hamdan & Lucarini 2013, 160.
38. Hayes 1965, 93.
39. Bard 1999, 20.
40. Hayes 1965, 94.
41. Shirai 2016, 1193.
42. Ibid.
43. Midant-Reynes 2000, 103.
44. Shirai 2016, 1190.
45. Shirai 2016, 1194.
46. McDonald 2002, 113.
47. McDonald 1998, 133.
48. McDonald 2016, 186.
49. McDonald 1998, 133.
50. McDonald 2016, 187.
51. McDonald et al. 2001, 9.

Chapter Five

1. McKim Malville 2015, 1080.
2. McKim Malville 2015, 1081.
3. McKim Malville, paper published online (Academia.edu), 3.
4. Ibid.
5. McKim Malville 2015, 1081.
6. The annual rising of a star on the eastern horizon at dawn, just before sunrise.
7. Schaefer 2000, 149.
8. McKim Malville 2015, 1082.
9. Bagnold 1931, 27.
10. McKim Malville 2015, 1082–1083.
11. Wendorf & Schild 1998, 111.
12. McKim Malville, paper published online, 7.
13. Wendorf & Schild 1998, 111.
14. Ibid.
15. McKim Malville et al. 2007, 4.
16. McKim Malville et al. 2007, 5.
17. McKim Malville 2015, 1086.

18. McKim Malville, paper published online, 8.
19. Bobrowski et al. 2012.
20. Avner 2018, 29.
21. The Natufian culture was first identified by the famous English archaeologist Dorothy Garrod in the 1930s and roughly dates from 13,000–10,000 BCE. The Natufians were a hunter-gatherer society but had a great influence on the emergence of the Neolithic in the Levant.
22. Avner 2019, 28.
23. Kobusiewicz et al. 2003, 572.
24. Kobusiewicz et al. 2003, 568.
25. Irish et al. 2002, 282.
26. Kobusiewicz et al. 2009, 151.
27. Kobusiewicz et al. 2003, 572–573.
28. Kobusiewicz et al. 2003, 573.
29. Kobusiewicz et al. 2009, 151.
30. Kobusiewicz et al. 2003, 569.
31. Zagórska 2008, 115.
32. Irish 2004, 645.
33. Irish 2004, 646.
34. Friedman & Hobbs 2002, 178.
35. Vermeersch 2000, 40.
36. Horn 2017, 85.
37. Kabaciński et al. 2018, 140.
38. Kabaciński et al. 2018, 141.
39. Friedman & Hobbs 2002, 188.
40. Ibid.
41. Osypiński & Osypińska 2016, 19–20.
42. Osypiński & Osypińska 2016, 9.
43. Osypiński & Osypińska 2016, 20.

Chapter Six

1. Thorpe 2000, 9.
2. Hoffman 1980, 86.
3. Becker & Wendorf 1993, 390.
4. Microwear analysis was carried out on these tools using a high-powered microscope, revealing that they had been used for various activities such as bone/antler working, wood/plant processing, hide-processing and meat-cutting.
5. Mostly from the heads and foreparts of the fish, perhaps suggesting that the bodies of the catfish were smoked over fires and consumed elsewhere.
6. Ferrill 1985, 23.
7. In the archaeological literature, fifty-nine skeletons are usually recorded as having been found at Site 117/Jebel Sahaba, although there seems to have been at least a few more people than this buried here.
8. Wendorf quoted in Hoffman 1980, 97.
9. Friedman, R., 14 July 2014. 'Violence and climate change in prehistoric Egypt and Sudan.' British Museum Blog. https://blog.britishmuseum.org/violence-and-climate-change-in-prehistoric-egypt-and-sudan
10. Ferrill 1985, 23.

11. Fred Wendorf generously donated the skeletal material and finds from Jebel Sahaba to the British Museum in 2002.
12. Friedman, R., 14 July 2014. 'Violence and climate change in prehistoric Egypt and Sudan.' British Museum Blog. https://blog.britishmuseum.org/violence-and-climate-change-in-prehistoric-egypt-and-sudan
13. Judd 2006, 162.
14. Marcus & Flannery 2016, 13.
15. Friedman, R., 14 July 2014. 'Violence and climate change in prehistoric Egypt and Sudan.' British Museum Blog. https://blog.britishmuseum.org/violence-and-climate-change-in-prehistoric-egypt-and-sudan
16. Marcus & Flannery 2016, 11.
17. Marcus & Flannery 2016, 12.
18. Ibid.
19. McDonald et al. 2007, 882.
20. Schild & Wendorf 2002, 10.
21. Quoted in Gayubas 2015, 9.
22. Quote taken from the Minutes of the British Museum's Standing Committee, 12 March 1898, in Taylor 2014, 105.
23. Taylor 2014, 106.
24. Snape 1998, 182.
25. Friedman et al. 2018, 120.
26. Several tattoos were also found on the body of 'Gebelein Woman', another one of the six mummies shipped home by Budge. These comprise an unidentified motif that looks like a long-handled axe or a throwing stick with a curved end and four S-shaped motifs, one above the other, on her upper right arm and shoulder respectively.
27. Friedman et al. 2018, 120.
28. Gayubas 2015, 47.
29. Hendrickx & Eyckerman 2012, 24.
30. Gayubas 2015, 9.
31. Gayubas 2015, 13.
32. Midant-Reynes 2000, 202.
33. Maish 1998, 6.
34. Ibid.
35. Dougherty & Friedman 2008, 309.
36. Gat 2006, 92.

Chapter Seven
1. Junker succeeded Ludwig Borchardt, the discoverer of the famous Nefertiti bust, as director of the German Archaeological Institute in Cairo. As Michael Hoffman has remarked (1980, 168): 'Junker's diplomatic disposition made him a natural candidate for the older scholar's position. While this trait is apparent in almost everything he did, its more negative aspects are apparent in the ease with which he accommodated himself to the Nazi government, in contrast to Borchardt's stubborn opposition to the new order – a capitulation that was not to endear Junker to his Western European colleagues.'
2. Hoffman 1980, 170.
3. Midant-Reynes 2000, 110.

4. Midant-Reynes 2000, 111.
5. Midant-Reynes 2000, 109.
6. Hayes 1965, 104. See pp.103–116 of this classic work for a more in-depth discussion of the fascinating archaeology of Merimde Beni Salama.
7. Hayes 1965, 105.
8. Midant-Reynes 2000, 115.
9. Ibid.
10. Hayes 1965, 106.
11. Vermeersch 2000, 38.
12. Hayes 1965, 107.
13. Pardo Mata 2004, 137.
14. Ibid.
15. Midant-Reynes 2000, 115.
16. Hoffman 1980, 192.
17. Sebakh refers to the deteriorated mud-brick found on many prehistoric and pharaonic sites in Egypt, and sebakh-diggers or Sebakhim have been targeting Egyptian archaeological sites for many hundreds of years, as not only does sebakh make an excellent fertilizer but can also be used as fuel for fires. Untold damage has been done to countless ancient sites in Egypt as the result of sebakh digging, although the same could be said for many of the nineteenth-century 'archaeologists' who, in truth, did little more than pillage Egyptian sites.
18. Hayes 1965, 119.
19. Ibid.
20. Shackleford et al. 2013, 4170.
21. Midant-Reynes 2000, 122.
22. Hayes 1965, 120.
23. Midant-Reynes 2000, 122.
24. Ibid.
25. Midant-Reynes 2000, 124.
26. Vermeersch 2000, 39.
27. Midant-Reynes 2000, 153.
28. This can be downloaded for free from the internet and contains much more information about the Badarian cemeteries and settlements: http://www.etana.org/sites/default/files/coretexts/15271.pdf
29. Brunton & Caton Thompson 14, 1928.
30. Ibid.
31. Jones et al. 2014, 1.
32. Ibid.
33. Vermeersch 2000, 41.
34. Midant-Reynes, 160.
35. Midant-Reynes 2000, 153.
36. The British Museum, Ancient Egypt: Ivory figure of a woman with incised features. https://britishmuseum.withgoogle.com/object/ivory-figure-of-a-woman-with-incised-features
37. Ibid.
38. Anderson 1992, 66.
39. Ibid.
40. Midant-Reynes 2000, 158.

Chapter Eight
1. Petrie & Quibell 1896, 59.
2. The First Intermediate Period (2181–2055 BCE) falls between the Old and Middle Kingdoms (2686–2181 and 2055–1650 BCE respectively) and marks a time of political instability in Dynastic Egypt when rival rulers or 'nomarchs' were jockeying for power as a result of a decline in royal authority and the creation of a power vacuum. The author has been fortunate to work at a notable site from this period: the tomb of Ankhtifi, which lies about 20 miles south of Luxor. A famous inscription from inside this atmospheric and charmingly-decorated rock-cut tomb hints that famine was not unknown during the First Intermediate Period.
3. Hoffman 1980, 107.
4. Petrie quoted in Spencer 2011, 19.
5. Midant-Reynes 2000, 46.
6. Petrie & Quibell 1986, 9.
7. Anderson 1992, 60.
8. Midant-Reynes 2000, 48.
9. Midant-Reynes 2000, 52.
10. Shaw & Nicholson 2008, 235.
11. Hikade 2003, 150.
12. Hendrickx 2011, 93.
13. Midant-Reynes 2000, 50.
14. Midant-Reynes 200, 54.
15. Stevenson 2011, 70.
16. Petrie & Quibell 1896, 50.
17. Other notable examples are the 'ritual knife' of the Brooklyn Museum, the 'Pitt-Rivers Knife' and the 'Gebel Tarif Knife'.
18. Kim 2013, 21.
19. Kim 2012, 6.
20. Josephson & Dreyer 2015, 167.
21. Vučković 2020.
22. Stevenson 2012.
23. Ibid.
24. Midant-Reynes 2000, 50.
25. Midant-Reynes 2000, 176.
26. Midant-Reynes 2000, 50.
27. Midant-Reynes 2000, 53.
28. Petrie & Quibell 1896, 32.
29. Ibid.
30. Hoffman 1980, 116.
31. Ibid.
32. Wilkinson, 52.
33. Judd & Irish 2008, 719.
34. Moll 2011.
35. Tassie & Wettering 2013/14, 66.
36. Petrie & Quibell 1896, 2.
37. Quoted in Adams 2002, 14.
38. Hendrickx & Förster 2010, 842.
39. Adams 2002, 14.

40. Kemp 1991, 80.
41. See Kemp 2000.
42. Kemp 1991, 80.
43. Linseele et al. 2009.
44. Friedman 2011, 34.
45. Friedman 2011, 34.
46. Clayton 1994, 18.
47. Bard 2000, 61.
48. O'Connor 2011, 147.
49. O'Connor 2011, 148.
50. Ibid.
51. Two Dog Palette: Real and fabulous royal beasts. https://www.ashmolean.org/two-dog-palette
52. Millet 1990, 53.
53. Ibid.
54. Ibid.
55. Bard 2000, 65.
56. Midant-Reynes 2000, 250–251.
57. Bard 2000, 65.
58. Midant-Reynes 2000, 52.
59. Midant-Reynes 2000, 207.
60. Midant-Reynes 2000, 208.
61. Josephson & Dryer 2015, 171.
62. Midant-Reynes 2000, 208.
63. Sumerian Shakespeare: The events portrayed on the mural of Tomb 100 in Hierakonpolis. https://sumerianshakespeare.com/748301/855901.html
64. Case & Payne 1962, 17.
65. Sadly, Michael Hoffman died from cancer in 1990, aged just 56.
66. https://www.hierakonpolis-online.org/index.php/history-of-exploration/michael-hoffman
67. This marked the resumption of excavations at the site by the American Museum of Natural History-Vassar College Expedition to Hierakonpolis under the directorship of Professor Walter Fairservis, which had ceased in 1969 because of the international political situation.
68. Hoffman 1989, 119–120.
69. Like Michael Hoffman, Barbara Adams also sadly died before her time, aged 57.
70. There is insufficient space here to mention the numerous fascinating finds made by the archaeologists of the Hierakonpolis Expedition, but for those readers who would like to know more about them, see the expedition's excellent annual online newsletter *Nekhen News*: https://www.hierakonpolis-online.org/index.php/nekhen-news
71. Friedman 2009, 3.
72. Friedman 2011, 38.
73. Friedman 2011, 39.
74. Ibid.
75. McNamara 2014, 8–9.
76. Friedman 2011, 42.
77. Friedman 2011, 35.

78. Friedman 2011, 36.
79. Hartung 2018, 319.
80. Hikade 2003, 146.
81. Hikade 2003, 147.
82. Dreyer 2011, 127.
83. Dreyer 2011, 133.
84. Dreyer 2011, 134.
85. MacArthur 2010, 119.
86. Ciałowicz 2011, 56.
87. Ciałowicz 2011, 57.
88. Watrin 2000, 163.
89. Midant-Reynes 2014, 4.
90. Hoffman 1980, 205.
91. Midant-Reynes 2000, 59.
92. Hayes 1965, 130.
93. Ibid.
94. Hoffman 1980, 213–214.
95. Quoted in Anđelković 2011, 29.

Bibliography

Adams, B., 2002, 'Petrie's Manuscript from Coptos.' *Topoi-Orient Occident*, Supplement 3. *Autor de Coptos*: https://www.persee.fr/doc/topoi_1764_-0773_2002_act_3_1_228

Anderson, W., 1992, 'Badarian Burials: Evidence of Social Inequality in Middle Egypt During the Early Predynastic Era', *Journal of the American Research Center in Egypt* 29, 51–66.

Antón, S.C., 2012, 'Early *Homo* – Who, When and Where?' *Current Anthropology* 53, 278–295.

Antón, S.C. & Swisher III, C.C., 2004, 'Early Dispersals of *Homo* from Africa', *Annual Review of Anthropology* 33, 271–296.

Avner, U., 1984, 'Ancient Cult Sites in the Negev and Sinai Deserts', *Tel Aviv* 11, 115–131.

Bagnold, R.A., 1931, 'Journeys in the Libyan Desert 1929 and 1930', *The Geographical Journal* 78, 13–33.

Bagnold, R.A., Myers, O.H. & Winkler, O.H., 1939, 'An expedition to the Gilf Kebir and Unweinat, 1938', *The Geographical Journal* 93, 281–312.

Bard, K.A., 1999, *Encyclopedia of the Archaeology of Ancient Egypt* (London, Routledge)

Bard, K.A., 1994, 'The Egyptian Predynastic: A Review of the Evidence', *Journal of Field Archaeology* 21, 265–288.

Bard, K.A., 2000, 'The Emergence of the Egyptian State' in Shaw, I. (ed.), *The Oxford History of Ancient Egypt*, 61–88 (Oxford, Oxford University Press)

Bard, K.A., 2015, *An Introduction to the Archaeology of Ancient Egypt* (Blackwell, Sussex)

Barich, B.E., 2008, 'Living in the Oases: Beginnings of Village Life at Farafra and in the Western Desert of Egypt' in Sulgostowska, Z. & Tomaszewski, A.J. (eds), *Man-Millennia-Environment, Studies in Honour of Romuald Schild*, 145–150 (Warsaw, Polish Institute of Archaeology and Ethnology, Polish Academy of Sciences)

Barich, B.E., 2014, 'The Wadi el Obeiyid Cave 1: The Rock Art Archive' in Barich, B.E., Lucarini, G., Hamdan, M.A. & Hassan, F.A. (eds), *From Lake to Sand: The Archaeology of Farafra Oasis Western Desert, Egypt*, 385–405 (Florence, Edizioni All'Insegna del Giglio)

Barich, B.E., 2014, 'Hidden Valley: A 7,000-year-old village in Wadi el Obeiyid' in Barich, B.E., Lucarini, G., Hamdan, M.A. & Hassan, F.A. (eds), *From Lake to Sand: The Archaeology of Farafra Oasis Western Desert, Egypt*, 167–208 (Florence, Edizioni All'Insegna del Giglio)

Barich, B.E., 2016, 'The Introduction of Neolithic Resources to North Africa: A Discussion of the Holocene Research between Egypt and Libya', *Quaternary International* 410, 198–216.

Barich, B.E. & Lucarini, G., 2002, 'Archaeology of Farafra Oasis (Western Desert, Egypt)', *Archeo-Nil* 12, 101–108.

Barich, B.E., Lucarini, G., Gallinaro, M. & Hamdan, M., 2012, 'Sheikh/Bir El Obeiyid: Evidence of Sedentism in the Northern Farafra Depression (Western Desert, Egypt)', Pre-history of North-Eastern Africa: New Ideas and Discoveries, *Studies in African Archaeology* 11, 255–278.

Bárta, M. & Frouz, M., 2010, *Swimmers in the Sand* (Dryada Publishing)

Bárta, M., 2015, 'The Oldest Mythological Run in Egyptian Desert? On the Possible Origins of the Sed Feast in Ancient Egypt' in Sázelová, S., Novák, M. & Mizerová, A. (eds), *Forgotten Times and Spaces: New Perspectives in Palaeoanthropological, Palaeontological and Archaeological Studies*, 487–493 (Brno, Institute of the Czech Academy of Sciences, Masaryk University)

Bar-Yosef, D.E., Vandermeersch, B. & Bar-Yosef, B., 2009, 'Shells and Ochre in Middle Palaeolithic Qafzeh Cave, Israel: Indications of Modern Behaviour', *Journal of Human Evolution* 56, 307–314.

Bar-Yosef, O. & Belfer-Cohen, A., 2001, 'From Africa to Eurasia – Early Dispersals', *Quaternary International* 75, 19–28.

Bar-Yosef, O. & Vandermeersch, B., April 1993, 'Modern Humans in the Levant', *Scientific American*, 94–100.

Bar-Yosef Mayer, D.E., Vandermeersch, B. & Beyin, A., 2006, 'The Bab al Mandab vs the Nile-Levant: An Appraisal of the Two Dispersal Routes for Modern Humans out of Africa', *African Archaeological Review* 23, 5–30.

Barzilai, O. & Gubenko, N., 2018, 'Rethinking Emireh Cave: The Lithic Technology Perspectives', *Quaternary International* 464, 92–105.

Baumgartel, E.J., 1965, 'What Do We Know about the Excavations at Merimda?', *Journal of the American Oriental Society* 85, 502–511.

Binneman, J. & Beaumont, P., 1992, 'Use-Wear on Two Acheulean Handaxes from Wonderwork Cave, Northern Cape', *Southern African Field Archaeology* 1, 92.97.

Bobrowski, P., Czekaj-Zastawny, A. & Schild, R., 2012, 'The Early Neolithic Offering Tumuli from Sacred Mountain (site E-06-1) in Nabta (Western Desert of Egypt)', *New Ideas and Discoveries: Studies in African Archaeology II*, Poznan Archaeological Museum, 409–420.

Bouzouggar, A., Humphrey, L.T., Barton, N., Parfitt, S.A., Clark-Balzan, L., Schweningger, J-L., El-Hajraoui, M.A., Nespoulet, R. & Bello, S.M., 2018, '90,000-year-old specialised bone tool technology in the Aterian Middle Stone Age of North Africa', *PLoS ONE* 13, 1–17. https://doi.org/10.1371/journal.pone.0202021

Bradshaw Foundation, 'Exploring the Fossil Record: Stone Tools', *Bradshaw Foundation Paleoanthropology*. www.bradshawfoundation.com/origins

Brass, M., 2003, 'Tracing the Origins of the Ancient Egyptian Cattle Cult' in Eyma, A.K. & Bennet, C.J., (eds), *Delta Man in Yebu: Occasional Volume of the Egyptologists Electronic Forum* No. 1, 101–110 (USA, Universal Publishers)

Brass, M., 2018, 'Early North African Domestication and its Ecological Setting: A Reassessment', *Journal of World Prehistory* 31, 81–115.

Brewer, D., 2012, *The Archaeology of Ancient Egypt: Beyond Pharaohs* (New York, Cambridge University Press)

Brunton, G. & Caton Thompson, G., 1928, *The Badarian Civilisation and the Predynastic Remains near Badari* (London, British School of Archaeology in Egypt; Bernard Quaritch)

Bubenzer, O. & Reimer, H., 2007, 'Holocene Climatic Change and Human Settlement between the Central Sahara and the Nile Valley: Archaeological and Geomorphological Results', *Geoarchaeology* 22, 607–620. DOI:10.1002/gea/20176.

Burton, R.F., 1879, 'Stones and Bones from Egypt and Midian', *Journal of the Royal Anthropological Institute of Great Britain and Ireland* 8, 290–319.

Carotenuto, F., Tsikaridze, N., Rook, L., Lordkipanidze, D., Longo, L., Condemi, S. & Raia, P., 2016, 'Venturing out safely: The biogeography of *Homo erectus* dispersal out of Africa', *Journal of Human Evolution* 95, 1–12.

Case, H. & Crowfoot Payne, J., 1962, 'Tomb 100: The Decorated Tomb at Hierakonpolis', *Journal of Egyptian Archaeology* 48, 5–18.

Caton Thompson, G., 1932, 'The Royal Anthropological Institute's Research Expedition to Kharga Oasis: The Second Season's Discoveries', *Man* 32, 129–135.

Caton Thompson, G., 1946, 'The Levalloisian Industries of Egypt', *Proceedings of the Prehistoric Society* 4, 57–120.

Chazan, M., 1995, 'Conceptions of Time and the Development of Paleolithic Chronology', *American Anthropologist* 97, 457–467.

Ciałowicz, K.M., 2011, 'The Predynastic/Early Dynastic Period at Tell el-Farkha' in Teeter, E. (ed.), *Before the Pyramids*, 55–64 (The Oriental Institute of Chicago, Oriental Institute Museum Publications)

Claassen, E., 2009, 'Djara – Cave Art in Egypt's Western Desert', *Archéo-Nil* 19, 47–66.

Clark, J.D., 1971, 'A Re-Examination of the Evidence of Agricultural Origins in the Nile Valley', *Proceedings of the Prehistoric Society* 37, 34–79.

Clayton, P., 1994, *Chronicle of the Pharaohs* (London, Thames & Hudson)

Close, A., 'Living on the Edge: Neolithic Herders in the Eastern Sahara', *Antiquity* 64, 79–96.

Corbey, R., Jagich, A., Vaesen, K. & Collard, M., 2016, 'The Acheulean Handaxe: More like a Bird's Song than a Beatle's Tune?' *Evolutionary Anthropology* 25, 6–19. DOI: 1002/evan.21467.

Crevecoeur, I., 2012, 'The Upper Palaeolithic Human Remains of Nazlet Khater 2 (Egypt) and Past Modern Human Diversity' in Hublin, J-J. & McPherron, S.P. (eds), *Modern Origins: A North African Perspective*, 205–218. Vertebrate Paleobiology and Paleoanthropology, DOI: 10:/1007/978-94-007-2929_14. Springer Science & Business Media B.V. 2012.

Crevecoeur, I. & Trinkaus, E., 2004, 'From the Nile to the Danube: A Comparison of the Nazlet Khater 2 and Oasis 1 Early Modern Human Mandibles', *Anthropologie* XLII/3, 203–213.

Crowfoot-Payne, J., 1973, 'Tomb 100: The Decorated Tomb at Hierakonpolis', *Journal of Egyptian Archaeology* 59, 31–35.

Czekaj-Zatawny, A., Irish, J.D., Kabaciński, J. & Mugaj, J., 2018, 'The Neolithic Settlements by a Paleo-lake of Gebel Ramlah, Western Desert of Egypt' in Kabaciński, J., Chłodnicki, M., Kobusiewicz, M. & Winiarska-Kabacińska, M. (eds.), *Desert and the Nile. Prehistory of the Nile Basin and the Sahara. Papers in honour of Fred Wendorf*, 515–538 (Studies in African Archaeology 15, Poznań Archaeological Museum)

Daniel, G., 1964, *The Idea of Prehistory* (Middlesex, Penguin)

Daniel, G., 1967, *The Origins and Growth of Archaeology* (Middlesex, Penguin)

Darnell, J.C., 2009, 'Iconographic Attraction, Iconographic Syntax and Tableaux of Royal Ritual Power in the Pre- and Proto-Dynastic Rock Inscriptions of the Theban Western Desert', *Archéo-Nil* 19, 83–107.

Dart, R.A. & Beaumont, P., 1969, 'Evidence of Iron Ore Mining in Southern Africa in the Middle Stone Age', *Current Anthropology* 10, 127–128.

Davies, O., 1970, 'Boucher de Perthes Centenary Lecture Delivered to the Witwatersrand Centre of the S.A.A.A.S.', *South African Journal of Science*, 143–150.

Debono, F., 1981, 'Prehistory in the Nile Valley' in Ki-Zerbo, J. (ed.), *General History of Africa: Methodology and Prehistory*, 634–655 (London, Heinemann)

De la Torre, I., 2016, 'The origins of the Acheulean: past and present perspectives on a major transition in human evolution', *Philosophical Transactions of the Royal Society* B 371: 201550245, 1–10. http://dx.doi.org/10.1098/rstb.2015.0245

D'Huy, J., 2009, 'New evidence of a closeness between the Abu Ra's shelter (Eastern Sahara) and Egyptian beliefs', *Sahara* 20,125–126.

D'Huy, J. & Le Quellec, J-L., 2009, 'From the Sahara to the Nile: the low representation of dangerous animals in the rock art of the Libyan Desert could be linked to the fear of their animation', *Notes of the AARS* 13.

Dibble, H.L., Aldeias, V., Jacobs, Z., Olszewski, D., Rezeck, Z., Lin, S.C., Alvarez-Fernández, E., Barshay-Schmidt, C.C., Hallet-Desguez, E., Reed, D., Richter, D., Steele, T.E., Skinner, A., Blackwell, B., Doronicheva, E. & El-Hajraoui, M., 2013, 'On the industrial attributions of the Aterian and Mousterian of the Maghreb', *Journal of Human Evolution* 64, 194–210 http://dx.doi.org/10.1016/j.jhevol.2012.10.010

Dougherty, S. & Friedman, R., 2008, 'Sacred or Mundane: Scalping and Decapitation at Hierakonpolis' in Reynes, B-M. & Trisant, Y. (eds), *Egypt at its Origins* 2, 309–335. Orientalia Lovaniensia Analecta 172.

Dreyer, G., 2011, 'Tomb U-J: A Royal Burial of Dynasty O at Abydos' in Teeter, E. (ed.), *Before the Pyramids*, 127–135 (The Oriental Institute of Chicago, Oriental Institute Museum Publications)

Ferrill, A., 1985, *The Origins of War* (London, Thames & Hudson)

Förster, F., Reimer, H. & Kuper, R., 'The "Cave of Beasts" (Gil Kebir, S-W Egypt) and its Chronological and Cultural Affiliation: Approaches and Preliminary Results of the Wadi Sura Project', *The Signs of Which Times? Chronological and Palaeoenvironmental Issues in the Rock Art of Northern Africa*. Royal Academy for Overseas Sciences, Brussels, 3–5 June 2010, 197–216.

Förster, F. & Scheid, M-H., 2015, 'Range and Categories of Human Representation in the "Cave of Beasts", S-W Egypt', *International Conference: Whatever Happened to the People? Humans and Anthropomorphs in the Rock Art of Northern Africa*. Royal Academy for Overseas Sciences, Brussels, 17–19 September 2015, 301–319.

Friedman, R., 2008, 'The Cemeteries of Hierakonpolis', *Archéo-Nil* 18, 9–29.

Friedman, R., 2009, 'Slow and Steady', *Nekhen News* 21, 3. https://www.hierakonpolis-online.org/nekhennews/nn-21-2009.pdf

Friedman, R., 2009, 'Locality HK29A: The Predynastic Ceremonial Center Revisited', *Journal of the American Research Center in Egypt* 45, 79–13.

Friedman, R., 2011, 'Hierakonpolis' in Teeter, E. (ed.), *Before the Pyramids*, 33–44 (The Oriental Institute of Chicago, Oriental Institute Museum Publications)

Friedman, R., 2014, 'The Masks of Hierakonpolis Cemetery HK6' in Jucha, M.A., Debowska-Ludwin, J. & Kolodziejczyk, P. (eds), 115–127. *Aegyptus Est Imago Caeli, Studies Presented to Krzystof M. Ciałowicz on his 60th Birthday*, Krakow.

Friedman, R. & Hobbs, J., 2002, 'A "Tasian" Tomb in Egypt's Eastern Desert' in Friedman, R. (ed.), *Egypt and Nubia: Gifts of the Desert*, 178–190 (London, British Museum Press)

Fuchs, G., 1989, 'Rock Engravings in the Wadi el-Barramiya, Eastern Desert of Egypt', *The African Archaeological Review* 7, 127–153.

Gamble, C. & Kruszynski, R., 2009, 'John Evans, Joseph Prestwich and the stone that shattered the time barrier', *Antiquity* 83, 461–475.

Garcea, E.A.A., 2004, 'Crossing Deserts and Avoiding Seas: Aterian North African-European Relations', *Journal of Anthropological Research* 60, 27–53.

Garcea, E.A.A., 2012, 'Successes and failures of human dispersals from North Africa', *Quaternary International* 270, 119–128.

Gautier, A., 1993, 'The faunal spectrum of the Middle Palaeolithic in Bir Tarfawi, Western Desert of Egypt' in Wendorf, F., Close Schild, R. & Close, A.E. (eds), *Egypt During the Last Interglacial*, 123–127 (New York, Springer)

Gayubas, A., 2015, 'Warfare and Social Change in Non-State Societies of the Predynastic Nile Valley', *Aula Orientalis de Estudios del Próximo Orienta Antiguo* 33, 43–49.

Gayubas, A., 'Warfare and Socio-Political Hierarchies: Reflections on Non-State Societies of the Predynastic Nile Valley', *Gladius* XXXV, 7–20.

Gibbons, A., 22 November 2016, 'Meet the frail, small-brained people who first trekked out of Africa', *Science Magazine* (*AAAS*), sciencemag.org/news/2016/11/meet-frail-small-brained-people-who-first-trekked-out-of-Africa

Goder-Goldberger, M., 2013, 'The Khormusan: Evidence for an MSA East African Industry in Nubia', *Quaternary International* 300, 182–194.

Gowlett, J., 1993, *Ascent to Civilization: The Archaeology of Early Humans* (London, McGraw-Hill, New York)

Gowlett, J.A.J., 2019, 'Boucher de Perthes: Pioneer of Palaeolithic Prehistory' in Hosfield, R.T., Wenban-Smith, F.F. & Pope, M.I. (eds), *Great Prehistorians: 150 years of Palaeolithic Research, 1859–2009, Lithics Special Volume* 30, 13–24.

Graves, R.R., Lupo, A.C., McCarthy, R.C., Wescott, D.L. & Cunningham, D.L., 2010, 'Just how strapping was KNM-WT 15000?' *Journal of Human Evolution* 59, 542–554.

Grine, F.E., 2016, 'The Late Quaternary Hominins of Africa: The Skeletal Evidence from MIS 62' in Jones, S.C. & Stewart, B.A. (eds), *Africa from MIS 6–2: Population Dynamics and Paleoenvironments*, 323–388 (New York, Springer)

Hartung, U., 2014, 'An Unusual Bone Comb from Cemetery U at Abydos' in Jucha, M.A., Dębowska-Ludwin & Kołodziejczyk J. (eds), *Aegyptus Est Imago Caeli: Studies Presented to Krzysztof M. Cialowicz on His 60th Birthday*, 151–1560 (Krakow, Institute of Archaeology, Jagiellonian University in Krakow)

Hartung, U., 2018, 'Cemetery U at Umm el-Qa'ab and the Funeral Landscape of the Abydos Region in the 4th Millennium BC' in Kabaciński, J., Chłodnicki, M., Kobusiewicz, M. & Winiarska-Kabacińska, M. (eds), *Desert and the Nile. Prehistory of the Nile Basin and the Sahara. Papers in honour of Fred Wendorf*, 313–335 (Studies in African Archaeology 15, Poznań Archaeological Museum)

Hassan, F.A., 'The Predynastic of Egypt', *Journal of World Prehistory* 2, 135–185.

Hayden, B. & Villeneuve, S., 2009, 'Sex, Symmetry and Silliness in the Bifacial World', *Antiquity* 83, 1163–1170.

Hayes, W.C., 1965, *Most Ancient Egypt* (Chicago, University of Chicago Press)

Hendrickx, S., 2011, 'Crafts and Craft Specialization' in Teeter, E. (ed.), *Before the Pyramids*, 93–98 (The Oriental Institute of Chicago, Oriental Institute Museum Publications)

Hendrickx, S. & Eyckerman, M., 2012, 'Visual representation and State development in Egypt', *Archéo-Nil* 22, 23–72.

Hendrickx, S. & Förster, F., 2010, 'Early Dynastic Art and Iconography' in Lloyd, A.B. (ed.), *A Companion to Ancient Egypt* (Vol. II), 826–852 (Oxford, Blackwell)

Hendrickx, S. & Vermeersch, P., 2000, 'Prehistory: From the Palaeolithic to the Badarian (700,000–4000 BC)' in Shaw, I. (ed.), *The Oxford History of Ancient Egypt*, 17–43 (Oxford, Oxford University Press)

Hendrickx, S. & Vermeersch, P., 2014, 'Neolithic and Predynastic Egypt' in Renfrew, C. & Bahn, P. (eds), *The Cambridge World Prehistory*, Vol. 1, 240–258 (Cambridge, Cambridge University Press)

Henneberg, M., Kobusiewicz, M., Schild, R. & Wendorf, F., 1989, 'The Early Neolithic, Qarunian burial from the Northern Fayum Desert (Egypt)' in Krzyzaniak, L. & Kobusiewicz, M. (eds), *Late Prehistory of the Nile Basin and Sahara*, Vol. 2, Studies in African Archaeology, 181–196 (Posnań, Posnań Archaeological Museum)

Hikade, T., 2003, 'Getting the Ritual Right – Fishtail Knives in Predynastic Egypt' in Myer, S. (ed.), *Ancient Egypt – Temple of the Whole World: Studies in Honour of Jan Assman*, 137–151 (Köln, Brill)

Hikade, T., 2010, 'Stone Tool Production' in Wendrich, W. (ed.), *UCLA Encyclopedia of Egyptology*, 1–17. Los Angeles: http://digital2.library.ucla.edu/viewItem/do?=2198/zz220025h6kk

Hikade, T., 2012, 'Egypt and the Near East' in Potts, D.T. (ed.), *A Companion to the Archaeology of the Ancient Near East*, 833–850 (Chichester, Blackwell)

Hill, C.L., 2001, 'Geological Contexts of the Acheulean (Middle Pleistocene) in the Eastern Sahara', *Geoarchaeology: An International Journal* 16, 65–94.

Hoffman, M.A., 1980, 'A Rectangular Amratian House from Hierakonpolis and its Significance for Predynastic Research', *Journal of Near Eastern Studies* 39, 119–137.

Hoffman, M.A., 1980, *Egypt Before the Pharaohs* (London, Routledge & Kegan Paul)

Holl, A.F.C., 2010, 'The Archaeology of Africa' in Hardesty, D.L. (ed.), *Archaeology Vol. II: Encyclopedia of Life Support Systems*, UK, EOLSS/Unesco.

Holmes, D.C. & Friedman, R.F., 1994, 'Survey and Test Excavations in the Badari Region, Egypt', *Proceedings of the Prehistoric Society* 60, 105–142.

Honoré, E., Raksa, T., Senut, B., Deruelle, P. & Pouydebat, E., 2016, 'First identification of non-human stencil hands at Wadi Sura II (Egypt): A morphometric study for new insights into rock art symbolism', *Journal of Archaeological Science: Report* 6, 242–247.

Horn, M., 2017, 'Re-appraising the Tasian-Badarian Divide in the Qau-Matmar Region: A Critical Review of Cultural Proxies and a Comparative Analysis of Burial Dress' in Midant-Reynes, B. & Ryan, T.Y. (eds), Proceedings of the Fifth International Conference: 'Origin of the State. Predynastic and Early Dynastic Egypt', Cairo, 13–18 April 2014, OLA, Leuven, Paris, Walpole (MA), 335–378.

Hublin, J.-J., Ben-Ncer, A., Bailey, S.F., Freidline, S.E., Neubauer, S., Le Cabec, A., Benazzi, S., Harvati, K. & Gunz, P., 2017, 'New fossils from Jebel Irhoud Morocco and the pan-African origin of *Homo sapiens*', *Nature* 546, 289–292. DOI.10.3038/nature22336.

Huyge, D., 2005, 'The Fish Hunters of El-Hosh: Rock Art Research and Archaeological Investigations in Upper Egypt (1998–2004)', *Mededelingen der Zittingen van de Koninklijke Académie voor Overzees Wetenschapen/Bulletin des Séances de l'Académie Royale des Sciences d'Outre-Mer* 51, 23–249.

Huyge, D., 2008, 'Lascaux along the Nile: The Palaeolithic Rock Art of Qurta (Upper Egypt)', *Bulletin des Séances de l'Académie Royale des Sciences d'Outre-Mer* 54, 281–296.

Huyge, D., 2009, 'Epipalaeolithic Rock Art in Egypt: Qurta and El-Hosh', *Archéo-Nil* 19, 31–46.

Huyge, D., 2009, 'Rock Art' in Wendrich, W. (ed.), *UCLA Encyclopedia of Egyptology*, 1–13 http://digital2.library.ucla.edu/viewItem.do?ark=21198/22001nf7fh

Huyge, D., 2013, '"Ice Age" Art at Qurta', *Ancient Egypt* 77, 32–41.

Huyge, D., 2013, 'Grandeur in Confined Spaces' in Bahn, P.G. & Fosatti, A. (eds), *Rock Art Studies News of the World* 2, 59–73 (Oxford, Oxbow)

Huyge, D., 2015, 'The "Headless Women" of Qurta (Upper Egypt): The Earliest Anthropomorphic Images in Northern-African Rock Art', *International Conference: Whatever Happened to the People? Humans and Anthropomorphs in the Rock Art of Northern Africa*, Royal Academy for Overseas Sciences Brussels, 17–19 September 2015, 419–430.

Huyge, D. & Claes, W., 2008, '"Ice Age" Art along the Nile', *Egyptian Archaeology* 33, 25–28.

Huyge, D., Vandenberge, Dimitri, A.G., D.A.G, De Dapper, M., Mees, F. & Darnell, J.C., 2011, 'First evidence of Pleistocene rock art in North Africa: securing the age of the Qurta petroglyphs (Egypt) through OSL dating, Antiquity' 85, 118401193.

Huyge, D. & Ikram, S., 2009, 'Animal representations in the Late Palaeolithic rock art at Qurta (Upper Egypt)' in Reimer, H., Förster, F., Herb, M. & Pöllath, N. (eds), *Desert Animals in the Eastern Sahara: Status, economic significance, and cultural reflections in antiquity*, 157–174 (Köln, Heinrich-Barth-Institut)

Huyge, D., Watchman, A., De Dapper, M. & Marchi, E., 2001, 'Dating Egypt's oldest "art": AMS ¹⁴C determinations on rock varnishes covering petroglyphs at El-Hosh (Upper Egypt)', *Antiquity* 75, 68–72.

Huyge, D. & Storemyr, P., 2012, 'A "masterpiece" of Epipalaeolithic rock art from el-Hosh, Upper Egypt', *Sahara* 23, 127–132.

Huyge, D. & Storemyr, P., 2013, 'Unique Geometric Rock Art at el-Hosh', *Ancient Egypt* 78, 24–30.

Huyge, D., Aubert, M., Barnard, H., Claes, W., Darnell, J.C., De Dapper, M., Figari, E., Ikram, S., Lebrun-Nélis, A. & Therasse, I., 2007, '"Lascaux along the Nile": Late Pleistocene Rock Art in Egypt', *Antiquity* 81 (Project Gallery)

Ikram, S., 2009, 'Drawing the World: Petroglyphs from Kharga Oasis', *Archéo-Nil* 19, 67–82.

Ikram, S., 2009, 'A desert zoo: An exploration of meaning and reality in the rock art of Kharga Oasis' in Reimer, H., Förster, F., Herb, M. & Pöllath, N. (eds), *Desert animals in the eastern Sahara: Status, economic significance, and cultural reflection in antiquity*. Proceedings of an interdisciplinary ACACIA workshop held at the University of Cologne 14–15 December 2007, Colloquium Africanum 4, 263–291 (Köln, Heinrich-Barth-Institut)

Ikram, S., 2013, 'A possible panel of arachnids in Kharga Oasis (Egypt's Western Desert)', *Sahara* 24, 95–100.

Ikram, S., 2013, 'Fat Ladies, Thin Men, Blobby People, and Body Parts: An Exploration of Human Representations in the Rock Art of the North Kharga Basin', International Conference, *Whatever Happened to the People? Humans and Anthropomorphs in the Rock Art of Northern Africa*. Royal Academy for Overseas Sciences, Brussels, 17–19 September 2015, 353–364.

Irish, J.D., 'A 5,500-Year-Old Artificial Human Tooth from Egypt: A Historical Note', *The International Journal of Oral and Maxillofacial Implants* 19, 645–647.

Jórdecska, M., Masojć, M., Królik, H. & Schild, R., 2007, 'Hunter-Gatherer Cattle-Keepers of Early Neolithic El Adam Type from Nabta Playa: Latest Discoveries from Site E-06-1', *African Archaeological Review* 30, 253–284.

Jórdecska, M., Masojć, M. & Schild, R., 2007, 'Here comes the rain again…the Early El Adam Occupation of the Western Desert, Nabta Playa Egypt', *Azania: Archaeological Research in Africa* 50. DOI: 10.1080/0067270X.2014.984969.

Jórdecska, M., Masojć, M., Królik, H. & Schild, 2011, 'Early Holocene Pottery in the Western Desert of Egypt: New Data from Nabta Playa', *Antiquity* 85, 99–115.

Jórdecska, M., Masojć, M., Królik, H. & Schild, 2012, 'Early Neolithic Settlements of El Adam Type from Nabta Playa. Site E-06-1', *Prehistory of North-Eastern Africa: New Ideas and Discoveries in African Archaeology* 11, Poznań Archaeological Museum, 365–407.

Josephson, J.A. & Dreyer, G., 2015, 'Naqada IId: The Birth of an Empire: Kingship, Writing, Organized Religion', *Journal of the American Research Center in Egypt* 51, 165–180.

Judd, M., 2006, 'Jebel Sahaba Revisited', *Archaeology of Early North-Eastern Africa: Studies in African Archaeology* 9, 153–166 (Poznan Archaeological Museum)

Judd, M. & Irish, J., 2008, 'Dying to serve: the mass burials at Kerma', *Antiquity* 83, 709–722.

Kabaciński, J., Schild, R. & Irish, J.D., 2004, 'Discovery of the first Neolithic cemetery in Egypt's Western Desert', *Antiquity* 65, 566–578.

Keeley, L., 1996, *War Before Civilization* (Oxford, Oxford University Press)

Kelany, A., 2012, 'More Late Palaeolithic Rock Art at Wadi Subeira, Upper Egypt', *Bulletin des Musées Royaux D'Art Histoire Parc Du Cincquantenaire, Bruxelles* 83, 5–21.

Kelany, A., 2014, 'Late Paleolithic Rock Art Sites at Wadi Abu Subeira and el-Aqaba el-Saghira, Upper Egypt', *Cashiers de l'AARS* 17, 105–115.

Kemp, B., 1991, *Ancient Egypt: Anatomy of a Civilization* (London, Routledge)

Kemp, B., 2000, 'The Colossi from the Early Shrine of Coptos in Egypt', *Cambridge Archaeological Journal* 10, 211–242.

Kim, P.E., 2012, *The Materiality and "Enchantment" of the Gebel el-Arak Knife and the Gerzean Flint Blade Production*. UC Berkley, Charlene Conrad Liebau Library Prize for Undergraduate Research. https://escholarship.org./uc/item/8bx0r2nr

Kindermann, K., 2000, 'Prehistoric links between the Desert and the Nile' in Hawass, Z. (ed.), *Egyptology at the Dawn of the Twenty-First Century: Proceedings of the Eighth International Conference of Egyptologists Cairo 2000* (Vol.1), 273–279 (Cairo, The American University in Cairo Press)

Kindermann, K., 2004, 'Djara: excavations and surveys of the 1998–2002 seasons', *Archéo-Nil* 14, 31–50.

Kindermann, K., 2003, 'Investigations of the Mid-Holocene Settlement of Djara (Abu Muhariq Plateau, Western Desert of Egypt)' in Krzyzaniak, L., Kroeper, K. & Kobusiewicz, M. (eds), *Cultural Markers in the Later Prehistory of North-Eastern Africa and Recent Research Studies* 8, 51–72 (Poznań, Poznań Archaeological Museum)

Kindermann, K., Bubenzer, O., Nussbaum, S., Reimer, H., Darious, F., Pöllath, N. & Smettan, U., 2006, 'Palaeoenvironmental and Holocene land use of Djara, Western Desert of Egypt', *Quaternary Science Reviews* 25, 1619–1637.

Kleimann, B., Horn, P. & Langenhorst, F., 2001, 'Evidence for shock metamorphism in sandstones from the Libyan Desert Glass strewn field', *Meteoritics & Planetary Science* 36, 1277–1282.

Klein, R., 2009, 'Hominid dispersals in the Old World' in Scarre, C. (ed.), *The Human Past: World Prehistory and the Development of Human Societies*, 84–123 (London, Thames & Hudson)

Kobusiewicz, M., Kabaciński, J., Schild, R., Irish, J.D. & Wendorf, F., 2009, 'Burial Practices of the Final Neolithic Pastoralists at Gebel Ramlah, Western Egypt of Egypt', *British Museum Studies in Ancient Egypt & Sudan* 13, 147–174.

Kohn, M. & Mithen, S., 1999, 'Handaxes: products of sexual selection?' *Antiquity* 73, 518–526.

Koopman, A., Kluiving, S., Wendrich, W. & Holdoway, S., 2012, 'Late Quaternary Climatic Change and Egypt's Earliest Pre-Pharaonic Farmers, Fayum Basin, Egypt', *eTopoi* 3, 63–69.

Kuper, R., 2007, *Archaeology of the Gilf Kebir National Park* (Cologne, Heinrich-Barth-Institut)

Kuper, R. (ed.), 2013, *Wadi Sura: the Cave of Beasts. A rock art site in the Gilf Kebir (SW-Egypt)*, (Africa Praehistorica 26, Cologne, Heinrich-Barth-Institut)

Kuper, R. & Kropelin, S., 2006, 'Climate-Controlled Holocene Occupation in the Sahara: Motor of Africa's Evolution', *Science* 313, 803–807. DOI: 10.1126/Science.1130989.

Leplongeon, A. & Pleurdeau, D., 2011, 'The Upper Palaeolithic Lithic industry of Nazlet Khater 4: Implications for the Stone Age/Palaeolithic of North-Eastern Africa', *African Archaeological Review* 28, 213–236.

Le-Quellec, J-L., 2008, 'Can One "Read" Rock Art? An Egyptian Example', *Iconography Without Texts*, Warburg Institute Colloquia 13, 25–42.

Le-Quellec, J-L., 2013, 'Two new Aterian sites in the Southern Gilf-Kebir (Western Desert, Egypt)', *Sahara* 24, 239–242.

Linseele, V., Van Neer, W., Thys, S., Phillips, R., Wendrich, W. & Holdaway, S., 2014, 'New Zooarchaeological Data from the Fayum "Neolithic" with a Critical Assessment of the Evidence for Early Stock-Keeping in Egypt', *PLOS One* 9, 1–22.

Linseele, V., Van Neer, W. & Friedman, R., 2009, 'Animals from a Special Place? The Fauna from KH29A at Predynastic Hierakonpolis', *Journal of the American Research Center in Egypt* 45, 105–136.

Linstädter, J. & Kröpelin, S., 2014, 'Wadi Bakht Revisited: Holocene Climate Change and Prehistoric Occupation in the Gilf Kebir Region of the Eastern Sahara, SW Egypt', *Geoarchaeology: An International Journal* 19, 753–778.

Lloyd, A.B., 2010, *A Companion to Ancient Egypt* (Vol. II) (Blackwell, Chichester)

Lubbock, J., 1873, 'Notes on the Discovery of Stone Implements in Egypt', *Journal of the Royal Anthropological Institute of Great Britain and Ireland* 4, 215–222.

Lycett, J. & Gowlett, J.A., 2008, 'On questions surrounding the Acheulean "tradition"', *World Archaeology* 40, 295–315.

Macarthur, E., 2010, 'The Conception and Development of the Egyptian Writing System' in Woods, C. (ed.), *Visible Languages: Inventions of Writings in the Ancient Middle East and Beyond*, 115–136 (Chicago, The Oriental Institute of Chicago Museum Publications)

Machin, A.J., 2008, 'Why handaxes just aren't that sexy: a response to Kohn & Mithen', *Antiquity* 82, 761–769.

Maheny, R.A., 2014, 'Exploring the Complexity and Structure of Acheulean Stone-Knapping in Relation to Natural Language', *Palaeoanthropology*, 586–606. DOI: 10.4207/PA.2014.ART90.

Maish, A., 1998, 'Trauma at HK43' in *Nekhen News* 10, 6–7.

Mandel, R. & Simmons, A.H., 2001, 'Prehistoric Occupation of Late Quaternary Landscapes near Kharga Oasis, Western Desert of Egypt', *Geoarchaeology: An International Journal* 16, 95–117.

Marshall, F. & Hildebrand, E., 2002, 'Cattle Before Crops: The Beginnings of Food Production in Africa', *Journal of World Prehistory* 16, 99–143.

McDonald, M.M.A., 1991, 'Technological Organization and Sedentism in the Epipalaeolithic of Dakhleh Oasis, Egypt', *African Archaeological Review* 9, 81–109.

McDonald, M.M.A., 1998, 'Early African Pastoralism: View from Dakhleh Oasis (South Central Egypt)', *Journal of Anthropological Archaeology* 17, 124–142.

McDonald, M.M.A., 2002, 'Dakhleh Oasis in Predynastic Times: Bashendi B and the Sheikh Muftah Cultural Units', *Archéo-Nil* 12, 109–120.

McDonald, M.M.A., 2009, 'Increased Sedentism in the Central Oases of the Egyptian Western Desert in the Early to Mid-Holocene: Evidence from the Peripheries', *African Archaeological Review* 26, 3–43.

McDonald, M.A.A., 2016, 'The Pattern of Neolithization in Dakhleh Oasis in the Eastern Sahara', *Quaternary International* 410, 181–197.

McDonald, J.J., Donlon, D., Field, J.H., Fullagar, R.L.K., Coltrain, B., Mitchell, P. & Rawson, M., 2007, 'The first archaeological evidence for death by spearing in Australia', *Antiquity* 81, 877–885.

McHugh, W.P., Breed, C.S., Schaber, G.C., McCauley, J.F. & Szabo, B.J., 1988, 'Acheulean Sites along the "Radar Rivers", Southern Egyptian Sahara', *Journal of Field Archaeology* 15, 361–379.

McKim Malville, J., 2015, 'Astronomy at Nabta Playa' in Ruggles, C.L.N. (ed.), *Handbook of Archaeoastronomy and Ethnoastronomy*, 1079–1091, New York, Springer. DOI.1007/978-4614-6141-8_101.

McKim Malville, J., Schild, R., Wendorf, F. & Bremner, R., 2007, 'Astronomy of Nabta Playa', *African Skies/Cieux Africains* 11, 1–7.

McNabb, J. & Cole, J., 2015, 'The mirror cracked: symmetry and refinement in the Acheulean handaxe', *Journal of Archaeological Science Reports* 3, 100–111.

McNamara, L., 2014, 'The Ivory Statuette from HK6 Tomb 72', *Nekhen News* 26, 7–9.

Mercier, N., Valladas, H. & Froget, L., 1999, 'Thermoluminecense Dating of a Middle Palaeolithic Occupation of Sodmein Cave, Red Sea Mountains (Egypt)', *Journal of Archaeological Science* 26, 1339–1345.

Mgeladze, A., Lordkipanidze, D., Mancel, M-H., Despriee, J., Chagelishvili, R., Nioradze, M. & Nioradze, G., 2011, 'Hominin Occupations at the Dmanisi site, Georgia, Southern Caucasus: Raw material and technical behaviours of Europe's first homonins', *Journal of Human Evolution* 60, 571–596.

Midant-Reynes, B., 2000, *The Prehistory of Egypt* (Oxford, Blackwell)

Midant-Reynes, B., 2000, 'The Naqada Period' in Shaw, I. (ed.), *The Oxford History of Ancient Egypt*, 44–60 (Oxford, Oxford University Press)

Midant-Reynes, B., 2014, 'Prehistoric Regional Cultures' in Grajetzki, W. & Wendrich, W. (eds), *UCLA Encyclopedia of Egyptology*, 1–13 (Los Angeles) http://digital12library.ucla.edy/viewItem.do?ark=21198/zz002hk251.

Millet, N.B., 1990, 'The Narmer Macehead and Related Objects', *Journal of the American Research Center in Egypt* 27, 53–59.

Mirazón Lahar, M., Rivera, F., Power, R.K., Mounier, A., Copsey, B., Crivelalaro, F., Edung, J.E., Maillo Fernandez, J.M., Kiare, C., Lawrence, J., Leakey, A., Muba, E.,

Miller, H., Muigai, A., Mukhongo, D.M., Van Baelen, A., Wood, R., Schweninger, J-L., Grün, R., Achyuthan, H., Wilshaw, A. & Foley, R.A., 2016, 'Inter-group violence among early Holocene hunter-gatherers of West Turkana, Kenya', *Nature* 529, 394–307.

Moll, M., 14 July 2011, *Archaeology of Ancient Egypt: Burial Practices at Naqada* http://anthropology.msu.edu/egyptian-archaeology/2011/07/14/burial-practices-at-naqada/

Nelson, K. & Khalifa, E., 2010, 'Nabta Playa Black-Topped Pottery: Technological and Social Change', *British Museum Studies in Ancient Egypt and Sudan* 16, 133–148.

O'Brien, E.M., 1981, 'The Projectile Capabilities of an Acheulean Handaxe from Olorgesailie', *Current Anthropology* 22, 76–79.

O'Connor, D., 2011, 'The Narmer Palette: A New Interpretation' in Teeter, E. (ed.), *Before the Pyramids*, 145–152 (The Oriental Institute of Chicago, Oriental Institute Museum Publications)

Olszewski, D.I., Dibble, H.L., Schurmans, U.A., McPherron, S.P. & Smith, J.R., 2005, 'High Desert Paleolithic Survey at Abydos, Egypt', *Journal of Field Archaeology* 30, 283–303.

Olszewski, D.I., Dibble, H.L., McPherron, S.P., Schurmans, U.A., Chiotti, L. & Smith, J.R., 2010, 'Nubian Complex Strategies in the Egyptian High Desert', *Journal of Human Evolution* XXX, 1–14.

Olszewski, D.I., McPherron, S.P., Dibble, H.L. & Soressi, M., 2001, 'Middle Egypt in Prehistory: A Search for the Origins of Modern Human Behaviour and Human Dispersal', *Expedition* 43, 31–36.

Osypiński, P. & Oyspińska, M., 2016, 'The Wadi Khashab ceremonial complex – manifestation of cattle-keepers in the Eastern Desert of Egypt before the end of the fifth millennium BC', *Azania: Archaeological Research in Africa*. DOI:10.1080/00672 70X.2016.11866335.

Pantalacci, L., 2012, 'Coptos', *UCLA Encyclopedia of Egyptology* 1 (Los Angeles) http://digital2.library.ucla.edu/viewItem.do?ark=21198/zz002dn8zx

Paulissen, E. & Vermeersch, P.M., 1987, 'Earth man and climate in the Egyptian Nile Valley during the Pleistocene' in Close, A. (ed.), *Prehistory of Arid North Africa, Essays in Honor of Fred Wendorf*, 29–67 (Dallas, Southern Methodist University Press)

Petrie, W.M. & Quibell, J.E., 1896, *Naqada and Ballas 1985* (London, Bernard Quaritch)

Pettit, P. & White, M., 'John Lubbock: Caves and the Development of Middle and Upper Palaeolithic Archaeology', Notes & Records, *The Royal Society Journal of the History of Science* 68, 35–48. DOI: 10.1098/rsnr.2013.0050. Published online 27 November 2013.

Phillips, R., Holdoway, S., Wendrich, W. & Cappera, R., 2012, 'Mid-Holocene occupation of Egypt and global climate change', *Quaternary International* 251, 64–76.

Polkowski, P., Kuciewicz, E., Jaroni, E. & Kobusiewicz, M., 2013, 'Rock art research in the Dakhleh Oasis, Western Desert (Egypt): Petroglyph Unit, Dakhleh Oasis Project', *Sahara* 24, 101–118.

Pope, M., Russell, K. & Watson, K., 2006, 'Biface form and structured behaviour in the Acheulean', Lithics: *The Journal of the Lithic Studies Society* 27, 44–57.

Postgate, N., Wang, T. & Wilkinson, T., 1995, 'The evidence for early writing: utilitarian or ceremonial?' *Antiquity* 69, 459–80.

Radford, T., 27 December 2000, 'The rock art from 6,000 years ago: British archaeologists uncover "the Sistine Chapel of predynastic Egypt" at 30 sites in the desert east of the Nile.' https://www.theguardian.com/science/2000/dec/27/archaeology.internationalnews

Reed, C.A., 1965, 'A Human Frontal Bone from the Late Pleistocene of the Kom Ombo Plain, Upper Egypt', *Journal of the Royal Anthropological Institute of Great Britain & Ireland* 65, 101–104.

Reeves, N., 2000, *Ancient Egypt: The Great Discoveries* (London, Thames & Hudson)

Reimer, H., 2009, 'Prehistoric Rock Art Research in the Western Desert of Egypt', *Archéo-Nil* 19, 31–46.

Rice, M., 2003, *Egypt's Making: The Origins of Ancient Egypt 5000–2000 bc* (London, Routledge)

Richter, D., Grün, R., Joannes-Boyau, R., Steele, T.E., Amani, F., Rué, M., Fernandes, P., Raynal, J-P., Geraads, D., Ben-Ncer, A., Hublin, J-J. & McPherron, S.P., 2017, 'The age of the hominin fossils from Jebel Irhoud, Morocco, and the origins of the Middle Stone Age', *Nature* 546, 293–299. DOI:10.1038/nature22335.

Richter, D., Moser, J., Nami, M., Eiwanger, J. & Mikdad, A., 2010, 'New chronometric data from Ifri n'Ammar (Morocco) and the chronostratigraphy of the Middle Palaeolithic in the Western Maghreb', *Journal of Human Evolution* 59, 672–679.

Richter, J., Hauck, T., Vogelsang, R., Widlok, T., Le Tensorer, J.M. & Schmid, P., 2012, '"Contextual areas" of early *Homo sapiens* and their significance for human dispersal into Eurasia between 200 ka and 70 ka', *Journal of Human Evolution* 274, 5–24. DOI: 10.1016/j.quaint.2012.04.017.

Rose, D.A., Olsen, J.W., Underwood Jr, J.R. & Giegengood, R.F., 1982, 'A handaxe of Libyan Desert Glass', *Antiquity* LVI, 88–92.

Rose, J.I. & Marks, A.E., 2014, '"Out of Arabia" and the Middle-Upper-Palaeolithic transition in the southern Levant', *Quartär* 61, 49–85. DOI:10.7485/QU 61 03.

Rots, V., Van Peer, P. & Vermeersch, P.M., 2011, 'Aspects of tool production, use and hafting in Palaeolithic assemblages from North-East Africa', *Journal of Human Evolution* 60, 637–664.

Rowland, J. & Tassie, C.J., 2014, 'Prehistoric Sites along the edge of the Western Nile Delta: Report on the Results of the Imbaba Prehistoric Survey 2013–2014', *Journal of Egyptian Archaeology* 100, 49–65.

Sackett, J., 2000, 'Human Antiquity and the Old Stone Age: The Nineteenth-Century Background to Palaeolanthropology', *Evolutionary Anthropology* 37, 37–49.

Sackett, J., 2014, 'Boucher de Perthes and the discovery of Human Antiquity', *Bulletin of the History of Archaeology* 24, 1–11. DOI:http//dx.doi.org/10.5334/bha.242.

Sample I, 7 June 2017, 'Oldest *Homo sapiens* bones ever found shake foundations of the human story.' https://www.theguardian.com/science/2017/jun/07/oldest-homo-sapiens-bones-ever-found-shake-foundations-of-the-human-story

Scerri, E.M.L., 2013, 'The Aterian and its place in the North African Middle Stone Age', *Quaternary International* 300, 111–130.

Scerri, E.M.L. & Spinapolice, E.E., 2019, 'Lithics of the North African Middle Stone Age: Assumptions, evidence and future directions', *Journal of Anthropological Sciences* 97, 1–36. DOI.10.4436/jass.97002.

Schaefer, B.E., 2000, 'The Heliacal Rise of Sirius and Ancient Egyptian Chronology', *Journal for the History of Astronomy* 31:2, 149–155.

Schick, K.D. & Toth, N., 1995, *Making Silent Stones Speak: Human Evolution and the Dawn of Technology* (London, Phoenix)

Schild, R. & Wendorf, F., 2002, 'Forty Years of the Combined Prehistoric Expedition', *Archaeologia Polona* 40, 5–22.

Shackelford, L., Marshall, F. & Peters, J., 2013, 'Identifying donkey domestication through changes in cross-sectional geometry of long bones', *Journal of Archaeological Science* 40, 4170–4179.

Shaw, I. & Nicholson, P., 2008, *The British Museum Dictionary of Ancient Egypt* (London, British Museum Press)

Shipton, C., 2010, 'Imitation and Shared Intentionality in the Acheulean', *Cambridge Archaeological Journal* 20, 197–210.

Shirai, N., 2002, 'Helwan Points in the Egyptian Neolithic', *Orient* XXXVII, 121–135.

Shirai, N., 2010, *The Archaeology of the First Farmer-Herders in Egypt: New insights into the Fayum Epipalaeolithic and Neolithic* (Leiden, Leiden University Press)

Shirai, N., 2013, 'Was Neolithisation a struggle for existence and the survival of the fittest or merely the survival of the luckiest? A case study of socioeconomic and cultural changes in Egypt in the Early-Middle Holocene' in Shirai, N. (ed.), *Neolithisation of North-Eastern Africa: Studies in Early Near Eastern Production, Subsistence and Environment* 16, 213–235. Berlin, *ex oriente*.

Shirai, N., 2016, 'The Desert Fayum at 80: Revisiting a Neolithic farming community in Egypt', *Antiquity* 90, 1181–1195.

Shirai, N., 2016, 'Establishing a Neolithic farming life in Egypt: A view from the lithic study of Fayum Neolithic sites', *Quaternary International* 412, 22–35.

Smith, P.E.L., 1976, 'Stone-Age Man on the Nile', *Scientific American* 235, 30–41.

Snape, S., 2104, *The Complete Cities of Ancient Egypt* (London, Thames & Hudson)

Spencer, A.J., 1991, *Death in Ancient Egypt* (London, Penguin)

Spikins, P., 2012, 'Goodwill Hunting? Debates on the "meaning" of Lower Palaeolithic handaxe form revisited', *World Archaeology* 44, 378–392.

Spikins, P.A., Rutherford, H.E. & Needham, A.P., 2010, 'From Homoninity to Humanity: Compassion from the Earliest Archaics to Modern Humans', *Time and Mind* 3, 303–325.

Stevenson, A., 2009, 'Palettes' in Wendrich, W. (ed.), *UCLA Encyclopedia of Egyptology*, 1–9. Los Angeles. http://digital12library.ucla.edy/viewItem.do?ark=21198/zz001nf6c0

Stevenson, A., 'Mace' in Wendrich, W. (ed.), *UCLA Encyclopedia of Egyptology*, 1–7. Los Angeles. http://digital12library.ucla.edy/viewItem.do?ark=21198/zz000sn3x

Stevenson, A., 2011, 'Material Culture of the Predynastic Period' in Teeter, E. (ed.), *Before the Pyramids*, 65–74 (The Oriental Institute of Chicago, Oriental Institute Museum Publications)

Stevenson, A., 2012, 'Predynastic Egyptian Figurines', *Semantic Scholar*. DOI:10.1093/OXFORDHB/9780199675616.013.004.

Stock, F. & Gifford, D., 2013, 'Genetics and African Cattle Domestication', *African Archaeological Review* 30, 51–73.

Storemyr, P., 2008, 'Prehistoric geometric rock art at Gharb Aswan, Upper Egypt', *Sahara* 19, 2008, 61–76.

Storemyr, P., 2009, 'A Prehistoric Geometric Rock Art Landscape by the First Nile Cataract', *Archéo-Nil* 19, 121–150.

Storemyr, P., 6 April 2012, *Wadi Abu Subeira, Egypt: Palaeolithic rock art on the verge of destruction*. Per-storemyr.net/2012/04/06/wadi-abu-subeira-egypt-palaeolithic-rock-art-on-the-verge-of-destruction

Storemyr, P., Kelany, A., Negm, M.A., & Tohami, A., 2008, 'More "Lascaux along the Nile"? Possible Late Palaeolithic Rock Art in Wadi Abu Subeira, Upper Egypt', *Sahara* 19, 155–158.

Stringer, C., 2003, 'Out of Ethiopia', *Nature* 432, 692–695.

Stringer, C., 2012, 'The Status of *Homo Heidelbergensis* (Schoetensack 1908)', *Evolutionary Anthropology* 21, 101–107.

Stringer, C. & Galway-Witham, J., 2017, 'On the origin of our species', *Nature (Notes & News)* 546, 212–214.

Stringer, C. & Galway-Witham, J., 2018, 'When did modern humans leave Africa?' *Science* 359, 389–390.

Svoboda, J.A., 2004, 'The Middle Palaeolithic of Southern Bahariya Oasis, Western Desert, Egypt', *Anthropologie* XLII, 253–267.

Svoboda, J., 2009, 'Action, Ritual and Myth in the Rock Art of the Egyptian Western Desert', *Anthropologie* XLVII, 137–145.

Thoma, A., 1984, 'Morphology and Affinities of Nazlet Khater Man', *Journal of Human Evolution* 13, 287–296.

Thorpe, N., 2000, 'Origins of War: Mesolithic Conflict in Europe', *British Archaeology* 52, 8–13.

Thorpe, I.J.N., 'Anthropology, archaeology and the origin of warfare', *World Archaeology* 25, 145–165.

Tobias, P.V., 1966, 'Fossil Hominid Remains from Ubeidiya, Israel', *Nature* 211, 130–133.

Tomassetti, M.C., Lucarini, G., Hamdan, M.A., Macchia, A., Mutri, G. & Barich, B.E., 2016, 'Preservation and Restoration of the Wadi Sura Caves in the Framework of the "Gilf Kebir National Park", Egypt', *International Journal of Conservation Science*, Special Issue 2, 913–934.

Torre, de la I., 2016, 'The origins of the Acheulean: Past and present perspectives on a major transition in human evolution', *Philosophical Transactions of the Royal Society* B 371, 1–13: 20150245.http://dx.doi.org/10.1098/rstb.2015.0245

Trinkaus, E., 2005, 'Early Modern Humans', *Annual Review of Anthropology* 34, 207–230.

Ucko, P.J., 1965, 'Anthropomorphic Ivory Figurines from Egypt', *The Journal of the Royal Anthropological Institute of Great Britain & Ireland* 95, 214–239.

Vance Haynes Jr, C., Maxwell, T.A., Johnson, D.C. & Kilani, A., 2001, 'Research Note: Acheulean Sites near Bir Kiseiba in the Darb el-Arab in Desert, Egypt: New Data', *Geoarchaeology: An International Journal* 16, 143–150.

Vance Haynes Jr, C., Maxwell, T.A., El Hawary, A., Nicoll, K.A. & Stokes, S., 1997, 'An Acheulean Site near Bir Kiseiba in the Darb el-Arab Desert, Egypt', *Geoarchaeology: An International Journal* 12, 819–832.

Van Peer, P., 1998, 'The Nile Corridor and the Out-of-Africa Model: An Examination of the Archaeological Record', *Current Anthropology* 39, 115–140.

Van Peer, P., Fullagar, R., Stokes, S., Bailey, R.M., Moeyersons, J., Steenhoudt, F., Geerts, A., Vermeersch, P. & Moeyersons, J., 1996, 'Palaeolithic Stratigraphy at Sodmein Cave (Red Sea Mountains, Egypt)', *International Journal of Geology, Geography and Tropical Ecology* 20, 61–71.

Van Peer, P., Vermeersch, P.M. & Paulissen, E., 2010, *Chert Quarrying, Lithic Technology and a Modern Human Burial at the Palaeolithic Site of Taramsa-1, Upper Egypt* (Leuven, Leuven University Press)

Van Peer, P. & Vermeersch, P.M., 2007, 'The Place of North-East Africa in the Early History of Modern Humans: New Data and Interpretations of the Middle Stone Age' in Mellars, P., Boyle, K., Bar-Yosef, O. & Stringer, C. (eds), *Rethinking the Human Revolution*, 197–198 (Cambridge, McDonald Institute for Archaeological Research)

Van Peer, P., Rots, V. & Vermeersch, P.M., 'A Wasted Effort at the Quarry: Wear Analysis and Interpretation of an MSA Lanceolate Point from Taramsa 8, Egypt', *Palaeoanthropology* 2008, 234–250.

Vanderbeken, T., De Dapper, M. & Geus, F., 2003, 'The Early to Middle Stone Age Transition and the Emergence of Modern Human Behaviour at Site 8-B-11, Sai Island, Sudan', *Journal of Human Evolution* 45,187–193.

Vekua, A. & Lordkpanidze, D., 2010, 'Damansi (Georgia) – Site of Discovery of the Oldest Hominid in Eurasia', *Bulletin of the Georgian National Academy of Science* 4, 158–164.

Vermeersch, P.M., 2002, 'Two Upper Palaeolithic Burials at Nazlet Khater' in Vermeersch, P.M. (ed.), *Palaeolithic Quarrying Sites in Upper and Middle Egypt*, 273–282 (Leuven, Leuven University Press)

Vermeersch, P.M., 2008, 'Egypt from 50–25 ka BP: a scarcely inhabited region?' in Camps, M. & Smidt, C., (eds), *The Mediterranean from 50,000–25,0000 BP: Turning-Points and New Directions*, 67–88 (Oxford, Oxbow)

Vermeersch, P.M., 2010, 'Middle and Upper Palaeolithic in the Egyptian Nile Valley' in Garcea, A.A. (ed.), *South-Eastern Mediterranean Peoples between 130,000 and 10,000 Years Ago*, 66–88 (Oxford, Oxbow)

Vermeersch, M., Paulissen, E., Ottem, M. & Gijselings, G., 2000, 'Nag El Khalifa, an Acheulean Site' in Vermeersch, P. (ed.), *Palaeolithic Living Sites in Upper and Middle Egypt*, 57–74 (Leuven, Leuven University Press)

Vermeersch, M.P., Paulissen, E., Gijselings, G. & Jansen, J., 1986, 'Middle Palaeolithic Exploitation Pits near Qena (Upper Egypt)', *Paléorient* 12, 61–65.

Vermeersch, P.M., Gijselings, G. & Paulissen, E., 1984, 'Discovery of Nazlet Khater Man, Upper Egypt', *Journal of Human Evolution* 13, 281–286.

Vermeersch, P.M., Paulissen, E. & Vanderbeken, T., 2002, 'Nazlet Khater 4, an Upper Palaeolithic Underground Chert Mine' in Vermeersch, P.M (ed.), *Palaeolithic Quarrying Sites in Upper and Middle Egypt*, 211–272 (Leuven, Leuven University Press)

Vermeersch, P.M., Van Peer, P., Moeyersons, J. & Van Neer, W., 1994, 'Sodmein Cave Site, Red Sea Mountains (Egypt)', *Sahara* 6, 31–40.

Vermeersch, P.M., Paulissen, E. & Van Peer, P., 1990, 'Palaeolithic chert exploitation in the limestone stretch of the Egyptian Nile Valley', *African Archaeological Review* 8, 77–102.

Vermeersch, P.M., Paulissen, E. & Van Peer, P., 1995, 'Palaeolithic chert mining in Egypt', *Archaeologia Polona* 33, 11–30.

Vermeersch, P.M. & Van Peer, P., 2005, 'A Middle Palaeolithic site with blade technology at Al Tiwayrat, Qena, Upper Egypt', *Antiquity* 79: Project Gallery.

Vermeersch, P.M., Linseele, V., Marinova, E., Van Neer, W., Moeyersons, J. & Rethemeyer, J., 2015, 'Early and Middle Holocene Occupation of the Egyptian Eastern Desert', *African Archaeological Review* 32, 465–503.

Vücković, A., 12 July 2020, 'Gebel El-Arak Knife – A Link to Ancient Egypt's Distant Beginnings.' https://www.ancient-origins.net/artifacts-other-artifacts/gebel-el-arak-knife-0013972

Warfe, A.R., 2003, 'Cultural Origins of the Egyptian Neolithic and Predynastic: An Evaluation of the Evidence from Dakhleh Oasis', *African Archaeological Review* 20, 175–202.

Wasylikowa, K., Mitka, J., Wendorf, F. & Schild, R., 1997, 'Exploitation of wild plants by the early Neolithic hunter-gatherers of the Western Desert: Nabta Playa as a case-study', *Antiquity* 71, 923–941.

Watrin, L., 2000, 'Copper Drops and Buried Buildings: Ma'adi's Legacy as a Predynastic Trade Capital', *Bulletin of the Egyptian Geographical Society* 73, 163–184.

Wenban-Smith, F., 2004, 'Handaxe typology and Lower cultural development: ficrons, cleavers and two giant handaxes from Cuxton', *Lithics* 25, 11–21.

Wendorf, F., Schild, R., Gautier, A. & Kobusiewicz, M., 1981, 'Research at Bir Tarfawi: Archaeological and Geological Investigations in the Egyptian Sahara', *Archaeologia Polona* XX, 177–189.

Wendorf, F., Close, A.E., Schild, R., 1987, 'Recent Work on the Middle Palaeolithic of the Eastern Sahara' in Phillipson, D.W. & Harris, J.W.K. (eds), *African Archaeological Review 5. Papers in honour of J. Desmond Clark*, 49–63 (Cambridge, Cambridge University Press)

Wendorf, F. & Schild, R., 1998, 'Nabta Playa and its Role in North-Eastern African Prehistory', *Journal of Anthropological Archaeology* 17, 97–123.

Wengrow, D., 2009, 'Predynastic Art' in Wendrich, W. (ed.), *UCLA Encyclopedia of Egyptology*, 1–7. Los Angeles.http://digital2.library.ucla.edu/viewItem. do?=21198/2001ndn3p

Wengrow, D., Dee, M., Foster, S., Stevenson, A. & Bronk Ramsey, C., 2014, 'Cultural Convergence in the Neolithic of the Nile Valley: A prehistoric perspective on Egypt's place in Africa', *Antiquity* 88, 95–111.

Whittaker, J.C. & McCall, G., 2001, 'Handaxe-Hurling Hominids: An Unlikely Story', *Current Anthropology* 42, 566–572.

Wilkinson, T., 2010, 'The Early Dynastic Period' in Lloyd, A.B. (ed.), *A Companion to Ancient Egypt* (Vol. 1), 48–63 (Sussex, Blackwell)

Williams, B., 1988, 'Narmer and the Coptos Colossi', *Journal of the American Research Center in Egypt* XXV, 35–59.

Williams, B., Logan, T.J. & Murnane, J., 1987, 'The Metropolitan Museum Knife-Handle and Aspects of Pharaonic Imagery before Narmer', *Journal of Near Eastern Studies* 4, 245–285.

Wurz, S. & Van Peer, P., 2012, 'Out of Africa, the Nile Valley & the Northern Route', *South African Archaeological Review* 67, 168–179.

Wynn, T. & Gowlett, J., 2018, 'The handaxe reconsidered', *Evolutionary Anthropology* 27, 21–29.

Yeshurun, R., 2017, 'Taphonomy of old archaeofaunal collections: New site-formation and subsistence data for the Late Palaeolithic Nile Valley', *Quaternary International* XXX, 1–20.

Zagorska, I., 2008, 'The Use of Ochre in the Stone Age Burials of the East Baltic' in Fahlander, F. & Oestigaard, T. (eds), *The Materiality of Death: Bodies, Burials, Beliefs*, 115–124 (Oxford, Archaeopress)

Zboray, A., 2012, 'An unpublished shelter with prehistoric engravings of a possible late Pleistocene date in the North-Central Sinai', *Sahara* 23, 163–166.

Zboray, A., 2013, 'Wadi Sura in the context of regional rock art' in Kuper, R. (ed.), 'Wadi Sura – The Cave of Beasts', *Africa Praehistorica* 26, 18–23 (Köln, Heinrich-Barth-Institut)

Index